# Military Statecraft and the Rise of Shaping in World Politics

# Military Statecraft and the Rise of Shaping in World Politics

Kyle J. Wolfley

ROWMAN & LITTLEFIELD
Lanham • Boulder • New York • London

Credits and acknowledgments for material borrowed from other sources, and reproduced with permission, appear on the appropriate page within the text.

Published by Rowman & Littlefield
An imprint of The Rowman & Littlefield Publishing Group, Inc.
4501 Forbes Boulevard, Suite 200, Lanham, Maryland 20706
www.rowman.com

The views expressed in this book are personal and do not reflect the policy or position of the US Military Academy at West Point, Department of the Army, Department of Defense, or US Government.

British Library Cataloguing in Publication Information Available

**Library of Congress Cataloging-in-Publication Data**

Library of Congress Control Number: 2021933053

Library of Congress Cataloging-in-Publication Data on File

ISBN 978-1-5381-5064-1 (cloth)
ISBN 978-1-5381-5066-5 (pbk)
ISBN 978-1-5381-5065-8 (electronic)

# Contents

# Preface

When I arrived at Cornell University to begin my graduate studies in preparation for teaching at West Point, I thought long and hard about my goals for the daunting experience ahead. Attempting to complete a PhD on an accelerated timeline required urgency in determining what would be a useful topic for my dissertation. I remember sitting on a bench outside of White Hall—which houses the Government department—overlooking Libe Slope and thinking to myself, "Why do militaries exist? What do they do on a regular basis to achieve their countries' goals?" These may seem like odd questions for an American military officer who led an infantry platoon in combat and commanded two companies in the storied 82nd Airborne Division, but I couldn't shake these thoughts. Sure, I knew that armies wage (or prepare) for war, but my experience had taught me that countries use their militaries in far more fascinating ways than anyone seemed to have a handle on. After extensive research, interviews, and data collection, I became certain that we were all missing a major development in contemporary statecraft.

This book is about the far-reaching ways in which the most powerful countries leverage their militaries to achieve the goals of foreign policy. The majority of scholarship—and conventional wisdom—imagines that the purpose of military power is to wage or threaten violence against others. Though this is generally true, what is remarkable is how, on a day-to-day basis, governments use their armed forces in ways that do not rely on the use or threat of violent force. When the US Army sends dentists to increase the welfare of Filipinos, when Chinese and Indian soldiers perform traditional dances together before maneuvers, or when the British invite foreign officers to train at their military schools, we begin to imagine military power as a different tool of influence unmoored from the traditional functions that we observe in history books or on the news. This book is the culmination of my attempt to understand why and how the most powerful states have increasingly relied on a way of military statecraft known as "shaping" and how this development will affect the future prospects for cooperation and competition in world politics.

This project was several years in the making, beginning first at graduate school and ending during my years teaching at West Point. I first thank God for the numerous opportunities he has provided me throughout my life: I am not worthy of his grace and still wonder why he has given me so much, especially my loving and dedicated family. I couldn't have written this book without the unending devotion of my best friend and wife, Danessa, who supports and encourages me in everything I do and who I know will always be there by my side. In addition to Danessa, our children Kolson and Lydia give me hope and strength when I feel in doubt; they are my joy and inspiration to keep moving forward. I am eternally grateful to Danessa's parents—Dennis and Pam—whose home serves as our permanent "home away from home" and provides my refuge for thinking and writing. I also want to thank my father for being my role model throughout my life and teaching me to never give up.

This project would not have been possible without the patience and dedication of my outstanding dissertation committee at Cornell: Matthew Evangelista, Sarah Kreps, Steven Ward, and Allen Carlson. Bryce Corrigan spent considerable effort helping me through the quantitative portions of this project, and I thank Vito D'Orazio for providing the sources for his exercise dataset which informed my own. I am grateful for the military officers and defense officials who were gracious enough to provide interviews so I could better understand shaping in practice. Saumitra Jha and Nancy Teeple provided great feedback on drafts of the article-version of this project. Carol Atkinson and Derek Reveron are among the few scholars who have explored this topic and whose work I admire and attempted to emulate. Teaching at West Point and learning from cadets, fellow instructors, and senior faculty has given me an opportunity to expand what began as a dissertation into this more comprehensive book. A special thanks goes to Max Margulies and Scott Limbocker who are not only outstanding instructors and mentors for our cadets at West Point, but whose early feedback and advice greatly shaped the direction of this book project. I owe a debt of gratitude to my editors at *Rowman and Littlefield*—Dhara Snowden and Rebecca Anastasi—for providing a wonderful home for this project. I hope the readers of this book—whether students, scholars, practitioners, or those generally interested in the shape of future competition and statecraft—will enjoy and learn from grappling with this topic as I have and will continue to do. Most importantly, I hope that practitioners wield shaping with wisdom to skillfully manage what appears to be an increasingly complex and dangerous international environment.

The views expressed in this book are personal and do not reflect the policy or position of the US Military Academy at West Point, Department of the Army, Department of Defense, or US Government.

*Chapter 1*

# Introduction: Shaping and the Broadening of Military Statecraft

In 2018, Russia announced that it was planning to conduct its largest military exercise since the Cold War, known as *Vostok*, involving roughly 300,000 troops along its eastern and southern borders. The size of the exercise is not what startled most observers: Russia regularly conducts large maneuvers and has been known to inflate troop numbers in the past. Instead, the most surprising feature was the Russian government's invitation of roughly 3,200 Chinese troops to join a training event that, during the Cold War, was part of an exercise program designed to deter the West *as well as China.*[1] Russia's use of this type of military exercise—first as a means to coerce China but now to engage with its southern neighbor—is representative of the surprising ways in which countries leverage military power to achieve their foreign policy objectives. Russia's attempt to attract China through military cooperation is an example of *shaping*, an instrument of military statecraft that is both common but not well-understood; one that relies less on threat or use of force, but more on the ability to manage military relationships and partners through attraction and legitimacy. Due to a complex international system, as well as contemporary changes in power and technology, shaping has the potential to become one of the most important instruments of statecraft in the coming decades.

This book explores the emergence of shaping in world politics and explains why it has become a major feature of great power statecraft and competition. National leaders have various foreign policy tools at their disposal to accomplish their aims, such as diplomatic missions, economic levers, propaganda, and military organizations. Although military statecraft is assumed to be synonymous with the threat or use of force, the most powerful states began to leverage different logics of military power more frequently after the end of the Cold War. Known as shaping, this use of the armed forces is intended to construct a more favorable environment by influencing the characteristics of other militaries, altering the relationships between them, or managing the behavior of allies. The goal of shaping is primarily to prevent the emergence of threats but also to be prepared and maintain and advantage if dangers do materialize. As opposed to the traditional instruments of military strategy, shaping relies less on threats, demonstrations, and uses of violence and more so on attraction, persuasion, and legitimacy; in other words, shaping relies on less hard power and more on soft power. Policymakers and military officers view shaping as a way to exert control over an ambiguous environment in which threats and allies are unclear through different activities, such as senior officer visits, exchanges, security assistance, forward presence, and certain types of military exercises. The analysis throughout the book reveals how major powers use shaping to manage a complex international environment of competition, costly war, and the persistent threat of violent non-state actors.

## STATECRAFT AND THE DIVERSE
## WAYS OF MILITARY POWER

According to David Baldwin, statecraft is the use of various national instruments to achieve the goals of foreign policy. Statecraft is conducted by national leaders and organizations to influence other actors and the goals are political: that is, to advance the country's interests, which often results in competition.[2] When discussing statecraft, scholars and practitioners often use the language of "military tools" as opposed to "nonmilitary tools," yet the rise of shaping and the broadening of the spectrum of military statecraft has often blurred these neat distinctions.[3] By military tools, we often think in terms of soldiers, tanks, bombers, aircraft carriers, and missiles. Yet these symbols are the only "means" of military power: the use of these instruments will vary based on the "ways" and "ends" of strategy.[4] Most observers would be quick to note that the purpose of military power is straightforward as the threat or use of violence; that is, inducing an adversary's submission through violent *warfighting* or changing an adversary's behavior through *coercion*. These traditional logics of military power are commonly on display during major military exercises, which, especially during the Cold War, were a primary instrument of deterrence between the United States and Soviet Union. Competition and statecraft today, however, seem more ambiguous and difficult to define. Students and policymakers are becoming interested in China's Belt and Road Initiative and Russia's skillful use of misinformation as attempts to gain asymmetric advantages over the United States using nonmilitary tools. Yet what is largely overlooked is how all major powers are also expanding how they use military organizations to carry out the state's foreign policy under the threshold of threats or violence.

Even a cursory observation of today's military activity reveals how major powers use their armed forces in far more fascinating ways than these traditional images of military strength reveal. Although a useful means to increase deterrence during the Cold War, US-led "Cobra Gold" biannual military exercises in Thailand today involve civic action projects, such as medical visits to local families and even the construction of schools, all carried out by American soldiers.[5] In 2014, the Chinese government deployed hundreds of soldiers to Sierra Leone and Liberia to treat Ebola patients, establish a treatment center, and train local medical professionals, declaring itself to be a "true friend" to Africa.[6] Russia is attempting to establish its first military base on the continent in Somaliland—a self-declared autonomous administration of Somalia—which would join United States and Chinese bases already established in the Horn of Africa in the last two decades.[7] In return for the base, the Russians have offered sovereign recognition, as well as future training for the local forces.[8] Although war and large-scale demonstrations of military might dominate our view of military power, the day-to-day activities of militaries often involve tasks usually carried out by diplomats or aid developers, which will have immense implications for world politics.

## MILITARY SHAPING: CONSTRUCTING A FAVORABLE ENVIRONMENT

These activities are examples of shaping: the use of military organizations to proactively build a more favorable environment by changing military relationships, the characteristics of other militaries, or the behavior of allies. The purpose of shaping is to prevent threats from emerging in the first place, which is less costly than reacting to adverse behavior through violent compellence or warfighting. There are four logics that express how major powers achieve their goals of shaping: attraction, socialization, delegation, and assurance. States use *attraction* to change international alignment patterns by creating warmer relations with neutral states, preparing some to become allies or coalition partners, or attempting to de-escalate tensions with rivals. *Socialization* is the attempt to change the practices or norms of other militaries, primarily to alter the role in which the military serves for its society, such as a regime-defender or democracy-promoter. Major powers *delegate* to pass the burden of security onto others, either by transferring the responsibility to deter to other major powers, or to fragile states to provide defense for themselves. Major powers, especially the United States with its vast alliance network, use *assurance* to reduce its allies' insecurity by promising protection through defense commitments and forward presence, which mitigates undesirable ally behavior and provides operational access in case of crisis or war. Chapter 2 compares these logics against the traditional uses of military organizations by exploring how each relates to different types of power and how they overlap with other instruments of statecraft.

Although the roots of shaping lie within classical military strategy, the concept became central to US foreign policy following the end of the Cold War. Faced with the collapse of its only competitor and the weakening of state control over non-state actors, US policymakers determined that the best way to manage their complex environment was by using its military to build relationships and modify the character of other militaries. These activities were prominent in the US-led Partnership for Peace program, which attempted to build closer ties to former communist states in Eastern Europe and even prepare a few for North Atlantic Treaty Organization (NATO) membership. Yet shaping is not only within the purview of the United States: China and Russia's impressive use of various shaping logics reveals how shaping is a tool not only prevent civil war, terrorism, or humanitarian disasters, but also to gain an advantage over other major powers.

Although theories of warfighting and coercion are well-established, the use of military organizations to construct a more favorable environment suffers from conceptual confusion as scholars and practitioners struggle how to define these non-conventional activities. Over the last three decades, the US military applied various terms to describe these missions in addition to shaping, such as "Military Operations Other Than War" (MOOTW), "cooperative security," "security cooperation," and "military engagement," exposing its discomfort in trying to define these nontraditional tasks. Proposals for US grand strategy often use the term "engagement" to describe a policy that relies heavily on military shaping, a concept that gained traction from the US President William Clinton administration's *National Security Strategy for Engagement and Enlargement*.[9] Non-US terminology also varies and reveals the overlap with the tool of diplomacy: British scholars and officers often use the terms "Defence Diplomacy" or "Defence Engagement";[10] Chinese doctrine and scholarship refers to them as "Military Diplomacy";[11] and the Indian government defines them as "Defence Cooperation."[12] Chapter 3 explores the evolution of how the American military understands and defines these activities and a goal of this book is to attempt to systematize how we describe these nontraditional military activities, making a case that the term "shaping" best represents the overall purpose and logics of these operations.

At its essence, shaping is more subtle than overt, more building than breaking, more Sun Tzu than Clausewitz, and more soft than hard power. These qualities render shaping seductive to state leaders, especially given shaping's underhanded nature and cost aversion. However, like deterrence, it is often difficult to determine whether shaping is "working" or "successful"; its measures of effectiveness are often elusive.[13] Does America's forward presence of troops abroad make America safer? Can exercises reduce mistrust between rivals such as China and India? The illustrative case studies only provide preliminary assessments, with the focus more on explanation than firm conclusions on effectiveness. For instance, although NATO's Partnership for Peace program in the 1990s—the subject of chapter 4—appears to have achieved its goals in attracting Eastern European partners, Russia's use of shaping in response to prevent Western democratic influence through such efforts—described in chapter 5—implies caution. Major powers sometimes regret inviting rivals to cooperative exercises: the United States even disinvited China to its biannual "Rim of the Pacific" (RIMPAC) maneuvers in 2018. While US officials cited Chinese aggression in the South China Sea as the reason, others worried about potential espionage given suspicions of spying during previous iterations of the exercise.[14] Shaping could alternatively lead to unintended consequences such as increased mistrust: as the logic of shaping is designed to both "prevent" and "prepare," one power's desire to change the characteristics of one state's army may appear threatening to another. Efforts to socialize armies or supply rebels against adversaries could result in "blowback" against the major power.[15]

The nontraditional nature of shaping is also controversial for statesmen and military officers alike: the overlap between shaping and the other tools of statecraft results in inevitable friction between diplomats and soldiers in terms of responsibility. Some military officers may even reject shaping as a distraction away from the traditional tasks of warfighting and coercion. This book explores not only the emergence of shaping in foreign policy, but also wrestles with the bureaucratic challenges and consequences of its implementation, which include the potential militarization of foreign policy and implications for US grand strategy. The increasing prominence of shaping, coupled with its contentious and paradoxical nature, requires an explanation about why, and under what conditions, this way of military statecraft becomes more attractive to policymakers. Given the lack of studies and theorizing on these nontraditional ways of military statecraft, this book offers one approach to understanding today's competition below the threshold of warfighting.

## THE EMERGENCE AND SOURCES OF SHAPING

### The Argument

The core argument of this book is that major powers prioritize shaping when strategic uncertainty is high; that is, when threats and allies become more ambiguous. A US military manual on shaping in 2008 captured the essence of this problem with a question: "How does a joint force commander (JFC) contribute to fostering a security environment favorable to U.S. interests as well as establish a solid base for effective crisis response given: . . . it is difficult to anticipate where and in what types of situations the United States will be involved".[16] The level of uncertainty is determined by two systemic forces: the distribution of international power and the consequences of globalization. First, the structure of the international system is comprised of the distribution of capabilities and is determined by the number and size of great powers in the system: structures can be bipolar, multipolar, or unipolar. Since bipolar structures are only comprised of two great powers, adversaries and alliances are more obvious than in other structures. Second, the consequences of contemporary globalization also influence the ability to predict threats and allies. Advances in transportation, communication, and information technology have provided violent non-state actors with an increased ability to coordinate, move, and support attacks against states from farther reaches of the globe, straining military planning to determine the location and the extent of these ambiguous threats. In addition to these two factors that impact strategic uncertainty, another systemic force increases the attractiveness of shaping: the balance of military technology. When defensive technology makes invasion prohibitively costly—such as nuclear weapons, advanced sensors, and air defense weapons—state leaders look for opportunities to compete below the threshold of open war. Although the dawn of nuclear weapons encouraged the superpowers to select deterrence as the primary military tool during the Cold War, shaping was also a useful non-warfighting tool to compete through proxies along the periphery.

As uncertainty increases, so do the incentives for shaping as the tool of choice of military statecraft. Shaping provides a means to reduce strategic uncertainty by attracting allies and partners, socializing practices in others, building the capacity of weaker states, and assuring weary allies. Compared to the relative certainty of the Cold War competition between the two superpowers, the unpredictable post-Cold War environment encouraged major powers to accelerate the use of shaping. Faced with the collapse of the Soviet Union, dissolution of communist states, proliferation of weapons, increased state fragility, and rise of terrorism, military planners began to reimagine the ways of military statecraft to create a more favorable environment and manage emerging threats. This sentiment of immense uncertainty is common among the US military's senior leaders. Comparing the current strategic environment to the Cold War, US Army Pacific Commander General Robert Brown noted in an interview:

> It's amazing how complex the world has become. I often would joke, "The last time I was bored was in the Cold War." I was a company commander, and I

had a responsibility in an area against the Soviets. You know, they could have come across but you kind of knew they wouldn't be that crazy. We had learned to fight outnumbered and win. We had almost 300,000 in Europe. We trained hard, but there was still time to get bored. I have not been bored since, and I don't think we'll be bored for another 50 years. The world is just so interconnected and complex.[17]

Agreeing with this assessment, Army General David Perkins writes in the preface to the US Army's 2014 Operating Concept: "The environment the Army will operate in is unknown. The enemy is unknown, the location is unknown, and the coalitions involved are unknown."[18] Marine General Joseph Dunford asked the graduating class of the National Defense University in 2016: "In the environment we are in today, with the complexity and volatility and variety of challenges we have, how do we assess risk? . . . How do we assess the capabilities or capacities that must exist in the joint force? A part of this is also how to prepare for the unexpected."[19] Although the United States originally emphasized shaping as a means to manage the threat posed by violent non-state actors, the recent emergence of a multipolar system has resulted in both the return of traditional tools as well as the use of shaping to attract allies as a form of balancing against competitors such as Russia and China. The diverse use of shaping—both against non-state actors and to gain an advantage over peers—begs for a better understanding in today's uncertain and competitive international system.

## Shaping in Practice through Military Exercises

As mentioned above, one of the most visible military activities is the multinational military exercise; that is, military training between two or more states. Often reported in the news and watched carefully by analysts and military officers, multinational exercises span the range of logics from traditional to shaping. NATO and the Warsaw Pact's frequent large-scale maneuvers during the Cold War served as an ostensible tool of deterrence and preparations for combat. The use of military exercises to prepare for combat and impress adversaries is as old as combat itself and would be unsurprising to Prussian King Frederick the Great, whose annual maneuvers awed the other great powers in the eighteenth century.[20] Interestingly, however, multinational military exercises increased substantially after the Cold War, which is puzzling given the end of superpower rivalry and incentives to enjoy the peace dividend, reduce overseas presence, and focus attention domestically. Yet as figure 1.1 reveals, when separated by logics, a new picture emerges: shaping exercises increased along with the post-Cold War strategic uncertainty. Another interesting puzzle appears in figure 1.2, which reveals the same data but separated

## Total Land-Based Multinational Exercises by Type

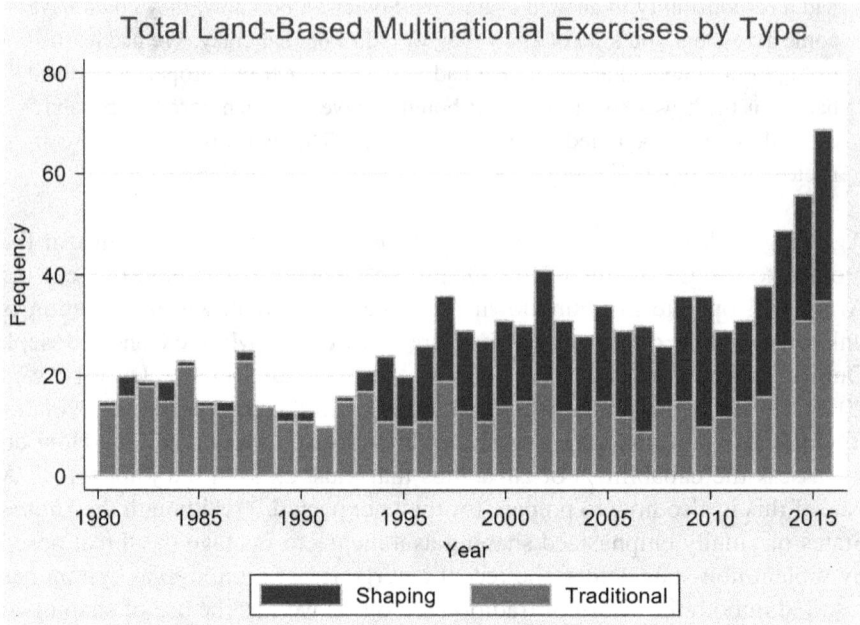

Figure 1.1   Number of Land-Based Multinational Military Exercises per Year Involving a Major Power, 1980–2016, by Exercise Type[22]

by types of allies: beginning in the early 1990s, major powers began engaging more non-allies than during the 1980s.[21] Yet exercises with non-allies create major opportunity costs, are oftentimes considered unnecessary or counter-productive by soldiers, and violate most military principles of secrecy and deception. The increased use of this common military tool, especially with non-allies, requires an explanation that this book seeks to provide.

   The figures underscore how multinational exercises have emerged as a prominent tool of military shaping. As opposed to merely prepare for combat or signal deterrence to an adversary, major powers use shaping exercises to proactively construct a more favorable environment. The case studies in the chapters that follow illustrate the four shaping logics through several major power-led multinational exercise programs. Chapter 4 explores the logic of attraction through the archetypal shaping exercise program—the US-led NATO Partnership for Peace—intended to recruit new partners for peacekeeping, promote democracy in post-communist Europe, and prepare select militaries for potential NATO membership. This chapter also highlights an initiative by the Chinese and India militaries since 2007—known as "Hand-in-Hand"—to reduce tensions along their shared ambiguous border. Chapter 5 investigates how Russia used Collective Security Treaty

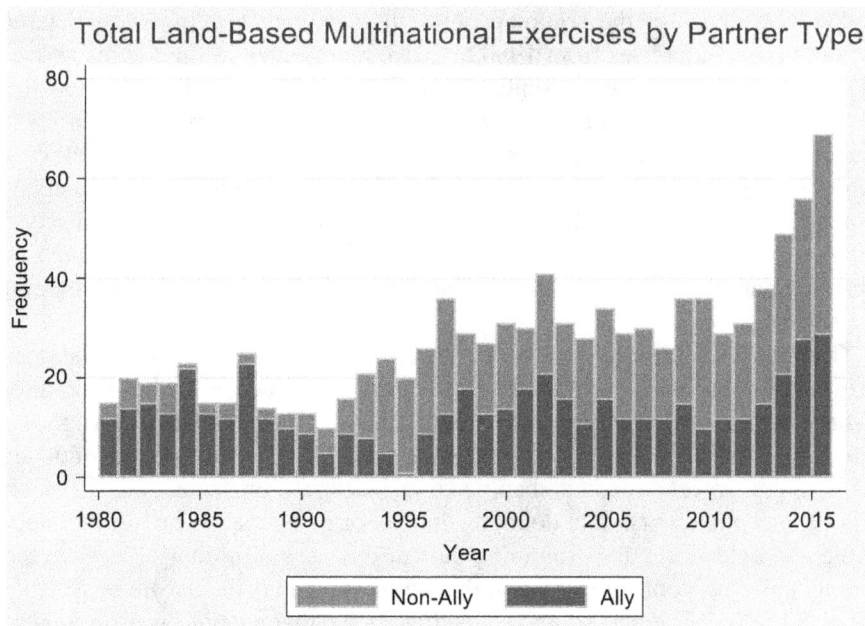

**Figure 1.2    Number of Land-Based Multinational Military Exercises per Year Involving a Major Power, Including Either Only Allies or at least One Non-Ally, 1980–2016**

Organization (CSTO) training events to socialize practices in bordering states to prevent political revolution in its near-abroad. The logic of delegation to pass the burden of responsibility is examined in chapter 6 through the British intervention and training program in Sierra Leone beginning in 2000. Finally, chapter 7 illustrates the logic of assurance through a US training event known as "Operation Dragoon Ride," which was intended to prevent Russia's sphere of influence from extending over a weary and uncertain European public.

## Contributions to Scholarship and Policy

Scholars, defense analysts, civilian and military practitioners, and those concerned with today's competitive international system would benefit from a broader understanding of why and how major powers use shaping to achieve their goals. This book builds on other important studies of the nontraditional use of military organizations by providing detailed case studies of shaping involving non-US major powers, such as China, India, Russia, and the United Kingdom.[23] In addition to the case studies, the appendix provides a more rigorous analysis of the argument through statistical tests of a new dataset of land-based exercises from 1980 to 2016, represented in the figures above. These statistical tests apply sentiment analysis of US military doctrine—the expressed "feeling" of uncertainty in army operational manuals—as a measure of strategic uncertainty. These tests are then expanded to include all current major powers. The results reveal that a rise in strategic uncertainty about threats and partners led all major powers to increase the number and scope of shaping exercises even when controlling for other explanations, such as military parochial interests, alliance interoperability, geography, and colonial or sovereign history.

This book also improves upon current theories of military power and doctrine prominent in the international relations and strategic studies literature, which largely imagine the military tool in the traditional sense of warfighting and coercion.[24] Moreover, by illustrating through case studies and statistics how major powers adapted shaping to an uncertain environment, this book challenges other works that doubt the impact of globalization on military doctrine and behavior.[25] By examining the various uses of military power in the context of other tools of statecraft, this book also enters the debate on the role of shaping in US grand strategy, making a case that shaping is a prominent tool for both active and restrained strategies.

## RESEARCH DESIGN AND BOOK OVERVIEW

In terms of methodology, this book offers two approaches to capture shaping in practice: qualitative case studies and quantitative tests. The purpose of the case studies is to illustrate both *why* these major powers chose shaping to achieve their goals (to reduce uncertainty), as well as *how* they used exercises to do so (through the four separate logics).[26] The cases were selected not only because they demonstrate the four different logics in action, but also to reveal how different types of major powers with various domestic systems, ideologies, and geographic positions reacted similarly to the same systemic forces. The cases were built from news reports, public affairs and other statements by national leaders, and several interviews with military officers and government officials by the author. The quantitative tests in the appendix offer a more rigorous political science test of the general argument: that the end of the Cold War marked a dramatic rise in strategic uncertainty, which resulted in major powers shifting from preparing for warfighting and coercing to shaping as the way to manage their security environments. These statistical tests employ sentiment analysis of US Army doctrine to gauge the impact of an organizational sense of uncertainty on the types of exercises conducted from 1980 to 2016, while controlling for alternative factors.

The next two chapters are dedicated to task of describing the emergence of shaping, while the others are designed to illustrate how shaping is carried out in practice. Chapter 2 explores the concepts of military power and statecraft more generally, situates shaping among the other ways of military statecraft (warfighting and coercing), and explains the three conditions under which shaping is more attractive to major powers. Chapter 3 traces the evolution of shaping from classical military strategy to a central component of US foreign policy, as well as the codification of the term in US military doctrine. This chapter also briefly discusses the operational and bureaucratic challenges of shaping given the overlap with other tools of statecraft.

Chapters 4 through 7 describe in more detail the four logics of shaping—attraction, socialization, delegation, and assurance—as well as provide one or two case studies of military exercise programs that illustrate the logics in practice. These case studies reveal how an increase in uncertainty about threats and partners led different major powers—the United States, China, India, Russia, and the United Kingdom—to employ shaping as an attempt to construct a more favorable environment. Chapter 8 concludes with a broader discussion of the significance of shaping by relating to theories of grand strategy, controversies over the "militarization of foreign policy," and the future of shaping in world politics. The following chapter begins the analysis by examining the diverse ways and unexpected sources of military statecraft.

# Chapter 2

# The Ways and Sources of Military Statecraft

Statecraft involves the use of various foreign policy tools to protect a state's interests, with security as the most vital. Statecraft emerged with the rise of large polities and the necessity to manage external relations: one historical study noted that the Roman Empire's rise required a more deliberate approach to foreign policy given its dangerous international environment.[1] The military instrument is one among several available to national leaders in pursuit of foreign policy goals, to include security. Scholars have found it useful to differentiate between these instruments using various frameworks, but the acronym "DIME"—representing diplomacy, information, military, and economics—is the most prevalent today.[2] By using the language of "instruments" or "tools" to describe these options, a common analogy emerges in which leaders select different devices for different types of foreign policy challenges. Generally speaking, diplomacy implies negotiations, treaties, agreements, and exchanges between national governments; information involves attempts to influence the perceptions and behaviors of foreign audiences through media such as print, television, and the internet; economic tools include the use of trade, assistance, and sanctions to attract or coerce; and the military appears to indicate the threat or use of violent force.

Yet the analogy of national instruments of power as "tools" suggests an assembly of statesmen huddled around a table, reaching into a toolbox to select the right hammer or screwdriver for a certain international problem. In an interview, former US chairman of the Joint Chiefs of Staff and Secretary of State Colin Powell bemoaned this model, noting that these tools are often interchangeable and complementary. As he argues, effective diplomacy often rests on the ability to use military force if necessary; his experience leads him to believe that national leaders pull out systems and combinations of tools to tackle difficult issues.[3] In fact, the overlap between tools is often more obvious than trying to imagine the tools in isolation. For example, when a country levies economic sanctions against another to prevent an atrocity—seemingly a role for the economic tool alone—one can imagine the complex orchestration of foreign ministry negotiations, financial sector policy compliance, information campaigns to convince allies into agreement, and the implicit (or explicit) threat of military force to cause an end to the undesirable behavior.

This unavoidable overlap in the tools of statecraft poses difficult challenges for state leaders: which combination of tools is appropriate for a certain international problem? Wars and interstate crises certainly require diplomacy and the military instrument, as these events conjure up images of massive aircraft carriers or armored tanks charging ahead in an assault or demonstration of power to intimidate an adversary. Yet this illustration belies the *other* ways in which countries employ military power to achieve their goals—especially as the international problem resembles less war and more peace—which often mimic the roles of diplomats, aid developers, and trade representatives. When the British army trains African soldiers to prevent rebellion, China sends its soldiers and medics on a humanitarian mission, and the United States invites cadets from Thailand to attend its military academies, it becomes obvious that the military tool extends beyond this conventional wisdom.

The purpose of this chapter is to better understand the three main ways of military statecraft—warfighting, coercing, and shaping—how they interrelate, and which types of power underly their logics. While warfighting and coercing comprise the most familiar tasks assigned to the military— "breaking" and "bending"—shaping is a rather surprising mission given the emphasis on "building" and its overlap with the other instruments of statecraft. These different logics vary in terms of how they apply power and the extent to which they share commonality with the other tools of statecraft. This chapter also describes the three systemic conditions that make shaping more attractive to policymakers: advances in defensive military technology, changes in the international distribution of power, and the consequences of globalization. The final portion of this chapter summarizes the overview of military statecraft to prepare for the next chapter's description of the evolution of shaping in strategy and US foreign policy.

## MILITARY POWER AND STATECRAFT

As noted in the introduction, military statecraft is a state's use of military means to achieve foreign policy ends. When state leaders and their subordinate organizations employ the means of national power to achieve political objectives (in cooperation or competition with other actors), they are engaging in *strategy*. That is, these actors attempt to achieve their goals by implementing the instruments of power at their disposal: sound strategy is the alignment of these "ends," "ways," and "means."[4] One could think of the military instruments or resources—the troops, tanks, ships, and planes—as the *means* of a particular strategy, while the logics—warfighting, coercing, and shaping—as the *ways*. In military planning, specific ways are often described as operational doctrine, concepts, or courses of action;[5] one could also describe ways as logics or mechanisms using common terms in political science.[6] The intersection of statecraft and power (described below) straddles both means and ways, as influence relies not just on material properties, but also how successfully they are implemented. Effective strategy not only draws on power, but also improves it. As Lawrence Freedman describes, strategy is the "art of creating power."[7]

In David Baldwin's seminal work on economic statecraft, he defines military statecraft as "influence attempts relying primarily on violence, weapons, or force," which nicely captures the conventional wisdom on the purpose of military organizations.[8] The most notable works in military power and doctrine also share this view of the value of military power. As the use of military power moves farther from the traditional role of warfighting, however, the overlap with the other instruments of statecraft—especially diplomacy and information—becomes more pronounced. Moreover, shaping relies on the effective use of both hard and soft power, which is unexpected and understudied in traditional theories of military power and doctrine. The sections below describe theories of military power and depict the surprising diversity of military statecraft available to national leaders.

## Power in International Relations

Any explanation of military power should begin with a discussion about what term "power" means when applied to international politics. A useful starting point is the simplified version Robert Dahl's definition of power: Actor A gets Actor B to do something Actor B wouldn't otherwise have done.[9] This definition, however, begs the question of how Actor A achieved this outcome. Simply by its material properties: resources such as its amount of wealth or size of its military? Or does the content and context of that relationship matter? David Baldwin distinguishes between these *property* and *relational* concepts of power: the former is concerned merely with each actor's possessions, while the latter requires knowledge of the relationship between the two.[10] The benefit of a property approach is the ability to easily measure and compare power; those actors with the most possessions will most likely prevail in causing an actor to change its behavior. At the same time, there are numerous instances of states with massive resources that are unable to achieve their goals in war or dispute. On the other hand, the relational approach observes the results of interactions between actors engaging in specific issue areas, which is useful when material comparisons are poor predictors of who "wins" during a dispute. The latter approach, however, is obviously limited by its ability to determine the outcome prior to the issue taking place.[11]

Most international relations theories define power in terms of material properties for reasons of convenience mentioned above. Overall gross domestic product (GDP) is one popular measure for material power, while others involve an aggregate of multiple indicators. For instance, the Correlates of War project began developing a dataset in 1972 that provides a numerical score for each state's "Composite Index of National Capabilities" (CINC), which is comprised of the following indicators: iron and steel production, military expenditures, military personnel, energy consumption, total population, and urban population.[12] Other scholars, such as Michael Beckley, have charged that any measures that rely on only the assets (such as overall GDP or population size) without taking into account the costs of providing welfare and security for a massive, impoverished population, severely inflates the power of certain countries.[13] Nevertheless, the idea that power is largely measured in terms of material capabilities is widely accepted, especially by those that work within the neorealist tradition.

*Soft Power*

However, other scholars note that a state's influence also rests on *soft power*; that is, the ability to persuade and attract through co-option rather than coercion or inducements. Instead of attempting to change another state's behavior through changing its cost-benefit calculation—through "carrots and sticks"—the possessor of soft power attempts to alter the other's underlying interests or preferences. As Joseph Nye explains, "Soft power rests on the ability to shape the preferences of others" through three main sources: culture, political values, and legitimacy in foreign policy.[14] Instead of forcing others to do what you want, soft power is getting others to *want* what you want. Nye notes elsewhere that military power rests primarily on *hard power*—through the threat or use of force—but also includes examples in which states leverage military soft power: for instance, by attempting to persuade locals to side with the government in a counterinsurgency campaign or delivering military assistance designed to attract partners.[15] This understanding of power acknowledges that overwhelming material capabilities and threats of force do not always lead to desired outcomes.

Although soft power is sometimes associated with the international relations traditions of liberalism and constructivism, several classical realists emphasize the importance of nonmaterial forms of power. E.H. Carr notes that a state's "power over opinion" rests on persuasion, the teaching of principles, and the use of propaganda to convince others of the legitimacy of one's cause.[16] Hans Morgenthau considered nonmaterial sources of power—a nation's quality of diplomacy, national morale, national character, and influence on opinion—as equally as important as weapons and wealth.[17] Although Arnold Wolfers separates the concept of power from influence—coercion vice benefits and persuasion—he admits that they are intertwined in practice and states must be effective in employing a mix of both to achieve their goals.[18]

The drawbacks in studying soft power, however, are similar to those that plague the relational approach to understanding power in general: that is, how to measure a country's soft power, as well as whether strategies that rely on soft power are "effective." As soft power rests on nonmaterial assets such as legitimacy, values, and culture, these sources are not only difficult to quantify, but are often not directly at the hands of a state government to manipulate. Nye originally offered several anecdotal metrics for soft power, such as levels of immigration, number of academic publications, enrollment in foreign universities, as well as public opinion polls that asked respondents to describe their views of the United States.[19] Carol Atkinson offered a more rigorous empirical test of the effect of student exchanges on the improvement of human rights in the target state.[20] More recently, the public consultancy firm Portland developed a "Soft Power Index" that combines polling with over 75 metrics along various categories of influence—digital, culture, enterprise, education, engagement, and government—to determine the top 30 soft power-wielding states.[21] Yet it is often difficult to observe the impact of these factors on specific state behavior, especially in the short term.[22] Despite these shortcomings, soft power is an essential and underrated component of military shaping, though the bulk of the literature on military power does not share this view.

## Military Power

Kenneth Waltz argues that in an international system without a central authority to protect states from one another, the possibility for war is always present; thus, military force is "*ultima ratio*" (last resort) of international politics.[23] The idea that war (or the threat of it) is a primary device of settling disputes places military power in a privileged domain of statecraft. Yet scholars of military statecraft often disagree about *which* aspect of force is most important in determining the outcome of violent interstate politics; that is, who will win in war. Stephen Biddle describes three theories of military power that are most prevalent in this debate: the size of military capabilities, the balance of military technology, or the type of tactical doctrine employed. Regarding size, John Mearsheimer measures state power in terms of military strength—the total number of troops, equipment, and weaponry a state possesses—and latent power—the amount of wealth and size of the population—which states can transform into military power when required.[24] Moreover, he argues that land armies are the most important indicator of military power, since ground troops are required to conquer and hold land: the ultimate goal for states in a world of scarce security.[25] Other scholars have argued instead that the balance of military technology, in addition to power, is necessary to understand military effectiveness: if weapon systems designed primarily for offensive operations outnumber those intended for defense, the success of attacks is more likely.[26] Scholars and military planners employ "net assessments" of the balance of technological superiority, as well as a host of other factors, when attempting to determine the potential outcomes of war.[27] Stephen Biddle occupies the third category by adding a nonmaterial factor to the calculus: instead of a preponderance of raw materials or advantages in technology, the ability for ground units to skillfully employ troops using the "modern system" of maneuver leads to victory.[28] There are, of course, other aspects not captured in these three perspectives that contribute to military power, such as strategic mobility, logistics, training, leadership, morale, intelligence, popular will, and alliances.[29]

Military power can also serve to *prevent* war through the demonstration of its ability to impose costs on an adversary. Robert Art differentiates between this "peaceful" use of military power from the "physical" (warfighting) use described above. By sustaining a strong military and signaling to adversaries the willingness to employ it, powerful states can prevent attacks from occurring in the first place.[30] For instance, the massive destructive capability of nuclear weapons has led to immense caution among state leaders when considering warfighting as a political option, which has led to what some scholars describe as a "nuclear peace" or a pacifying effect on great power war.[31] Another stabilizing element of military power is the ability to protect international commerce, enforce blockades of illegal weapon shipments, and assure allies. Barry Posen argues that the US command of the "global commons"—the air, sea, and space that belong to no single country—is the foundation of American military power and hegemony. Through its ever-present naval and air assets, as well as its geographic command structure and prepositioned stocks, the United States is able to defend shipping lanes and deter aggression throughout the world.[32] Some scholars have pointed out that force is "fungible" and can be useful in policy domains other than the military—for example, a strong, forward-deployed American military as a calming presence for oil markets and balance of payment deficits—yet the reliance on hard power to achieve these goals remains paramount.[33]

The major perspectives on military power above reveal how scholars view military power as synonymous with hard power. As Carol Atkinson notes, the use of the military to increase a state's soft power is surprising given the usual association of armed force to hard power.[34] Two of the tools of military statecraft described below—warfighting and coercing—certainly rely on hard power. Using this type of power to predict outcomes is enticing given the ease at which one can compare relative forces, technological superiority, and doctrine. Yet, the ability to attract, persuade, and change the preferences of others often relies on the effective use of soft power, which is one of the main goals of shaping. Because shaping sometimes involves the transferal of material possessions (such as military aid) to build the power of others, however, shaping relies on the effective use of both soft and hard powers to get other states to change their behavior or preferences.

## THE WAYS OF MILITARY STATECRAFT: WARFIGHTING, COERCING, AND SHAPING

To understand the diverse ways in which states use military power to achieve their goals, the many tools of military statecraft can be categorized into three general, overlapping categories: warfighting, coercing, and shaping.[35] These categories are overlapping because distinguishing them in practice—let alone theoretically—is often difficult and some types of military operations transcend single categories: for instance, wartime compellence straddles the first two, while deterrence spans the latter two.[36] However, in order for students and practitioners to truly understand the range of military statecraft, there is value in attempting to draw conceptual distinctions among these various logics. The categories can be situated along a continuum by the degree in which each instrument relies on violence to achieve its goals, the source of power employed, and the extent to which there is overlap with the other tools of statecraft (see figure 2.1). As one moves from left to right along the spectrum

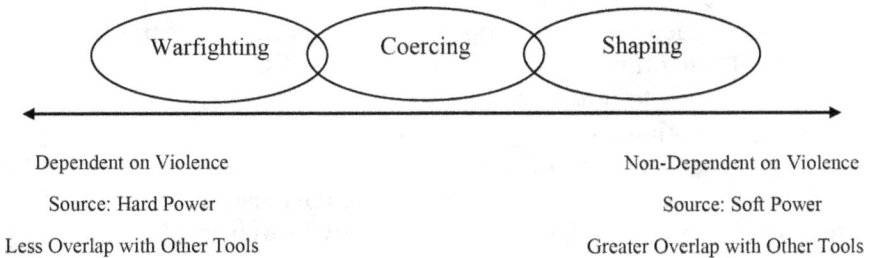

| Warfighting | Coercing | Shaping |

| Dependent on Violence | Non-Dependent on Violence |
| Source: Hard Power | Source: Soft Power |
| Less Overlap with Other Tools | Greater Overlap with Other Tools |

**Figure 2.1   *Ways of Military Statecraft, in Relation.***

(from warfighting to shaping), it appears that the role for the military becomes less traditional and thus, less expected. Each of the categories is described below, with a brief discussion to what degree the tools of statecraft overlap for each.[37]

## Warfighting: The Use of Violent Force

Warfighting, at its core, is the use of military organizations to overcome an adversary through violence to achieve a political objective. Renowned strategic theorist Carl von Clausewitz provides the hallmark definition, noting that the goal of war is to "compel an enemy to do our will" through physical force: in order to do so, an army must "render the enemy powerless."[38] He encourages us to imagine a "duel on a larger scale" or "a pair of wrestlers" attempting to prevent the opponent from resisting.[39] Warfighting is still politics, but through other means: "a policy conducted by fighting battles rather than by sending diplomatic notes."[40] Of course, the political goals of wars vary: total wars demand unconditional surrender from the adversary, while others are more limited by territory, objectives, or types of weapons employed.[41] American war aims against Japan and Germany during World War II are examples of the first, while the state's objectives during the Gulf War are representative of the second.

In US military doctrine, warfare is divided into two major categories: "traditional" and "irregular."[42] When waging traditional, interstate warfare, states employ their lethal forces for conquest or protection: that is, they can leverage military force *offensively* to seize territory or defeat enemy troops, or *defensively* to guard the same type of assets that an enemy seeks to capture.[43,44] Violence can be manipulated by or against non-state actors that employ asymmetric tactics with the goal of winning the loyalty of a population: what the US military labels "irregular warfare,"[45] or others have labeled "low intensity war" or "guerilla warfare."[46] States can employ their own irregular or "special" forces against both states and non-state actors in a counterterrorism or counterinsurgency campaign, the latter of which requires combat operations in addition to measures designed to win the population's support, such as restoring the government's legitimacy or essential services.[47] Governments can also leverage violence to initiate regime change or alleviate human suffering through interventions.

If one of the main goals of traditional diplomacy is to negotiate a settlement short of war, then warfighting is an activity that draws the greatest distinction between the diplomatic and military instruments.[48] The primary objective of all militaries is to be prepared to fight wars: though violent conflict is considered a last resort, war is sometimes necessary when states fail to reach a compromise through diplomacy.[49] Of course, diplomacy between warring states may continue throughout the course of the war in an attempt to end it; however, especially for total wars, this may not always be the case.

## Coercing: The Threat of Future Pain

The emergence of nuclear weapons and peacetime alliances following World War II gave rise to the prominence of the second tool of military statecraft, known as coercion. The goal of coercion is to convince an actor—be it state or non-state—to do something it does not want to do by manipulating costs, benefits, and risks.[50] As opposed to what Thomas Schelling labeled "brute force" (warfighting), military coercion is largely a state's *threat* of future pain, which can take the form of deterrence or compellence.[51] *Deterrence* is the attempt to convince an opponent, through overt or implicit threats, that the costs of invasion—or some other undesirable action—outweigh the potential benefits. There are two primary ways by which states persuade an adversary that an attack would be prohibitively costly: by signaling the strength and resolve to fend off an attack (deterrence by denial) or by threatening to retaliate after the attack (deterrence by punishment).[52] Patrick Morgan notes that states produce general deterrence by maintaining a "broad military capability" with the implied threat of pain to dissuade any would-be attacker, or they can signal immediate deterrence during a crisis with more overt threats of punishment if an attack was perceived to be imminent.[53] Most scholars agree that successful deterrence rests on the ability to communicate the capability and credibility (or resolve) to impose costs on the attacker, though they differ about whether a reputation for standing firm is a necessary component of credibility.[54]

While the goal of deterrence is to maintain the status quo, coercers can also *compel* others to alter their behavior by threatening, demonstrating, or using limited force. Compellence thus could involve the exercise of violent force *or* the threat of force with the goal of changing an adversary's undesirable behavior. Short of violence, states could mobilize troops as a costly signal to persuade an adversary to back down during a crisis;[55] they could also employ a naval blockade to impose unacceptable costs to force a concession from the target. States may also apply selective violence through strategic bombing to deny an adversary its military means or to punish its population to generate demands for surrender.[56] Robert Art and Kelly Greenhill distinguish between this "wartime compellence" and "coercive diplomacy": the former usually combines both violent force and economic sanctions, the latter of which takes place short of open warfare between two or more actors.[57] Compellence is not only an option for recognized governments: violent non-state actors

also rely on violent terrorist tactics—such as improvised explosives or suicide bombings—to convince a more powerful actor to end an occupation or
acquiesce more territory.[58] Although peacekeeping often relies on assurances
and inducements, effective peacekeeping relies to some degree on the threat
of force or pain: peace is only sustainable because the warring sides fear the
consequences of resuming arms against an international force.[59] As the first
UN Secretary General Dag Hammarskjold argued, "Peacekeeping is not a
soldier's job, but only a soldier can do it."[60]

Since coercion necessarily involves bargaining between two actors, the
overlap between the diplomatic and military domains becomes more prou-
nounced. However, some of the most prominent theories of coercion attempt
to differentiate the two realms in order to highlight the minimal costs of coercion as opposed to warfighting. For instance, Alexander George describes
coercive diplomacy as a "nonmilitary," defensive strategy that attempts to
prevent an adversary from changing the status quo. For George, the role of
force (if used at all) is secondary to the use of diplomacy: "if force is used at
all it is not part of conventional military strategy but rather a component of a
more complex political-diplomatic strategy for resolving a conflict of interests, which is why *coercive diplomacy* is an appropriate description."[61] Thus,
the instruments begin to overlap.

## Shaping: The Construction of a Favorable Environment

As a military activity that relies as much on soft power as hard power, shaping is the least expected role for the armed forces. In fact, the term "shaping"
is usually associated with the other tools of statecraft. In the first sentence of
Henry Kissinger's well-known tome on diplomacy, he notes that every century
seems to produce a great power that attempts to "*shape* the international system in accordance with its own values."[62] When Joseph Nye argues that "Soft
power rests on the ability to *shape* the preferences of others," he is largely
referring to the resources necessary for effective public diplomacy; that is,
efforts by governments to use information to attract and persuade the publics
of other countries.[63] As discussed in the following chapter, the expression
"shaping the international environment" actually emerged from economic policies developed during the Ronald Reagan administration. The ability for states
to manipulate their military instrument to attract and build rather than defeat
or compel seems, at first, counterintuitive. Yet, shaping through the armed
force has become more frequent in recent years and, as the final section below
reveals, may become one of the most prominent tools in the years to come.

Military shaping is the state's use of military organizations to cause its
environment to be more favorable by changing military relationships, the
characteristics of other militaries, or the behavior of allies. The goals of

shaping are to prevent threats from emerging but being prepared and maintaining an advantage in case dangers do arise. Major powers use shaping to proactively manage allies, friends, and adversaries in the hope to avoid the need for warfighting or costly coercion. Through the effective use of shaping, these powers hope to obviate the need to react under disadvantageous conditions in the future. Shaping can be used either to build or to maintain: that is, it can be leveraged to change the current environment (in terms of partners or their characteristics), or it can be used to maintain the status quo if the environment is already favorable. The overarching goal of shaping is to avoid crises, threats, and violence and, as recent US military operational manual explained, to keep "adversary activities within a desired state of cooperation and competition."[64] Shaping relies primarily on attraction, legitimacy, persuasion, and positive incentives and less on uses or threats of force. As Derek Reveron notes, shaping is "different in fundamental ways from warfighting. Shaping is about managing relationships, not command and control; it is about cooperation, not fighting; and it is about partnership, not dominance."[65]

Given shaping's focus on prevention, there is considerable overlap between the logics of shaping and the coercive logic of deterrence; however, there are also several differences worth noting. The targets of shaping are primarily partners and allies, while the targets of deterrence are adversaries; since shaping is about relationships, it is necessarily multilateral and cooperative, while deterrence is not. Moreover, shaping's primary focus is on precluding threats from emerging in the first place; if shaping is effective, there is little need to convince an adversary that the costs of unwanted behavior outweigh the benefits. At the same time, deterrence can be improved by shaping through the attraction or delegation of partners. As a 2008 US joint manual notes, the shaping and deterrence concepts are "distinct but mutually supporting."[66]

## LOGICS OF SHAPING: ATTRACTION, SOCIALIZATION, DELEGATION, AND ASSURANCE

In order to achieve the goals of shaping, major powers focus on two targets: the partner's characteristics or the partner's relationship with the major power. By *relationships* I refer to the status of relations between the partners: friendly, neutral, or adversarial. By *characteristics*, I refer to both the partner's combat power and the "role" partner's military serves for its society, such as an institution to inculcate national values, an armed force to defend its state from external and/or internal threats, or an organization that defends a certain regime or set of political interests.[67] States achieve the goals of shaping through four main logics: attraction, socialization, delegation, and assurance. To change characteristics such as the partner military's coercive power or practices, major powers reach for the logics of socialization and delegation; to manage relationships, major powers employ attraction and assurance. Yet these logics also vary by their reliance on soft power characteristics such as legitimacy, persuasion, and values: attraction and socialization rely heavily on these attributes, while assurance and delegation do not. Although the terms are sometimes used interchangeably, the US military's categories of operations into "military engagement" and "security cooperation" could be loosely applied to this distinction.[68] Figure 2.2 below graphically depicts the logics separated by these variables and chapters 4–7 describe each in more detail.

## Engagement Logics: Attraction and Socialization

The first two logics are similar in that they rely more on persuasion and values than the building or transferring of material capabilities. These logics can be considered "engagement" activities, which Evan Resnick defines as attempts to influence other states through the establishment and enhancement of contacts across diplomatic, military, economic, and cultural domains.[69] *Attraction* is a military's attempt to create new allies or coalition partners, detract from an adversarial alliance or coalition, or reassure a rival. Major powers use attraction to persuade neutral states into a defense-pact alliance or multinational coalition, as well as to drive a wedge between an adversary and any potential partners. The targets of attraction are certain domestic actors, such as politicians, military officers, or the general public, who are skeptical of becoming allies with the major power. Attraction oftentimes relies on public diplomacy to convince an uncertain public that security cooperation is beneficial, but this logic could also rely on offering the "stick" of greater security and military effectiveness.[70] Attraction to build trust with a potential

|  | | **Reliance on Soft Power** | |
|---|---|---|---|
|  | | High Reliance on Soft Power | Low Reliance on Soft Power |
|  | | "Military Engagement" | "Security Cooperation" |
| **Target of Shaping** | Relationship | *Attraction*<br>to change international alignment | *Assurance*<br>to reduce ally insecurity and manage its behavior |
|  | Partner Characteristics | *Socialization*<br>to transform values and practices | *Delegation*<br>to pass the burden |

**Figure 2.2　*Logics of Shaping.***

rival through increased contacts is similar to what Janice Gross Stein labels a strategy of "reassurance."[71] By cooperating with a rival, major powers hope to reduce tensions and the likelihood of inadvertent war.

*Socialization* is the use of military organizations to instill values, norms, or practices into other militaries through persuasion, teaching, and the building of habits.[72] The goal is to change the partner military's identity and role to one that is viewed more favorably by the major power. For instance, militaries may encourage values such as democracy or respect for human rights in other armies; conversely, militaries may value state security and teach others to protect autocratic regimes against violent protests. By creating more democracies or stable regimes, major powers hope to reduce a source of uncertainty in their environments. State leaders and policymakers leverage international exchanges, workshops, enrollment in military academies, and military training to impart values and roles. Although the logic of socialization overlaps with attraction—especially to spread democracy in the belief that democracies do not fight one another—the former is focused on transforming the values and character of the partner, while the latter is not.

## Security Cooperation Logics: Delegation and Assurance

The other side of shaping—which can be described as security cooperation—relies more on material power and threats of force than the mechanisms of engagement described above. *Delegation* is when major powers attempt to transition the responsibility of security to another military, against both state and non-state threats. Partner states that are unable to provide for their own protection suffer from what Derek Reveron describes as "security deficits," which the major power attempts to fill through weapons, training, and other forms of assistance.[73] Especially since 9/11, Western powers have attempted to build the coercive and administrative capacity of weaker states with the goal of creating more stability and preventing the emergence of terrorism and civil war. Additionally, major powers may send advisors, funding, and equipment to "pass the buck" to another major power in order to avoid the responsibility for deterring or fighting a powerful opponent.[74] Delegation shares the desire to relieve security deficits with the logic of assurance below; however, they differ in that delegation attempts to pass this burden to the partner, while assurance assumes the responsibility for it.

*Assurance* is a major power's attempt to reduce an ally's sense of vulnerability by promising protection through defense commitments and the forward presence of soldiers. Major powers may be concerned that without such signals of support, an ally may act in ways counter to the major power's interest by acting aggressively, developing a more independent foreign policy, or considering closer alignment with a rival. One way to limit this adverse behavior is to reduce the ally's insecurity by sending signals of commitment through treaties, troop deployments, arms transfers, and multinational exercises.[75] By promising protection, major powers hope to influence domestic opinion in favor of the patron and limit the severity of the security dilemma; that is, when one's states accumulation of security (via increases in weapons or territory) threatens another's.[76] By removing the necessity for the ally to build up its military strength to become threatening, the provider serves as a pacifying force for the region. Of course, there is substantial overlap between the concepts of deterrence and assurance, given that the latter involves the extension of security commitment to an ally. Yet assurance is different from the types of deterrence covered under the tool of coercion: not only is the logic of assurance primarily aimed at the *ally* rather than the adversary, but also because security commitments often dampen the fears of the *rival* that the ally will act aggressively. Robert Art argues that America's core alliance commitments and permanent stationing of soldiers in Europe, Asia, and the Persian Gulf "help keep the peace and dampen security competitions," through this logic.[77] In this sense, major powers manipulate alliance pacts to restrain aggressive allies as much as deter rivals, even during crises, by changing the bargaining behavior of their partners.

## SOURCES OF SHAPING: POWER, GLOBALIZATION, AND MILITARY TECHNOLOGY

As state leaders look to their arsenal of military instruments to improve their security, shaping becomes more appealing under certain conditions. Specifically, three systemic forces—that is, external forces that impose constraints and opportunities to all units or actors in a system[78]—make shaping more attractive: imbalances in the distribution of power, the consequences of globalization, and dominant defensive military technology. The first two forces determine the level of strategic uncertainty—that is, the degree to which friends and threats are clear—in which major powers must operate. Higher levels of uncertainty increase the incentives for shaping. When the balance of military technology favors the defense, shaping (as well as some forms of coercion) becomes more desirable. While the discussion below describes theoretically why these factors matter, the illustrative case study and the quantitative models in the appendix provide tests for the argument.

### Strategic Uncertainty

The concept of "uncertainty" in international relations is common but oftentimes underspecified. However, my use of uncertainty is most closely aligned with Knight's; that is, the inability to confidently assign probability values to outcomes or consequences. This understanding of uncertainty is separate from "risk": the potential for an undesirable outcome or event, which can often be assessed in terms of probability and severity.[79] When adversaries and allies are relatively known, traditional ways of military statecraft are useful for limiting the potential for failure or an undesirable outcome; that is, reducing risk. Major powers can signal capability and resolve to reduce the risk of invasion by an adversary; they may also signal commitment to assure an ally that the risk of abandonment is low. However, warfighting and coercion are less useful under high levels of strategic uncertainty in which threats and allies are relatively unknown. Especially given the unpredictable nature of non-state threats (such as terrorism, social protest movements, and transnational crime) as well as expansive potential locations of threats (e.g., failed states, overpopulated cities, impoverished regions), military planners are faced with a complex strategic environment. When militaries are uncertain about who is a *threat*, locations from which threats will appear, and who will be a *partner* against these threats, they are unable to properly plan for contingencies and develop an appropriate conventional doctrine to address this uncertainty. In this type of environment, planners rely on shaping.

## The Distribution of Power

The first factor that affects strategic uncertainty is the structure of the international system—that is, the distribution of capabilities among the great powers, also known as the "balance of power." When attempting to determine the balance, Hans Morgenthau observes, "The crowning uncertainty, however, lies in the fact that one cannot always be sure who are one's own allies and who are the opponent's."[80] Distributions are based on the number and size of great powers in the system: systems can be unipolar (one great power), bipolar (two great powers), or multipolar (more than two great powers). Different distributions influence the ability of major powers to identify friends and adversaries: in short, bipolar systems produce the lowest strategic uncertainty while unipolar systems create the highest.

According to Kenneth Waltz, bipolar systems are the most stable since there are only two great powers. Threats are obvious: because there are only two powers, the main adversary is the other power. Under bipolar systems, great powers attempt to attract allies; however, since these minor powers have little impact on the overall distribution of capabilities, great powers are not as concerned about which side the minor power is attracted.[81] The paradigmatic example of a bipolar system is the Cold War between the United States and Soviet Union: though both great powers constructed treaty alliances, the preponderance of power between the two meant that defection by an ally would not significantly affect the overall balance of power.

The stability and relative certainty of bipolar systems is contrasted with multipolar structures, which are more uncertain since more than two great powers dwell in the system. In this type of environment, great powers have difficulty locating which state is an adversary and which is a potential ally because these states are roughly the same size. For instance, Robert Jervis notes that Great Britain worried more about France than Germany following World War I in spite of the fact that Germany became the clear adversary during the war.[82] Moreover, major powers have the option of switching sides before or even during war: although Italy signed a mutual defense treaty with Austria and Germany prior World War I, not only did the country not meet this obligation and instead declared neutrality after the outbreak of war, Italy consequently joined the side of the opposition. In multipolar systems, great powers may also attempt to "pass the buck" and expect another to be responsible for checking an adversary; alliance politics between France and the United Kingdom against Germany in the 1930s illustrate this problem well.[83] Thus, threats and allies are more fluid in a multipolar system, which increases strategic uncertainty for military planners.

Finally, a structure can be unipolar, meaning that only one great power comprises a system. Scholars, even neorealists, disagree about the stability of unipolar systems. From one perspective, unipolar structures are both peaceful and durable since other states have little choice but to accept the domination by the single great power; any attempt at resistance would be futile.[84] Others take issue at both assertions. First, some doubt the longevity of unipolar systems: at some point, other powers should emerge to reestablish the balance that is necessary to protect themselves in an anarchic system.[85] Second, rather than producing peace, unipolar systems create incentives for conflict, either between the great power and other states or between other states. The type of war depends on the great power's grand strategy: offensive and defensive dominance results in war against vulnerable minor powers, while disengagement leads to fighting between other states.[86] Given the empirical record of the post-Cold War era (the only instance of unipolarity in modern history), the second camp seems more persuasive: although great power war in this environment is unlikely, unipolarity is both short-lived and conflict-prone as the unipole attempts to maintain its place in the system and minor powers fear its power. This lack of durability and instability results in the highest level of strategic uncertainty: both the unipole and other emerging powers struggle to identify both threats and allies in this highly uncertain system.

## Globalization

In addition to the international distribution of power, advances in communications and transportation technology also have an impact on the level of strategic uncertainty. As the ease of movement and coordination between goods, ideas, and people increases, so does the difficulty for great powers to predict threats and attract allies to reduce these threats. This increase in connectivity is known as globalization. Although several definitions exist, for my purpose globalization is essentially a set of forces that are felt by states, but produced and exploited by non-state actors.[87] Interstate trade and capital flows are important components of globalization, but are not the only aspects of this phenomenon. Especially in the "contemporary" age of globalization, advances in transportation, communication, and information technology have accelerated the speed at which humans can travel and interact apart from mere business transactions. As Kenneth Waltz points out, if we define and compare ages of globalization in terms of only trade and capital mobility, the 1990s appear to be similar to the 1910s.[88] However, when we consider the ability for people to share ideas, organize, plan, and move, the contemporary age is unprecedented. Advances in overland and sea shipping have increased the geographic dispersion of production and progress in information technology has made capital markets more efficient. Benign non-state actors, such as multinational corporations and nongovernmental organizations, benefit from the consequences of globalization such as the ability to connect, organize, and share ideas as well as resources with greater ease. Although these technological changes have decreased the incentives for territorial conquest among states,[89] violent non-state actors (such as insurgents, separatists, and terrorists) enjoy an increased ability to achieve their goals against states.

There are two categories of technology that increase the power of non-state actors vis-à-vis the state: communication and transportation. During the modern era of globalization (1850–1945), the use of telegram and telephones increased the opportunity for individuals to connect globally, yet the owners of phones were largely wealthy.[90] The contemporary wave involved faster communications: almost every individual on the earth owns a smartphone, which decrease the costs to communicate verbally and send information almost instantaneously. Advances in information technology, especially the internet, increase the opportunities for non-state actors to collaborate, plan, and organize operations, sometimes anonymously.[91] Violent non-state actors, such as Islamic State and Al Qaeda, not only harness the power of computers to coordinate attacks, they use the social media to encourage violence and recruit members to its cause.[92] Advances in transportation also make the identification of the location of threats more problematic. During the modern wave, steamships and railroads provided increased opportunities to move people and goods farther distances. However, progress in sea and air travel substantially decreased the time that individuals could cross oceans.[93]

Karl Mueller notes that globalization is a "paradox" for US national security: although Americans enjoys the benefits of open trade and access to new markets abroad, the transmission of American values and culture creates resentment against perceived imperialism and support for transnational terrorism.[94] Audrey Kurth Cronin agrees that globalization was both a cause and a consequence of radical terrorism: Al Qaeda resented the increased exposure to Western ideas in traditionally Muslim regions of the world, a consequence of the power of communications technology. Subsequently, Al Qaeda exploited another consequence of globalization—the advent of commercial aircraft—to respond and attack the United States.[95] The possibility for a few individuals from distant ends of the world to coordinate and conduct a large-scale attack on a major power's soil was largely a surprise to intelligence and military officials. Thus, the number of places and the number of potential actors (not just other states) from which threats may emanate increase, causing a problem for military planning.

Although globalization—at least in terms of economic openness and the spread of cultural values—is often associated with the United States, the ability for non-state groups to exploit technology and plan attacks against major powers is not limited to America or the West. The Islamic State claimed responsibility for the death of 224 people in a downed Russian commercial airplane in 2015,[96] while two suicide bombers killed 38 people in a Moscow subway in 2010.[97] By one count, 3,500 people have died in Russia from terrorist attacks since 1970.[98] China suffered a vehicle-born explosive attack in Beijing's Tiananmen Square in 2013,[99] while the attack on the Taj hotel in Mumbai in India killed 166 people.[100] As the ability for violent non-state actors to plan and coordinate attacks against major powers increases, so does the level of strategic uncertainty for military planners.

## Defensive Military Technology

The final factor that influences the selection of shaping is the balance of military technology; that is, whether the dominant military technology makes invasion the most cost-effective route to security. As described in the introduction, war is extremely costly in terms of both lives and treasure, even for "irregular" wars against far weaker non-state actors. According to one study, the post-9/11 wars have cost the United States about $5.4 trillion with an additional $1 trillion obligated to care for wounded veterans over the next several decades.[101] This economic cost is in addition to the hundreds of thousands of military and civilian deaths caused by the wars.[102] Yet, large scale war would impose even greater financial and human costs on states and certain types of military technology make conventional invasion riskier. As mentioned in the discussion on military power, one theory holds that as military technology favors the defense (by making attack more costly), war becomes less likely. The massive destructiveness of nuclear weapons has encouraged immense caution among national leaders against interstate war as the primary instrument of foreign policy crises.[103] Even technological advances in conventional weapons—such as surface-to-air missiles and sensors—over the last decade has made conquest more challenging and provided at least a marginal advantage to the defense.[104] Because shaping does not require the actual use of violent force, states will be attracted to this less costly option to achieve their goals. Several theories of "hybrid warfare" emphasize how this strategy is becoming more attractive due to the high normative and material costs of war. Alexander Lanozska defines this strategy as an approach in which states combine subversive tactics with conventional deterrence to achieve their goals short of open war by the major power.[105] Thus, as the state of contemporary military technology makes warfare appear more costly, shaping becomes more appealing.

## SUMMARY

This chapter provided a framework for understanding shaping in relation to other logics and ways of military statecraft. As leaders attempt to advance the national interest through effective statecraft, they choose among systems of instruments, often arranged in the DIME structure familiar to practitioners. Although the military tool is often conflated with warfighting and coercion, states leverage their militaries in diverse ways that may rely as much on soft power as hard power. The four logics of shaping—attraction, socialization, delegation, and assurance—vary in their targets and reliance on the attributes of soft power; yet they all are designed to prevent threats from emerging and build a more favorable environment through cooperation with other states, militaries, and publics. Several structural forces make shaping more attractive: when there is an imbalance in the distribution of international power, when the consequences of globalization increase the reach of non-state actors, and when the balance of military technology favors the defense. The first two sources make threats and allies less obvious, while the third increases the desire to avoid the costs of warfighting and violent compellence. Although this chapter's structure was largely theoretical, the following chapter paints a more detailed picture of shaping's emergence in military strategy and US foreign policy.

*Chapter 3*

# The Evolution and Challenges of Shaping

During an event hosted in Huntsville, Alabama in 2015, the commander of the US Army Training and Doctrine Command articulated the Army's new operating concept; that is, a description of how the land force anticipates it will compete in the future. He argued, "You're either winning or losing. We define winning as exploiting the initiative to get to a position of relative advantage." He continued, "You have to always be moving forward and repositioning yourself because the world has changed and poses very complex problems for us. A complex world has unknowns—it is unknowable and is constantly changing."[1] The document that captured this Army concept—entitled "Win in Complex World"—began with a foreword by the Army Chief of Staff General Ray Odierno: "The Army Operating Concept (AOC) describes how future Army forces will prevent conflict, shape the security environment, and win wars while operating as a part of our Joint Force and working with multiple partners."[2] This language may sound odd for an organization dedicated to warfighting and coercing, yet shaping would be no surprise to military thinkers over the centuries that emphasized the use of militaries to create advantage short of threats or violence.

Despite shaping's relatively recent emergence in military doctrine, the idea of states leveraging their armies to build a more favorable environment reaches back to the classical strategists on warfare. Often held in contrast to Clausewitz, the writings of Sun Tzu contain the seeds of shaping that would be exercised in statecraft for millennia. This chapter explores the practice of shaping and offers a detailed look at the emergence of this way of statecraft in US foreign policy and military doctrine. Historically, shaping was apparent in the use of military attachés to increase cooperation and intelligence collection, military and economic assistance to partner forces, and the training of foreign officers. Shaping is more common in environments in which strategic uncertainty is high—such as multipolar Europe—yet bipolar systems also incentivize certain logics of shaping, especially delegation.

After the Cold War, US foreign policy officials began to articulate ideas for how to create advantages in America's newfound primacy. The complexity of the threat environment required policymakers and military officers to reimagine how the military tool would be waged. The US military's discomfort with shaping is apparent in its variety of terms used to describe these activities over the last three decades, such as "Military Operations Other Than War (MOOTW)," "preventive defense," "engagement," "cooperative security," and "security cooperation." This chapter explores the evolution of shaping by examining US national strategy and "joint" doctrine—involving land, sea, air, and other branches of the military—over the last three decades. The chapter concludes by describing an inherent tension in the exercise of shaping: the fact that shaping involves substantial overlap with the diplomacy, information, and economics creates problems for governments in practice, given the fact that different agencies are responsible for these instruments.

## EARLY AND MODERN SHAPING

### Shaping in Classical and Modern Strategy

If warfighting is a tool of military statecraft most commonly associated with strategist Carl von Clausewitz, then the origins of shaping—and to a large extent, coercing—can be drawn from the writings of another well-known theorist of strategy: Sun Tzu ("Master Sun," or *Sun Zi* in certain translations). Although originally believed to be penned by a single author, scholars now agree that *The Art of War* was a compilation of multiple writers.[3] Though the authors' focus was on explaining methods warfighting, there are numerous references throughout the work of how statesmen and generals can subdue their enemy "without having to fight a battle."[4] Sun Tzu acknowledges the immense costs of war—the "great of affair of the state. The field of life and death"—and how engaging in prolonged violent battle is detrimental in terms of both lives and treasure.[5] Because of these potential losses, the preferred approach to defeating one's adversary is to first "stymie the enemy's plans" and "his alliances," before attacking "his troops" or, reluctantly, "his walled cities" when there is no other option.[6] As one scholar of Chinese strategy explains, "Thus in the *Art of War*, Sun Tzu treats warfare, from its preparation to execution and termination as first and foremost a contest of wisdom. Use of force is secondary."[7]

If warfighting is necessary, the authors emphasize the concept of *shi*— developing a favorable configuration of power or strategic advantage prior to battle—a term so important that it occurs fifteen times throughout the short book.[8] As Arthur Waldron explains, to husband precious resources, "configuration must be assessed with great precision, and the moment to expend force must be chosen with care." Thus, Sun Tzu's "ideal war is one in which the fighting diminishes to zero."[9] David Lai applies the analogy of board games to differentiate Sun Tzu's approach from that of Clausewitz: while the game of chess represents the latter with its use of direct force to eliminate adversaries, the millennia-old Chinese game of *go* to acquire territory by creating advantageous spheres of influence intersects with Sun Tzu's teachings. Given the different game designs, the use of military statecraft also varies: "As a prolonged and complex game, *go* players focus on building or creating rather than chess players' emphasis on removal and destruction."[10] Sun Tzu's writings have had an immense impact on contemporary military planning and strategy, and many of the tools of shaping are informed by the concerns outlined above.[11] Lawrence Freedman notes that *The Art of War* is a work of "statecraft as well as war," which reveals the substantial overlap between the diplomatic and military tools involved with shaping.[12]

In addition to Sun Tzu, strategies that involve shaping are also located in the works of British strategist B.H. Liddell Hart; the British military thinker even wrote a foreword for Samuel Griffiths' translation of *Art of War* in 1963.[13] Although charged by other scholars for excessive self-promotion and distorting history in his scholarship,[14] Hart's ideas are well known and his preference for avoiding warfighting calls for a focus on coercing and shaping, especially through his preferred policies of the "indirect approach" and "limited liability."[15] Revising his book on strategy after World War II, Hart was sensitive to the costs imposed by war, an aversion he adopted after suffering a poison gas attack in World War I. His revulsion toward the horrors of combat accelerated after the advent of atomic weapons, which promised the ability to kill hundreds of thousands of combatants and civilians.[16] After observing a North Atlantic Treaty Organization (NATO) table-topic exercise in 1955 simulating a devastating nuclear war between the alliance and the Soviet-led Warsaw Pact, he reportedly concluded, "Victory [had] lost its point."[17] Hart criticized Clausewitz for narrowing strategy down to "the pure utilization of battle, thus conveying the idea that battle is the only means to the strategical end."[18] Like Sun Tzu, for Hart victory can be attained by weakening the opponent through deception and misdirection, with the ultimate goal of reducing losses to lives and treasure.

Hart's broader view of military statecraft includes several elements of coercion and shaping, especially his encouragement of buck-passing to avoid losses. Although his book *Strategy* is focused on the warfighting strategy of exhaustion and psychological dislocation to compel the enemy to submit, he prefers to avoid decisive battles and favors coercion and deterrence. He

argues that instead of fighting costly battles against superior foes, governments would be wise to wait until the balance becomes more favorable by
attracting stronger allies. By distinguishing military strategy from *grand
strategy* (or "higher strategy") he contends that the latter incorporates a plan
for creating a sustainable peace after the war, which implies the importance
with which he places in constructing a favorable environment.[19] In a separate
work, he advocated fiercely for a British foreign policy of "limited liability"
in which Britain would restrain itself from committing to any European ally,
lest Britain be pulled into another continental war in which it would have
little to gain.[20] This policy envisioned that Britain would achieve its goals
indirectly through economic coercion, using its navy to seize its adversary's
colonial possessions, and delegate responsibility for a continental balance to
others—likely France—to minimize harm to itself.[21]

## Shaping in Practice in Multipolar and Bipolar Systems

Though the term "shaping" does not emerge in official foreign policy discussions until at least the end of the Cold War, shaping in practice—in addition
the theories described above—holds a long pedigree. Three of the most common historic shaping activities are the stationing of military attachés abroad,
providing training and financial assistance to other militaries, and using
education to socialize practices in foreign officers. One of the oldest forms of
shaping is the use of military attachés: liaison officers deployed to the capitals
of other nations to observe the military developments of other states, provide
advice to ambassadors, and cooperate with host militaries. Though the term
and diplomatic status of "attaché" was codified in the 1850s, the deployment
of military officers for political or diplomatic purposes can be dated back
to the Roman empire.[22] The practice of dispatching military officers abroad
to increase cooperation and collect intelligence became more common after
the Thirty Year's War and the dawn of the new state system and balance of
power. Napoleon Bonaparte ordered several of his generals to be diplomats
abroad and is credited by some to have designated the first officer to serve
in an official advisory capacity at a diplomatic mission in Vienna in 1806.[23]

Another common shaping activity is the use of military assistance and
advisers to help create stronger foreign militaries. Historical examples of
military assistance include French covert support to undermine the British in
the early years of the American Revolution, as well as the early experience
of Helmuth von Moltke—later the Prussian Chief of the General Staff—who
as a young captain advised the Sublime Porte in Turkey against Egypt.[24]
Another common shaping practice is the training of foreign officers through
military education. The UK's Imperial Defence College was established in
1922 to educate and develop officers from across its colonies to defend the

empire against internal and external threats; the French Ecole Supérieur de Guerre played a similar role.[25] The US military education system has hosted thousands of foreign officers, though it has been criticized for training would-be leaders of coups and authoritarian governments.[26]

As noted in the previous chapter, shaping—especially the logics of attraction, socialization, and delegation—is more common in environments in which strategic uncertainty is high: that is, when threats and allies are less obvious. Multipolar systems, in which there are more than two great powers in a system, result in an increase in strategic uncertainty since alliance options become more numerous and less firm. The rapidly changing alliance systems from the dawn of the Westphalian system to the end of World War II provided opportunities for great powers to use military shaping as a way to attract or disrupt alliances. Even Napoleon Bonaparte, well known for his warfighting prowess, integrated shaping into his statecraft to divide his opponents: by convincing Prussia into neutrality in 1805, he was better situated to defeat the allied Austrians and Russians through his impressive maneuver tactics.[27] Despite the reduced need to attract allies in bipolar systems, major powers often use delegation to compete with one another by providing assistance to proxies as was common during the Cold War. Below are two illustrations of shaping in multipolar and bipolar systems, while the appendix to this book provides a more systematic test of how a rise in strategic uncertainty results in an increase in the use of shaping activities.

### Shaping in Nineteenth Century Europe: The Franco-Russian Alliance

George Kennan's account of the emerging Franco-Russian defense pact in the 1890s—what he labeled the "fateful alliance" and major contributor to the outbreak of World War I—provides an apt illustration of shaping in a multipolar system. As the neutrality pact between Germany and Russia ended in 1890 (coinciding with Bismarck's retirement), French and Russian states-men were considering new partners that would increase their security in a fluid European system comprised of six great powers. Though both states shared a mutual interest in deterring German expansion and the French public largely supported a treaty with Russia, several obstacles to alliance forma-tion existed. For instance, Russian Foreign Minister Nikolai Giers feared that an alliance with France would open up adventurism from France in the Alsace-Lorraine and even his own country in the Balkans, as well as divide Europe into two "warring camps" leading to impending conflict.[28] Britain was considered a possible alliance candidate by both, though mutual suspi-cion precluded any agreements with Britain until the early 1900s. Moreover, the potential for a Franco-Russian Alliance was made more difficult by the divergent French and Russian domestic systems and state ideology: while the former symbolized the republican revolution, the latter represented one of Europe's most autocratic monarchies.[29] Other major powers feared the formation of this alliance and took actions to prevent it: after only three months of invading Paris in 1971, Prussian Chief of the General Staff Helmuth von Moltke described this potential alliance as the "most dangerous threat to the new German Empire."[30]

Yet in 1890, Russian Tsar Alexander III sent a personal invitation to a French military officer formerly assigned to the French embassy in Russia, General Raoul le Mouton de Boisdeffre, to attend the annual Russian maneuvers in Narva.[31] This set of military exercises also included German officers— as well as the Kaiser—and the inclusion of General Boisdeffre was viewed as a counterweight to the public's anticipation of a renewal of the Reinsurance Treaty. General Boisdeffre spent the several weeks meeting with Russian Chief of the General Staff General Nikolai Obruchev, other government officials, and even a personal meeting with the Tsar. Although specific accounts of the encounter with Alexander III are elusive, Kennan argues that after the meeting, the Tsar was "greatly reassured about the quality of a republican France as a possible partner in an alliance."[32] Additionally, a growing friendly relationship between General Boisdeffre and General Obruchev culminated in closer military cooperation between the two powers over the years. The importance of this personal military-to-military relationship cannot be understated, as Kennan argues: "Without this personal bond between the two men and without the collaboration that it made possible, it is hard to imagine how the Franco-Russian Alliance could ever been achieved."[33]

## Shaping during the Cold War

Shaping also occurs in environments of higher certainty, such as bipolar systems, though it holds a lower priority than the other military tools such as warfighting and coercing. As mentioned in the previous chapter, in bipolar systems alliances coalesce around the two great powers: uncertainty is relatively low given that threats are obvious (the other great power) and the overall balance of power would not fundamentally shift if one weaker ally defects to the other side. Given the mutual threat and the relatively fixed alliances, the great powers use their resources to prepare for warfighting and leverage deterrence and compellence against one another. The Cold War represents one of the few truly bipolar systems in history and illustrates how great powers focus their military statecraft on one another. Both superpowers planned for conventional war in Europe, evidenced by both strategic planning documents and the balance of forces that were prepared for an invasion through the Fulda Gap between East and West Germany.[34] Lawrence Freedman notes that great powers' military planning "all took place within a cold-war context, in which the enemy was both well known and substantial, and the problem to be solved was deterring and if necessary resisting aggression across the inner German border. The focus was therefore on a classic great power confrontation between large armies in the center of Europe."[35]

However, shaping is still useful in these environments, especially through the logics of delegation and assurance. During the Cold War, the United States and Soviet Union provided funding to allies and non-allied proxies in order to develop spheres of influence and prevent the ideological expansion of the other superpower, especially in the developing world.[36] US military assistance to South Vietnam to prevent the expansion of communist North Vietnam is illustrative of delegation in action. In the 1950s, the Eisenhower administration's "New Look" policy attempted to increase American security and conserve precious resources by relying on nuclear weapons to deter a conventional attack in Europe. Yet the administration began to fear not just Soviet conventional strength, but also "communist subversion" to compete with the West under the threshold of open war. According to William Rosenau, "The Eisenhower approach went beyond simply reacting to Soviet thrusts. Rather . . . the administration policy emphasized the proactive use of foreign aid, covert intelligence activities, and propaganda to keep Moscow off balance."[37] Southeast Asia became one of these covert battlegrounds and the US government began sending foreign aid, military officers, and even police advisors to develop the internal security forces and institutions of South Vietnam under a Military Assistance Advisory Group (MAAG). These programs were expanded under the John F. Kennedy administration to include a new Military Assistance Advisory Command (MACV) and the enlargement of modern Special Forces to train the South Vietnamese security forces against the guerilla tactics of the north.[38] In response, the Soviet Union provided military equipment such as jet fighters and missiles to the North, as well as trained its officers at Soviet military schools.[39]

The bipolar structure also gave way to two competing alliances led by the two superpowers: NATO and other US bilateral alliances on the one hand, and the Warsaw Pact on the other. The sprawling US alliance system in Europe and East Asia, reinforced by the presence of hundreds of thousands of American troops abroad, reassured allies and extended deterrence against its rival. The Soviet Union also stationed troops in the Warsaw Pact, though often through armed intervention to prevent the overthrow of the ally's ruling communist regime.[40] The emergence of nuclear deterrence by the mid-1950s increased the incentives to move away from warfighting and more toward coercing and shaping. Yet both the practice and articulation of shaping would accelerate as the Soviet Union fell and the United States entered a novel security environment following the end of the Cold War.

## SHAPING IN US FOREIGN POLICY
## AFTER THE COLD WAR

The story of the US focus on shaping its environment—primarily expressed in strategy documents and operational doctrine—begins in the late 1980s as policymakers looked to reinvent American power and manage a rapidly changing international system. The collapse of communist regimes, the consequences of globalization, and the rise of non-state threats forced American policymakers to conceptualize and articulate a need to proactively construct a favorable system instead of merely reacting to external forces. The section below describes how national-level security and defense strategy began to place shaping as a central focus, while the American military grappled with how to manage these nontraditional threats given its primary mission of warfighting.

### Shaping an Economic Environment

One of the earliest applications of the term "shaping" to describe US foreign policy initiatives began during the last few years of the Ronald Reagan administration. Instead of military doctrine or diplomacy, however, the expression was used to articulate international economic policy. In written testimony to the US Senate Committee on Finance in February 1987, US Treasury Secretary James H. Baker laid out the president's six goals for increasing US economic competitiveness, the last of which was "shaping the international economic environment."[41] The hearing was the final in a series entitled "Mastering the World Economy," designed to develop an international economic policy that answered two main questions: "What should be our international economic objectives as a nation?" and "How is our country going to earn its way in the new global economy that is upon us?"[42] The atmosphere among the committee members was that the United States was declining in terms of economic strength to its competitors, trade was stagnating, and the United States needed a new policy that could change the emerging international economic system in favor of US interests. As Senator Bob Dole remarked, "Now we must return to our rightful place in the world economic competition."[43]

To increase its competitive edge, the members argued that the United States needed to become more proactive internationally. The Committee Chairman Senator Lloyd Bentsen argued that for the US economy to flourish, "world trade must grow." He claimed that "our trading partners have to open their economies" and that the United States "must lead the world trading system."[44] Secretary Baker outlined the president's six-part strategy to increase American economic competitiveness, spanning initiatives from increasing human capital to reducing the budget deficit. However, the sixth part of the strategy, which involved the majority of the written testimony, was "shaping the international environment." Baker focused on the consequences of globalization for the US economy: how trade, capital flows, exchange rates were creating vulnerabilities for the US economy. In order to create foreign markets for US businesses, Baker suggested that the US strengthen economic cooperation with other advanced economies and aggressively pursue open markets through trade negotiations.[45] Baker's idea of a major power shaping the environment would become far more common following the unexpected fall of the Soviet Union and end of the Cold War.

## The Shaping "Moment" in the George H.W. Bush Administration

The opportunity for American policymakers to proactively influence the world around them was accelerated when the Soviet Union collapsed unexpectedly and the "unipolar moment" emerged. By early 1990, the George H. W. Bush administration was the at the helm of American foreign policy as major changes were underway within the Soviet Union: a rapidly declining economy, proclamations of arms and troop reductions, and destabilizing independence movements in the Soviet Republics and other Warsaw Pact states. As National Security Advisor Brent Scowcroft recalls, "The President made clear that he wanted to take charge of the agenda and try to shape events rather than be shaped by them."[46] Yet the rapid decline of the Soviet empire and America's newfound primacy's were met with other immediate crises—the reintegration of Germany, Iraq's invasion of Kuwait, and the growing violence in Southern Europe—which required the administration to develop a strategy to construct the environment to suit US interests and liberal values.[47] As Scowcroft writes in the postscript of his memoir with President George H.W. Bush, "We were suddenly in a unique position, without experience, without precedent, and standing alone at the height of power. It was, it is, an unparalleled situation in history, one which presents us with the rarest opportunity to *shape* the world and the deepest responsibility to do so wisely for the benefit of not just the United States but all nations."[48] In a speech to the Chicago Council on Foreign Relations, then-Secretary of State James H. Baker agreed: "Either we take hold of history or history will take hold of us."[49]

Yet translating this desire to create a more favorable environment into strategy documents become more elusive, even controversial. The 1992 *National Military Strategy* sought to imagine future competition by depicting a "spectrum of conventional conflict" that imagined military operations from peace to war: forward presence was the only nontraditional military tool to prevent crises from emerging.[50] The leaked 1992 draft version of the

Defense Planning Guidance—supervised by Undersecretary of Defense for Policy Paul Wolfowitz—was more expansive in terms of maintaining US troop presence abroad, promoting free markets and democracy, and preventing the emergence of rivals to US power, even among allies such as Japan and Germany.[51] The language of the document was noticeably unilateral and aggressive (the final version was softened by Lewis "Scooter" Libby, a Wolfowitz aide) yet, as Hal Brands points out, many of the themes from the planning document would be emphasized in speeches by key administration officials.[52] The US-led coalition to repel Iraqi aggression out of Kuwait, the hand of US policymakers in the reunification of Germany, and the decision to maintain and possibly expand NATO pointed to a new era of American leadership in international affairs.

## The Expansion of Shaping in the Clinton Administration

Because of the Bush administration's impressive foreign policy achievements, observers were surprised when he lost the 1992 election to a relatively inexperienced William Clinton. The former Arkansas governor's campaign strategy of focusing on the economy rang true with voters who grew tired of stagnant wages and a large budget deficit, and his extension of economic issues to international ones was natural. Yet critics charged that his sole focus on international trade and finance neglected the more important aspects of foreign policy, as Council on Foreign Relations president Leslie Gelb remarked: "A foreign economic policy is not a foreign policy and it is not a national security strategy."[53] Cold War-era government officials such as Henry Kissinger and Jeane Kirkpatrick accused the novice president of being too reactive to crises in Somalia, Haiti, and Bosnia without a grand strategy.[54] Reaction and crisis management appeared ad hoc and ill-conceived: the administration would need to find a way to get *ahead* of these issues rather than become victim to them.

Before his UN General Assembly speech in the fall of 1993, Clinton asked his National Security Advisor Anthony Lake to gather a group to determine a phrase that would capture Clinton's approach to foreign policy much like the renowned George Kennan's policy of "containment." Known as the "Kennan Sweepstakes," the team within the national security council debated different expressions to capture the general liberal approach of expanding the number of democracies, opening other states to free trade, and emphasizing the role of international institutions. With a belief that representative democratic governance and economic liberalization go hand in hand, Lake's team settled on the term "enlargement" to describe the goal of increasing the number of free-market democracies abroad.[55] They would combine this term with "engagement" in the 1995 National Security Strategy—appropriately entitled

*National Security Strategy of Engagement and Enlargement (NSS)*—to explain the new US strategic approach to a novel environment void of super-power rivalry but a seeming acceleration of non-state threats, such as ethnic wars, humanitarian crises, and rising terrorism.

The 1995 *NSS* emphasized many non-warfighting roles for the armed forces in addition to the traditional military functions of "deterring and defeating aggression." These activities included a credible overseas presence to deter conflict and underwrite regional stability, contribute to peacekeeping operations, provide advice and training to friendly governments, deliver humanitarian aid, and encourage democracy in post-communist and fragile states.[56] Specifically, the strategy called for the use of engagement to help transition the former Soviet Republics and Warsaw Pact members into market democracies.[57]

## Shaping Becomes the Focus of American National Security

US defense strategy in the 1990s adjusted to this new environment, attempting to translate national security goals to the military instrument of power. Defense policy underwent at least three major force structure reviews to determine the appropriate size of the four military services to implement. Importantly, these reviews took place during an environment of declining defense expenditures and troop reductions as the administration attempted to balance the budget and enjoy the "peace dividend" afforded to a single superpower. The 1993 Bottom-Up Review (BUR) focused on sizing the force structure to plan for two simultaneous "Major Theater Wars," as well as to plan for smaller contingencies and peace operations. The BUR departed from previous defense reviews with its greater emphasis on engagement; however, a RAND report found that the defense strategy and budget proposals under-estimated how frequent these peace operations would become.[58] Through four budget submissions, the BUR was implemented into defense policy from 1995 to 1998. The *1995 National Military Strategy* also applied the language of engagement to describe peacetime, non-warfighting activities such as military-to-military contacts, nation assistance, humanitarian operations, and peacekeeping.[59]

Clinton's reelection in 1996—with turnovers in the role of national security advisor and leadership of the Department of Defense—resulted in the release of new strategy documents in the first year of his second term. The year 1997 was a hallmark in the history of shaping in national and defense strategy, with three major US security documents emphasizing the concept as a central aspect of US strategy: the *NSS*, *Quadrennial Defense Review (QDR)*, and the *National Military Strategy (NMS)*. The first two documents—designed by the National Security Council and Department of Defense, respectively—were released in May of 1997, while the NMS—prepared by the Joint Chiefs of Staff—was published in September after incorporating the guidance from the first two.[60]

The 1997 *NSS* painted a picture of the contemporary security environment, which involved both the promise of greater international peace, economic openness, and democracy abroad, yet also the peril of numerous non-state threats: ethnic conflict, transnational crime, proliferation of weapons of mass destruction, and environmental damage.[61] To manage this complex environment, the national strategy called for an "Imperative of Engagement," an approach that eschewed isolationism in favor of active American leadership abroad to deter aggression, encourage democracy, open foreign markets, and help resolve international conflicts.[62] In order to implement this strategy and protect the first core interest of enhancing American security, the document identified three mechanisms: shaping the international environment, responding to crises and major wars, and preparing for an uncertain future.[63] The strategy document described the preventive logic of shaping, which applies all the instrument of power to increase American security: "When signs of potential conflict emerge, or potential threats appear, we undertake initiatives to prevent or reduce these threats."[64] Shaping was viewed as a way to obviate the need for "responding to crises" through coercion or war, which is why this logic was placed prior to the other two.

## Shaping Translates to Defense and Military Strategy

The 1997 *QDR* was the DoD's attempt to translate the *NSS* principles into decisions on force structure, acquisition, and modernization. The defense strategy largely reaffirmed many of the strategic principles in the 1993 BUR, including the need to structure for two major wars as well as prepare for smaller contingencies. Yet, the *QDR* developed a more detailed defense strategy that emphasized the "shape, respond, prepare" framework laid out by the *NSS*. The *QDR* reads: "A strategy of engagement presumes the United States will continue to exercise strong leadership in the international community, using all dimensions of its influence to shape the international security environment. This is particularly important to ensuring peace and stability in regions where the United States has vital or important interests and to broadening the community of free-market democracies."[65] Other goals of shaping were to "promote regional stability, prevent or reduce conflicts and threats, and deter aggression and coercion on a day-to-day basis" through the use of military activities such as forward stationed troops, military exercises, and officer exchanges.[66]

This central role for shaping was also translated into the 1997 *National Military Strategy*, released under the supervision of chairman of the Joint

Chiefs of Staff General John Shalikashvili, which depicted a similar approach by summarizing the three ways of the strategy: "shape, respond, prepare now." Although the military's primary focus would be on warfighting—as the chairman notes in his preface, *"we fight,"*—he also acknowledges that the military instrument of power would need to contribute to the grand strategy of engagement, "helping to shape the international environment in appropriate ways to bring about a more peaceful and stable world."[67] The strategy laid out the two main objectives for the armed forces: to "promote peace and stability," and, "when necessary, to defeat adversaries." Shaping would contribute to stability through deterrence, peacetime engagement, overseas presence, and even by encouraging democracy to "help keep some countries from becoming adversaries tomorrow."[68] Shaping was now a central focus of US strategy, yet translating these principles to military doctrine and practice would become far more difficult.

## SHAPING EMERGES IN US MILITARY
## OPERATIONAL DOCTRINE

The US military's evolution on thinking about shaping can be traced through the updates of its joint operational doctrine, which provides a sense of what military leaders believe are the most important characteristics of the security environment and for which types of operations the military should plan. Two sections within these operational manuals are salient in understanding how shaping relates to other types of operations over time: the "range of military operations" (referred to as ROMO) and the "phasing" construct for joint operations, which grew out of national strategy documents noted above in the early 1990s.[69] The former depicts the *types* of military operations in which the military may engage (spanning from peace to war), while the latter describes the *sequence* of these operations in an imaginary competitive relationship with an adversary. By observing the US military's range and phases of operations, a picture emerges in which an organization dedicated primarily to warfighting is adjusting to its requirement to engage in nontraditional, shaping activities. As Lauren Fish points out, the "Phase I" of early 1990s construct imagined an aggressor such as Iraq or North Korea invading another state. Yet by 2001, this phase was redesignated as "Deter/Engage" to express the desire to prevent war, and by 2006 a "Phase 0" emerged in which shaping attempts to prevent threats from emerging in the first place.[70] What begins in the early 1990s as a focus on leveraging precision technology to defeat state adversaries in potential war, by the end of the decade emerges more detailed guidance on how to shape the environment in America's favor.

## The Warfighting Focus

Despite the end of the Cold War and superpower rivalry, military operational planning during the 1990s was dominated by thinking on the impact of new technologies on future conventional war, what became known as the "Revolution in Military Affairs." According to Dmitry Adamsky, only by the early 1990s were US defense officials beginning to realize the disruptive potential of technological advancements that emerged in the 1970s and early 1980s, such as precision-guided munitions, computerized command-and-control systems, and improvements in intelligence, reconnaissance, and surveillance.[71] The emphasis on precision technology and operational concepts that leveraged network-centric warfare appeared confirmed by the overwhelming success of the US military against Iraq's relatively ill-equipped and backward forces during the Gulf War in 1991. Memoranda written by planners in the Department of Defense's Office of Net Assessment (ONA) began circulating to the broader defense community the need to incorporate the consequences of long-range fires and information technology in planning for future war.[72]

This thinking was enshrined in the US Joint Staff's Joint Vision 2010 (published in July 1996), which served as a "conceptual template" for how the American warfighting services—in tandem—would leverage this new technology and their innovative soldiers to achieve dominance across all domains of warfare.[73] The focus of the Joint Vision was clearly on warfighting and violent coercion: the only use of the term "shape" was to describe the role of precision engagement to set conditions for battle and protect the force (what I label "coercive shaping," described below); the term "peacetime engagement" was not used at all.[74]

### "Military Operations Other Than War"

This focus on precision warfighting against state militaries belied the challenges of addressing novel complex threats, which were accelerated by the collapse of the Soviet Union and its client states, as well as the destabilizing effects of globalization for weak states. In the preface to the first military strategy since the end of the Cold War, Chairman of the Joint Chiefs of Staff (CJCS) General Colin Powell wrote, "For most of the past 45 years the primary focus of our national military strategy has been containment of the Soviet Union and its communist ideology—we met that challenge successfully." Despite the triumph of this strategy, however, Powell warns: "Future threats to US interests are inherent in the uncertainty and instability of a rapidly changing world." Moreover, "But the real threat we now face is the threat of the unknown, the uncertain. The threat is instability and being unprepared to handle a crisis or war that no one predicted or expected."[75] Given the unique nature of the threat environment, the US military increased its use of nontraditional activities around the globe, though it struggled with how to define these types of operations. Although the first edition of the hallmark joint operational manual—*Joint Publication (JP) 3-0*—was not published until 1993,[76] even the US Army's Cold War operational manual—*Field Manual 100-5: Operations*—in 1982 and 1986 did not discuss how to use military power in non-warfighting ways.[77]

This discomfort by the military to prepare for non-warfighting activities is evident in the label applied. The 1993 edition of *JP 3-0* distinguished between two main military activities: "War" and "Military Operations Other than War" (MOOTW). The publication noted that MOOTW were focused on "deterring war and promoting peace," intended to "keep the day-to-day tensions between nations below the threshold of armed conflict," and desired to "maintain influence in foreign lands." Thus, MOOTW could be based on the threat of force (deterrence), the use of force (e.g., counterterrorism or peace enforcement), or no threat/use of force at all (e.g., nation assistance).[78] The document acknowledges that as a nontraditional military mission, MOOTW is not usually led by the military; therefore, combatant commanders should work with other agencies including the Department of State, Agriculture, and Commerce, as well as nongovernmental organizations such as the Red Cross.[79] Common MOOTW included arms control, counterterrorism, counterdrug operations, nation assistance, noncombatant evacuation operations, peace operations, and support to insurgencies.[80]

In the first publication of the operational manual dedicated solely to MOOTW, the idea that these were odd activities for militaries was obvious in the CJCS's introduction: "While we have historically focused on warfighting, our military profession is increasingly changing its focus to a complex array of military operations—other than war." He acknowledges the anticipated uneasiness with these operations when he notes, "Although the goals and endstates may not be crystal clear, you should spare no effort in planning and executing MOOTW."[81] The manual asserts that one of the defining characteristics of MOOTW is the extensive overlap between political objectives and military operations; thus, the manual urges commanders to fully understand the strategic nature of these operations and that oftentimes the military will not be the "lead" agency for these missions.[82] Given the highly political nature of MOOTW, the manual urges commanders to constantly assess the consequences of their tactical decisions on the political context. The next editions of the publication in 1995 and 2001 left this conceptualization largely unchanged, though the latter included additional types of MOOTW to the list of typical operations, such as consequence management, enforcement of exclusion zones, ensuring freedom of navigation, and shows of force.[83]

*The US Army and "Preventive Defense"*

Interestingly, it was the US Army that began envisioning an important role for shaping with its own version of the operating concept, Army Vision 2010. The document introduced the concept of "preventive defense," which laid out that "Through peacetime engagement, land forces are active and dominant players in the preventive defense activities ranging from nation building to military-to-military contacts." The focus on liberal values was apparent: "Through their presence, they provide a unique capability to impart American/democratic values as they interact with nations' armies and peoples to favorably shape the world environment and help keep potential dangers to our security from becoming full-blown threats."[84] What will become a doctrinal confusion (described below), the term shaping was primarily applied to preparing the battlespace for ground forces using weapons such as precision fires or tactics such as deception and feints, though the conclusion notes that the Army will most likely be called to shape the environment through "continuous contacts around the world."[85]

Despite the Army's growing adoption of shaping logics, joint doctrine also needed to align with the new 1997 *QDR* defense strategy of "shape, respond, prepare": thus, the Joint Staff's May 1997 "Concept for Future Joint Operations" (also published in May 1997) was the first major joint document that articulated the concept of shaping. In the forward, the doctrine writers note that "America's Armed Forces must be able to shape the strategic environment to prevent war, respond when deterrence fails, and begin now to prepare for an uncertain and challenging environment."[86] The doctrine adds that overseas presence have a "stabilizing effect" that allows for peacetime engagement to positively shape the environment.[87] However, the use of shaping was largely superficial, designed more to incorporate the language of the *QDR* and *NMS* rather provide operational guidance and details for shaping operations.

## After 9/11: From MOOTW to Shaping in the Mid-2000s

If the fall of the Soviet Union and end of the Cold War provided the impetus for military officers to imagine the military instrument differently, then the Al Qaeda terrorist attacks of September 11, 2001, solidified it. Although warfighting would remain the priority focus for the invasion of Afghanistan, there was a sense that military units need to get *ahead* of these problems in the future. The military began expressing its ideas for operations along a timeline in its 2001 publication of *JP 3-0* by laying out four sequential "phases" in which peace, war, and then peace again would take place, expressed in the following phases: (1) "deter/engage"; (2) "seize initiative";

(3) "decisive operations"; and (4) "transition."[88] However, military planners wanted to create an environment that would preclude threats from emerging. As the primary practitioners of operational shaping, military commanders at US Geographic Combatant Commands began to imagine the usefulness of this form of military statecraft. General Charles Wald, the deputy commander for US European Command (EUCOM) in the mid-2000s, described the need to develop a "Phase Zero" prior to combat operations in order to prevent the need for costly military intervention following a future terrorist attack. For him, the four-phase campaign model depicted in the pre-9/11 edition of *JP 3-0* was insufficient to properly shape the environment and "prevent conflicts from developing in the first place."[89] In order to obviate the need for costly warfighting, he described how European Command imagined Phase Zero as an opportunity for "building capacity in partner nations that enable them to be cooperative, trained, and prepared to help prevent or limit conflict." Instead of measuring victory in terms of enemy combatants killed during war, success would be determined by how many conflicts were avoided, which would save both American lives and treasure.[90] As another senior leader, General Anthony Zinni of Central Command (CENTCOM), noted about the purpose of shaping operations as proactive influence: "When I assumed command of CENTCOM and had the ability to choose between fighting fires or preventing them, I chose prevention. If there was any possible approach to making this a less crisis-prone, more secure and stable region, I wanted to try it through shaping operations."[91]

*Phase Zero: Shaping*

By 2006, this desire to prevent threats from emerging and preclude the need for warfighting was enshrined in two major joint military manuals: The Capstone Concept for Joint Operations (CCJO) and the 2006 edition of *JP 3-0*. The CCJO, published in August 2005, argued that "although the future joint force must maintain a focus on waging and winning our Nation's wars, it must also be capable of supporting national efforts to shape the environment to prevent conflict."[92] The concept explained that shaping operations "might be aimed at spreading democracy, creating an environment of peace, stability, or goodwill or even aimed at destabilizing a rogue regime."[93] The capstone concept described shaping as its own set of operations (or "Line of Effort"), apart from deterrence and warfighting, that would span the entire duration of operations before, during, and after combat operations.[94]

This understanding of shaping was then implemented in the update for the 2006 edition of *JP 3-0*, which expanded the phasing model by including a

Phase Zero as described by General Wald. Some of the goals of this phase were to "enhance international legitimacy," "gain multinational coopera-tion," "assure success by shaping perceptions and influencing the behavior of both adversaries and allies," as well as increase partner capability, assure operational access, and dissuade undesirable behavior through general deter-rence.[95] This edition deliberately discontinued the use of MOOTW in favor of disaggregating these types operations into two other groups of activities.[96] The version also extended the range of military operations by replacing the binary operational types "war" vs. "MOOTW" with three clusters of activi-ties, replacing MOOTW with the first two clusters: (1) military engagement, security cooperation, and deterrence; (2) crisis response and limited contin-gency operations; and (3) major operations and campaigns.[97] The inclusion of the word "shape" or "shaping" was generally dedicated to this first cluster to describe how Joint Force Commanders could influence their environments before combat operations were necessary.

Despite the introduction of shaping in strategy and doctrine, the use of non-traditional terms remained contentious. In a speech to the National Press Club in 2004, Under Secretary of Defense for Policy Doug Feith explained how Secretary of Defense Donald Rumsfeld wanted to "move beyond the rela-tively unfocused practice of 'engagement'—which sometimes amounted to little more than 'showing the flag' abroad."[98] Instead, Rumsfeld encouraged the combatant commanders to use the term "security cooperation" instead of "engagement" to emphasize how these efforts contributed to protecting America's vital interests.[99] Yet both terms are still defined and applied in cur-rent US military doctrine today, revealing further confusion about how best to describe these nontraditional activities.

## How the US Military Views Shaping Today

The doctrinal application of shaping has ebbed and flowed in US military doc-trine since the term was codified in the 2005 CCJO and 2006 *JP 3-0*. A 2008 joint concept introduced the term "cooperative security" to describe shaping operations, while the 2011 version of *JP 3-0* emphasized shaping as a means to prepare for potential warfighting by including the need to "set conditions" for future operations, a phrase that was retained in the 2018 update.[100] The joint phasing construct has also come under scrutiny: CJCS General Joe Dunford questioned the utility of a linear numbered-sequence construct, noting that it was ineffective in modeling competition that stops short of evolving into traditional war.[101] The Joint Staff subsequently removed the phasing construct in its planning doctrine, though retained it in *JP 3-0*.[102] General Dave Perkins, mentioned in the introduction, has advocated for understanding competition not as a linear progression from peace to war (and back to peace again), but as a circle of competition, conflict, and a return to competition. As he notes, "There is and always will be strategic competition."[103] The use of shaping has continued in joint doctrine, though the term has varied in its meaning.

Current US military usage of the term can be described in two ways: "non-coercive" and "coercive" shaping. The first aligns with how the term is used throughout this book, while the second is closer aligned to the logics of warfighting and coercing. At the level of strategy and higher level operations, shaping is often viewed in the first category: the non-warfighting use of force to construct a more favorable environment. Using the most recent version of *JP 3-0* as a guide, the category of military operations described as "military engagement, security cooperation, and deterrence" is viewed as the way to "establish, shape, maintain, and refine relations with other nations."[104] As mentioned in chapter 2, "military engagement" generally refers to the logics of attraction and socialization, while "security cooperation" overlaps with delegation and assurance.[105] Defense officials also apply security cooperation to describe programs, lines of budgeting and accounting, and offices (such as the Defense Security Cooperation Agency), yet the term often suffers from conceptual confusion as noted by several reports.[106]

Coercive shaping, by contrast, is an operation or tactic to support the main effort of a mission, such as preparatory fires to ensure the enemy is degraded before ground soldiers attack, or obscuring the enemy's observation of friendly forces.[107] In earlier doctrine, this task was often described as a "supporting" effort to increase the odds of success for the "main" effort in battle.[108] The purpose of coercive shaping is similar to the *prepare* logic described above, intended to set the conditions for future tactical success in combat. A recent article depicted shaping at the strategic level similarly, which was described as a coercive strategy to "complicate an adversary's calculus and target his strategic intentions, not just his forces. The objective is to create a sharp deterrent effect by removing the adversary leadership's sense of control of the crisis or conflict."[109] This type of shaping is more similar to coercion and especially military deception (MILDEC) in which one actor attempts to mislead and confuse the other, albeit with the intention to prevent an attack rather than improve one's own.[110] Despite the diverse use of terms to describe nontraditional military activities over the last three decades, shaping seems to be the most consistent.

## THE BUREAUCRATIC AND OPERATIONAL CHALLENGES OF SHAPING

The description of the evolution of shaping provided above indicates the uneasiness in which MOOTW were adopted by military officers given that these missions are often the purview of other agencies. As is clear from the previous chapter, shaping is a military approach that intersects significantly with other tools of statecraft, especially diplomacy and information. Because of this overlap, various departments and agencies must achieve a high level of coordination to ensure that the goals of shaping are achievable, what is often referred to as a "whole of government approach." In fact, the American military views shaping as the primary responsibility of departments that oversee the other instruments of power: as the most recent version of *JP 3-0* acknowledges, "Shaping activities are largely conducted through other interorganizational participants (e.g., [United States Government] departments and agencies, [Partner Nations]), with DOD in a supporting role."[111] Yet, by applying James Q. Wilson's seminal work on bureaucracy, it is clear that interagency coordination is remarkably difficult to achieve. Government bureaucracies are complicated organizations that often differ from private firms in terms of interests and objectives. In order to survive, bureaucracies attempt to define a critical task, seek autonomy to independently achieve this critical task, and defend their "turf" against external rivals.[112] Achieving these parochial interests oftentimes preclude cooperation and interdependence between two or more major government bureaucracies. For instance, within the US government, the Department of Defense is primarily responsible for the military instrument, while the Department of State is responsible for diplomacy and information. Since shaping involves a complex blend of these instruments, one can imagine the difficulty in requiring defense officials, military officers, diplomats, aid workers, and information specialists to agree on which tools to use, from which budgets these should derive, and how much to rely on one another for mission success.

As warfighting is another form of politics, there is, of course, overlap between the various instruments when a state engages in violent force. Yet history is replete with instances in which war planning was conducted without the effective oversight of civilian leaders. Barry Posen argues that because of military organizational and bureaucratic preferences for offensive doctrines, civilians are often forced to intervene to reintegrate military policy into grand strategy.[113] Jack Snyder argues that prior to World War I, European militaries imbued with a "cult of the offensive" were unchecked by civilian leaders, resulting in the onset of that devastating war.[114] After learning about a costly military offensive during the war, French Prime Minister Georges Clemenceau purportedly argued, "War is too serious a matter to entrust to military men."[115] Given the military's expertise and experience with war, the possibility for military planning to become the sole domain of the military is unsurprising. Yet, shaping, given the intersection between multiple instruments, involves such overlap that it would unimaginable for this way of statecraft to be "left to the generals."

Even some military officers view shaping as antithetical to the warrior ethos and a distraction from the primary missions of the armed forces. As opposed to offensive doctrines that allow militaries to instill a "warrior spirit" and aggressive initiative in its soldiers, shaping operations are oftentimes viewed by officers and troops as unnecessary, incompatible with the traditional role of the armed forces, or even counterproductive to the military's ability to wage large-scale war.[116] For instance, Morton Halperin's seminal work on bureaucratic politics and foreign policy notes that the US Army's organizational essence prefers ground combat to other peripheral roles, such as "Military Assistance Advisory Group (MAAG) missions, air defense, and the special Green Beret, Delta, or counterinsurgency forces"; in other words, shaping activities are considered "peripheral" to the US Army's core mission.[117] As shaping is a task that contrasts heavily with warfighting and is often under the purview of nonmilitary agencies, bureaucratic and operational challenges are sure to emerge.

## Shaping in AFRICOM

An illustration of the bureaucratic challenges of American shaping in practice is the creation of the most recent US Geographic Combatant Command, US Africa Command (AFRICOM). Despite attempts to uniquely design the command to fully integrate nonmilitary government officials into leadership positions—from agencies such as USAID and the Departments of State, Commerce and Treasury—the creation of the command in 2007 drew suspicion and even hostility from outside the Department of Defense.[118] As a Government Accountability Office report noted, US government and nongovernmental organizations were concerned that "AFRICOM could blur traditional boundaries between diplomacy, development, and defense," especially given the outsized budget of the military instrument.[119] Despite assurances by the AFRICOM Commander General William "Kip" Ward that "The U.S. military is not an instrument of first resort in providing humanitarian assistance but supports civilian relief agencies," criticism from outside the military grew. In testimony to the Senate Committee on Foreign Relations, Mark Malan, the head of peacekeeping at Refugees International, feared that because of the vast disparity in resources between the Departments of Defense and State, "[there is a] fear that AFRICOM will marginalize and/or subordinate long-term development goals to short term political and security imperatives."[120]

Derek Reveron describes other accounts of pushback by US lawmakers and State Department officials, including a retired US ambassador who argued, "We do not permit our military to train our own police and law enforcement personnel and do economic development work in the US," which challenges the assumption that the military should do so abroad.[121] Reveron also notes how attendees at a National Defense University conference about AFRICOM were concerned "that Africa Command risked becoming simply another competitor in the interagency race for scarce resources, and part of an improper trend in the militarization of US foreign aid."[122] The consequences of this overlap between the instruments of power—namely, the potential for a "militarization of foreign policy"—will be examined in more detail in the concluding chapter, but it is important here to understand how the nature of shaping creates problems for actual policy implementation.

## SUMMARY

Before the event in which General Perkins depicted the new Army operating concept (AOC) (described in the introduction), an article that transcribed an interview with the senior officer captured the essence of shaping nicely: "If a chessboard was ever an accurate analogy for the global security environment, the board has been upended. Tomorrow's Soldiers will play a different game."[123] This sentiment that militaries should anticipate and prepare for a different game—perhaps more *go* and less chess—is well founded in the classical works of Sun Tzu. Yet shaping's theoretical origins lie not only in the ancient Chinese text, but also in more modern interpretations by Western strategists such as B.H. Liddell Hart. The practice of shaping was common throughout history in the use of military diplomats, foreign assistance, and the education of foreign officers, though these military activities receive far less attention than battles or crises. However, the codification of shaping in US foreign policy and military doctrine emerged only after the end of the Cold War as leaders grappled with how to influence a complex environment. This chapter explored the story of shaping through US military concepts and manuals, revealing how difficult it was to define these activities. This chapter also considered the bureaucratic and operational challenges of shaping, given the unavoidable overlap with other tools of statecraft. The following chapter describes and illustrates the first logic of shaping used to change international alignment through persuasion and claims to legitimacy.

## Chapter 4

# Attraction

## *Shaping to Change International Alignment*

In 1995, at a remote base in the swamps of Louisiana, a journalist asked an Albanian Army officer about his recent experience training with American soldiers in a multinational exercise. He responded, "America, for us, has been the great enemy of the world . . . Now America is our best friend."[1] Three years later, an American noncommissioned officer participating in a different exercise in Uzbekistan remarked, "This is history being made . . . If you'd told me 10 years ago that we were going to have an exercise in what used to be the Soviet Union, I'd have told you you [sic] were crazy."[2] For soldiers who trained to prepare for conflict against their Cold War adversaries, conducting military exercises alongside those same former enemies would be surprising, if not absurd. Yet during these training events, soldiers from previously rival countries fired each other's weapons, maneuvered together, and simulated evacuating casualties as fellow comrades. These exercises were designed as part of the North Atlantic Treaty Organization's (NATO) Partnership for Peace (PfP) program, an initiative led by the United States to build positive relations with the former European communist states, attract participation for peacekeeping missions in Southern Europe, and prepare a few states for NATO membership.

NATO's PfP program illustrates the logic of attraction in practice: how a major power leverages increased personal contacts, persuasion, shared values, and claims to legitimacy to draw other states into closer military relationships. Attraction serves as a gravitational pull from a distant to a closer relationship: from adversarial, to neutral, friendly, or even allied. Through this mechanism, major powers attempt to create new partners and allies, disrupt adversarial alliances, or reassure rivals. As mentioned in chapter 2, major powers use attraction to convince the target state's military officers, government officials, or even its public that cooperation is beneficial for its national interest. If the major power and the target state are generally neutral, the major power may increase contacts to persuade this neutral state to join a traditional military alliance or a coalition for a humanitarian mission. If the two states are current or former rivals, the major power could use attraction to reduce tensions by reassuring the competitor of its benign security-seeking intentions, or to prevent the rival from joining a future adversarial coalition. This chapter provides in-depth descriptions of the logic below and illustrates these mechanisms through two case studies: first, NATO's PfP as introduced above, and second, India and China's "Hand-In-Hand" exercise program, an initiative by two bordering major power rivals to reassure one another of their security-seeking intentions.

## ATTRACTION AND ALLIANCE POLITICS

### Recruiting New Allies and Partners Under Uncertainty

The first purpose of attraction is the attempt to build new alliances or coalitions. Major powers often seek alliances—that is, security commitments to come to the aid of the other in case of attack—with others to balance against and deter what they perceive as the greatest threat.[3] Major powers have good reason to seek defense pacts: studies reveal that defensive alliances are more likely to deter both threats and attacks from potential challengers.[4] Although under certain conditions alignment decisions are obvious, states sometimes fail to form effective balances due to misperception or domestic reasons, as was the case for Britain and France against Nazi Germany in the 1930s.[5] Especially in multipolar systems, great powers become more uncertain about which "side" another state will support in the event of war.[6] Thus, attraction is a tool by which states use their militaries to cooperate and draw potential allies closer. Even when considering employing force against non-great powers or for humanitarian purposes, there are both practical and normative incentives to assemble a coalition: partners provide legitimacy and, as long as operational and threat time horizons allow, beneficial resources for military operations.[7] Since interventions are costly and usually do not pose a threat to the partners' core national interests—especially when conducted for humanitarian reasons—major powers usually convince partners to join the mission in order to share the burden with others.

To attract new allies and partners, major powers increase contacts through interactions such as high-level military officer visits, port calls, education programs, security assistance, or multinational exercises. These interactions are intended to convince not only reluctant government officials and military officers, but also the general public, which may grow skeptical of increased cooperation with the major power. In this sense, attraction employs public diplomacy to attract and persuade the citizens of the other country who may otherwise oppose the warming relationship. For a historical example, chapter 3 described an anecdote of how military officers helped develop the Franco-Russian Alliance in the early 1890s. Another crucial development in this relationship was when the French navy expanded its campaign for a Franco-Russian alliance by dispatching a squad of French ships for a port visit at Russia's Cronstadt base in July 1891. The French officers aboard the vessels were met by jubilant crowds, fine dining with Russian aristocracy, and even the singing of the French hymn "Marseillaise" by the Tsar, a marching song that George Kennan points out "a hundred years before, had beheaded a king."[8] Cultural activities by both the French and the Russians to showcase their cooperation and expose one another to their societies were clear attempts at attraction.

Since public diplomacy largely relies on soft power, the military applies tools such as persuasion, attraction, agenda-setting, and serving as a role model rather than by leveraging threats and payments.[9] As Carol Atkinson notes, the US military frequently employs public diplomacy by inviting foreign officers to attend its military schools in order to not only expose them to democratic values (which falls in line more with the socialization logic in the following chapter), but also to build friendships and networks between senior military leaders that could be leveraged in the future.[10] The American military is genuinely concerned with how its image and legitimacy affect its ability to develop relationships, which is apparent in its most comprehensive manual on shaping to date. The 2008 Joint Operating Concept provides a five-step plan for developing relationships with new partners, first by establishing informal contact and building confidence through limited gestures, then by encouraging partners to view their interests "in a different light" and nudge the partner toward cooperation.[11] The manual calls on commanders to strengthen their units' security posture abroad, which is supported by the "legitimacy, image, influence, and popular support of the command and the United States as a whole."[12] The doctrine instructs regional commanders to establish an identity for America's forward presence—such as "protector," "advocate for international cooperation," or "preserver of the human condition"—instead of allowing its role to be defined as an "occupier" or "neo-imperialist" by the adversary. The manual notes that relationships and forward presence improve the odds of gaining operational access during a crisis, a shaping goal that is further explained in chapter 7.[13] Although the United States employs the most well-known attraction programs, other major powers are also increasing their use of this tool, discussed in more detail below.

## Managing Opposing Alliances and Rivals

In addition to building new security commitments or coalitions, major powers also manipulate attraction to disrupt adversarial alliances by drawing in one of the opposing states. When a major power fears that an adversarial coalition is in the making, attraction serves as a tool to break up this alliance. As Sun Tzu urges, "When [the enemy] is united, divide him . . . Sometimes drive a wedge between a sovereign and his ministers; on other occasions separate his allies from him. Make them mutually suspicious so that they drift apart. Then you can plot against them."[14] Timothy Crawford labels these types of logics "wedging strategies" that are intended to separate opponents that are currently in an alliance or prevent the relationship from emerging in the first place. Major powers could employ "dealignment" to encourage one of the opponents into neutrality, or "prealignment" to discourage a neutral state from joining an adversary's alliance.[15] Although Crawford focuses on inducements such as concessions or endorsements of the target's territorial claims, the logic can extend to efforts to attract others through soft power.

The use of wedging strategies to draw one rival closer is similar to a policy of reassurance, which Janice Gross Stein defines as a set of strategies intended to reduce the risk of miscalculation or war between adversaries. Through exercising restraint, developing norms of competition, making irrevocable commitments, or creating security regimes that encourage reciprocity and transparency, rivals rely on cooperation rather than the manipulation of threats to protect themselves against one another.[16] These types of reassurance strategies sometimes require sending "costly signals"—such as removing troops along a border to reduce a threatening posture—or increasing transparency by announcing in advance the size and duration of a large-scale military exercise, what is known as a Confidence and Security Building-Measure (CSBM).[17] Strategies to reassure rivals do not rest solely on material capabilities, however. Stacie Goddard notes how rising powers—even Bismarck's Prussia—often use rhetoric and legitimation strategies to justify that their behavior fits within the existing norms and rules of the international system.[18] Other attempts at reducing tensions rely on changing perceptions and social relations to create zones of stable peace through increased diplomatic contacts between two rivals, especially among those that share similar cultures or domestic social orders.[19]

A related concept to reassurance is *dissuasion* in which the sender of deterrent signals offers not just threats but also inducements to better persuade the target to avoid an unwanted course of action. A team at RAND describes this strategy as a broader approach to deterrence that attempts to avoid spirals of mistrust that may result from a threatening posture intended to deter: a classic intensification of the security dilemma.[20] Effective deterrence requires not only communicating a credible threat against a target state, but also that the sender will refrain from fulfilling this threat if the target complies. This definition of reassurance is the flip side of deterrence, yet it emphasizes the security rewards involved in complying with demands.[21]

## Chinese Attraction Through "Friendship" Exercises

Although the United States has maintained the longest-standing attraction exercise programs—through NATO's PfP but also several exercise programs with Asian allies and partners—China's increasing use of "Friendship" military exercises since the early 2000s demonstrates the various attraction logics by an emerging power. China conducts annual exercises with most of its neighbors, either through the multilateral Security Cooperation Organization (SCO) or through other bilateral exercise programs. Among these attraction initiatives, two stand out. First is China's "Hand-in-Hand" exercise program with the Indian army, which is explored in a case study below. The second is the potential attempt to drive a wedge between the United States and one of its Asian allies: Thailand. The United States and Thailand began an exercise program in 1982 known as "Cobra Gold" that now includes several other militaries such Japan, South Korea, Indonesia, Malaysia, and Singapore. In addition to conducting maneuvers, US soldiers also engage in civic action projects, such as medical visits to local families and even the construction of schools.[22]

China's military cooperation with Thailand expanded in the mid-2000s, just before the Thai military seized power from the civilian government. The first major Chinese-Thai exercise took place in 2005, which simulated a joint search and rescue mission, and military officers began planning for more exercises in the future.[23] After a military coup in September 2006, the United States reduced the size of the Cobra Gold exercise in May 2007, while Chinese and Thai officials signed an agreement to boost military cooperation including a second exercise in July 2007 involving training with special forces against a simulated drug-trafficking organization.[24] In 2009, China invited Thailand to begin a new exercise program designed similarly to the US-Thai Cobra Gold program. Thai defense officials acknowledged how the small exercises—involving only several hundred soldiers—were designed to accelerate a partnership as one Thai defense official explained: "This will be the first step as Thailand and the US took more than 20 years to develop their joint exercise to the Cobra Gold scale."[25] China offered to pay for Thai participation, but since the exercise was small, the Thai government insisted on providing its own resources.[26] Thai officials realized how the United States would view this growing military relationship with skepticism, which is why US officers were invited as observers.[27] The section below describes how attraction—by China as well as other major powers—is possible through cooperative training events by increasing interoperability and personal relationships.


## EXERCISES TO RECRUIT PARTNERS
## AND MANAGE RIVALS

### Recruiting New Allies and Partners

Military exercises serve as a useful attraction tool because in addition to increasing interoperability—that is, the ability for two or more military forces to execute each other's doctrine, conduct joint planning, and ensure that technologies are compatible—these exercises offer the opportunity to build relationships at the soldier and senior officer level.[28] Multinational training events brings soldiers together, become familiar with one another, and serve as a symbol of positive military relations for those who decide to deploy troops abroad: governments and their publics. As these exercises are largely symbolic, they include few troops—usually about 100 to 500 total—and involve many opportunities for soldiers from different countries to interact on a friendly, personal level. Given the small number of soldiers involved, the events are sometimes "scripted" in that there is little battlefield realism to the scenario; instead, they are designed to demonstrate "solidarity" among partners and can be understood as "symbolic flag-waving."[29] The adherence to strict, unrealistic training scenarios makes these types of exercises seem "nonmeaningful" and "unnatural" as compared to large-scale maneuvers.[30]

In addition to building friendly relations between military officers and soldiers, major powers leverage these types of exercises to persuade skeptical government officials and positively affect public opinion. This aspect of attraction is essentially public diplomacy: the attempt to promote a positive image of one's country to attract and persuade the publics of other countries.[31] For instance, one attempt to reduce hostility and build cooperation between former adversaries occurred between the United States and Russia in the mid-1990s. Russia hosted US Army soldiers for the first time at a military base near the Ural Mountains in 1994. The exercise was planned to be small in scale and focused on peacekeeping tasks. In the run up to the event, however, anti-Western sentiment from ultranationalists in the Russian parliament grew to such an extent that US Senators proposed moving the exercise to the United States to rescue the cooperative initiative. Nevertheless, Russian foreign minister, Andrei Kozyrev, insisted that the exercise remain in Russia to demonstrate the fledgling power's commitment to international security, so the exercise took place in October.[32] The training event was repeated in 1995 at Fort Riley, Kansas, which marked the first time that Russian soldiers were invited to train in the United States. Some locals were skeptical, as one told a reporter: "The Russians being a recent enemy, I am a little leery—don't bring them in too close." Yet others favored the exercise as a positive step toward peaceful relations.[33] One participating Russian military officer remarked: "I never expected to take part in such a historic event . . . I think the more our armies get training like this, the easier it will be for us to settle our problems without military force."[34] A dispute between the United States and Russia over American bombing in Bosnia almost derailed the exercise, yet military officers and government officials insisted that it remain.[35] These exercises reveal how both Russian and American government officials and military officers attempted to highlight the benefits of cooperation while reassuring weary publics and lawmakers.

Although more common after the Cold War, the United States and Soviet Union used attraction through exercises to achieve greater military cooperation with partners: the biannual US-Egypt "Bright Star" exercise program was largely an attempt by the United States to strengthen ties to Egypt not only to continue to maintain peace with Israel, but also as a counter to Soviet influence in the region.[36] Conversely, the Soviet Union extended beyond the Warsaw Pact in an exercise with Syria in 1981 to maintain tight military relations and naval bases with the non-ally.[37] After the Cold War, the United States and European powers attempted to attract and prepare former Warsaw Pact and Soviet countries for eventual NATO membership or to practice for peacekeeping missions. India also leverages attraction through exercise programs such as the "SAMPRITI" and "SHAKTI" training events "to develop good relations" with Bangladesh and France, respectively.[38]

## Managing Rivals Through Reassurance

Exercises may also be intended to reduce tensions between current major power rivals and prevent the onset of inadvertent war. They achieve this by demonstrating a focus on non-state threats, usually terrorism or transnational crime, and creating opportunities for soldiers from rival armies to view each other as comrades. Since all military exercise scenarios require an "enemy" to fight, planners create a third-party adversary, such as insurgents or even natural disasters, that is the focus of the soldiers' training. By providing opportunities for rival soldiers to view each other as fellow troops, major powers hope that as these soldiers advance throughout their careers, they will perceive each other's need for security as legitimate and within the bounds of responsible competition. By changing perceptions of soldier attitudes toward each other, major powers expect that their troops are able to overcome the assumption that all military behavior from a rival is hostile; by not assuming the worst, officers and soldiers may be able to manage small crises and prevent escalation into open war.

Both of these mechanisms are intended to change perceptions between rival militaries to prevent future small crises from conflagrating into open conflict. For instance, when rival troops come in contact in the ocean, along a border, or in the skies, these soldiers may better understand each other's complex environment and need for security and, thus, not assume these military actions are necessarily hostile. Instead, this military behavior would be viewed as largely defensive in nature, allowing lower-level units to reduce the risk of large-scale war. For example, when surface ships pass each other in the ocean, a crisis may ensue if actions appear threatening. If troops and their superiors automatically assume the rival action is hostile, the crisis may escalate; troops and their superiors may decide to conduct threatening maneuvers, mass more units, or even fire weapons as a warning to their rivals. Military leaders fear that this scenario is possible especially in the South China Sea, where both China and the United States —along with Brunei, Malaysia, the Philippines, Taiwan, and Vietnam—conduct consistent patrols.[39] Rivals that share a border (or whose allies share a border) also experience troop interactions that may result in standoffs, as is common between China and India. Major powers hope that if a crisis occurs between units at the small-unit level, the soldiers, or their superiors, are able to de-escalate the crisis because they better understand each other as humans who desire to provide security for their country.

The two case studies below demonstrate how major powers use multinational exercises to entice new partners and reduce tensions with rivals through personal contacts, the emphasis on shared values or culture, and claims to legitimacy and benign intentions. NATO PfP is one of the most well-known attraction exercise programs intended to recruit new allies and partners, as well as reduce tensions with former communist states. On the other hand, the case of Sino-Indian "Hand-in-Hand" exercises reveals how even non-Western, non-liberal powers manipulate attraction to achieve their objectives. As mentioned in chapter 2, although determining the effectiveness of shaping is difficult, I briefly assess how effective these programs were in achieving their goals following the case studies.

## CASE STUDY I: NATO'S PARTNERSHIP FOR PEACE

As mentioned above, one of the most well-known and expansive exercise programs is NATO's PfP developed in the early 1990s, which served as both political and military initiatives designed to groom partners for NATO membership, as well as to generate support for potential peacekeeping missions in response to the ethnic wars in the Balkans. The main political goals of PfP were to demonstrate NATO's commitment to potential members—notably Poland, Hungary, and the Czech Republic—as well as build diplomatic support for possible multilateral operations. Although some US and NATO officials preferred offering NATO membership to former communist states, PfP was viewed as an acceptable compromise to preclude antagonizing a reforming Russia. The specific mechanisms by which the United States recruited post-communist and neutral European states through military exercises were interoperability and the development of strong military relations. Thus, PfP served as an opportunity to both prepare potential members for ascension and recruit help for potential missions.

## Origins of NATO's Partnership for Peace: Security through Democracy and Multilateralism

The origins of NATO's PfP coincided with America's newfound primacy after the end of the Cold War. As noted in chapter 3, when US President William Clinton ascended to the oval office in January 1993, his priority was to deliver on his campaign promise of focusing on the domestic economy. His predecessor, President George H.W. Bush, had presided over the collapse of the Soviet Union and the end of Cold War hostilities. Despite Clinton's inheritance of a unipolar international order and understandable desire to focus on the economy, he could not escape America's unique opportunity to shape a fragile post-communist Eurasia. The collapse of communism and political disintegration of both former Soviet and Yugoslav states resulted in some of the worst European ethnic conflicts in decades. With no existing policy toward the growing crisis in the Balkans and no framework to answer the question of European security, his foreign policy needed an overarching strategy to address these pressing international problems.[40]

Clinton's team approached these issues with a faith in democracy promotion and multilateralism. In his address to the UN General Assembly in September 1993, Clinton declared, "In a new era of peril and opportunity, our overriding purpose must be to expand and strengthen the world's community of market-based democracies. During the Cold War, we sought to contain a threat to survival of free institutions. Now we seek to enlarge the circle of nations that live under those free institutions."[41] Speaking to Congress in his 1994 State of the Union address, Clinton argued, "Ultimately the best strategy to insure our security and to build a durable peace is to support the advance of democracy elsewhere. Democracies don't attack each other; they make better trading partners and partners in diplomacy."[42] In line with Clinton's stated beliefs and the language used in the security strategy, Clinton's team, especially his first national security advisor, Tony Lake, advocated for the promotion of market-based democracies and an emerging post-communist Europe appeared to be the ideal region to execute the policy.[43]

To realize this objective of enlarging the number of capitalist democracies committed to the liberal order, one tactic the Clinton's team discussed was NATO enlargement. When the topic of whether to leave, remain in, or expand NATO came to the forefront of policy debates, those in the administration pointed to the fact that the organization was not only intended as an alliance against a great competitor, but also to serve, "as an institution of shared values (promotion of democracy and peaceful relations among its members)."[44] By recasting NATO as a vehicle to promote the liberal international order, the administration would ensure the organization's relevance post-Cold War. In fact, this new mission for NATO had deep roots in the organization's founding. Thomas Risse-Kappen argues that the political goal of NATO to support and protect democracies predated the military policy of containment: the Soviet threat, manifested through a totalitarian ideology and aggression toward Eastern Europe, was an assault on the liberal community's identity established prior to and not dependent on the USSR.[45] Even at the end of the Cold War, NATO's task of protecting the liberal democratic order was championed as its vital mission. Only a month before the dissolution of the Soviet Union in December 1991, NATO produced a strategic concept that reaffirmed the organization's original mission: "Based on common values of democracy, human rights and the rule of law, the Alliance has worked since its inception for the establishment of a just and lasting peaceful order in Europe. This Alliance objective remains unchanged."[46] NATO's commitment to democracy, human rights, international law, and UN principles were crucial to the organization's mission before and after the Cold War.

Clinton's team initially desired to use prospective NATO membership as an incentive for the emerging Central and Eastern European states to reform their political and economic policies to mirror market-based democracies. Secretary of State Warren Christopher believed that by setting a high bar for inclusion, the United States could shape these emerging states into democracies. In an Op-Ed entitled, "NATO Plus," Warren insisted that these countries would have to show that they adhere to, "the principles of democracy, individual liberty and respect for human rights, the rule of law, the peaceful settlements of disputes, the inviolability of national boundaries."[47] These democratic benchmarks, later known as the "Perry Principles" after further articulation by then Secretary of Defense William Perry, would serve as the tool for democracy promotion through NATO. However, US policymakers were acutely aware that expanding NATO would cause problems for democratic reform in Russia.

The Clinton administration also sought to develop an international framework to conduct multilateral peacekeeping operations, which key officials believed would help share the burden of stabilizing Europe and legitimize the use of force. The increasing calls for the deployment of military force came in response to the crisis in the Balkans, which by the summer of 1992 developed into the worst fighting in Europe in forty years. Uproar over Serbian-sponsored ethnic cleansing and fears over possible spill-over into other parts of Europe increased pressure on the administration to "do something." Clinton's team struggled to respond to the growing violence: Secretary Christopher called the crisis "the problem from hell," while the lack of US response was characterized by assistant secretary of state for European and Eurasian Affairs Richard Holbrooke as "the greatest collective security failure of the West since the 1930s."[48] The desire to intervene in the ethnic war was most salient in Lake, who told reporters in a 1994 press briefing: "When I wake up every morning and look at the headlines and the stories and the images on television of these conflicts, I want to work to end every conflict. I want to work to save every child out there."[49] The vexing security problem caused divisions within the administration: Lake encouraged intervention while Secretary of Defense Les Aspin and Chairman of the Joint Chiefs of Staff Colin Powell wanted to limit the use of military force.[50] The ambiguous nature of ethnic war and difficultly in crafting a response led the Clinton team to look to NATO as a possible solution.

The only existing mechanism the administration possessed for connecting NATO with former Warsaw Pact countries was the North Atlantic Cooperation Council (NACC), announced at the 1991 Rome Summit as a ministerial body that would promote cooperation among all NATO and Eurasian states. The Rome Summit was also significant in its illustration of new post-Cold War non-state threats and how similar they sounded to the Clinton team's description: "Risks to Allied security are less likely to result from calculated aggression against the territory of the Allies, but rather from the adverse consequences of instabilities that may arise from the serious economic, social and political difficulties, including ethnic rivalries and territorial disputes, which are faced by many countries in Central and Eastern Europe."[51] Yet the NACC did not guarantee security for non-NATO states, a problem Clinton's administration considered to rectify by enlarging NATO. When Secretary of State Warren Christopher prepared for his June 1993 NATO meeting in Athens, key officials were pressuring him to give more muscle to NACC or to acquiesce to states pushing for membership, such as Hungary, Poland, and the Czech Republic.[52]

However, the topic of enlarging NATO was met with resistance, especially outside the White House. There were few in Congress interested in enlargement and the military was not eager to extend formal commitments to defend new, militarily weak members in a possible attack. Moreover, the military and some policy officials feared the move would alarm a fledgling Russia and possibly inhibit security cooperation between the two countries.[53] Russian president Boris Yeltsin opposed expansion and in mid-September 1993 he wrote a letter to Clinton and other NATO leaders arguing that although he understood the sovereign right of states to freely seek their own alliances, "relations between [Russia] and NATO should be several degrees warmer than relations between the alliance and Eastern Europe."[54] Given the multiple obstacles and issues associated with NATO enlargement during the early 1990s, the United States had to find a way to encourage democratization and generate support for peacekeeping short of offering membership.

## The Need for Multilateral Partners and the Problem of NATO Enlargement

Given the question of NATO expansion still unanswered and the increasing instability in Southern Europe, US Army General John Shalikashvili, the Supreme Allied Commander Europe, asked his staff to look into how NATO would respond to conflicts outside its borders. He noticed there was no command structure for these sorts of operations, which up to this point did not affect the traditional alliance. He then determined that a flexible Combined Joint Task Force (CJTF) command was necessary in order to integrate both NATO and non-NATO partners—including former communist states as well as neutrals such as Sweden—in future multilateral missions, which could be "handed off" to other organizations such as the United Nations or Western European Union. This CJTF would establish a "common set of practices and understanding" between NATO and non-NATO partners.[55] He knew that eventual NATO enlargement was inevitable, yet he also understood the political and military sensitives associated with expansion. He began to envision the possibility of a compromise between these two camps: NATO should develop "patterns of cooperation" with non-NATO militaries that were not "just talk" like the NACC. Though effective in increasing communication between NATO and Warsaw Pact countries, the NACC was largely deemed ineffective at practical cooperation on the ground.[56]

General Shalikashvili discussed these ideas with assistant secretary of defense for Regional Security Affairs Charles Freeman Jr., who, with the help of his aides, developed a concept labelled "Peacekeeping Partnership" that they pitched to Secretary of Defense Les Aspin in September 1993. Not only would this program develop a CJTF to solve the problem of joint command for potential out-of-sector peacekeeping missions, the partnership would create stronger military-to-military ties between NATO and post-communist Eurasian states. A month later, to distance the program from the failed Somalia operation that gave peacekeeping a politically divisive name, one of Freeman's deputies suggested the program be renamed the "Partnership for Peace."[57] Secretary Aspin first discussed the initiative internationally at the NATO Defense Ministers meeting in Travemuende, Germany in October 1993. His delegation circulated a paper among the NATO staff that de-emphasized NATO enlargement but highlighted the benefits of defense cooperation through PfP: "Rather than forcing a premature consideration of formal membership at the time, the partnership focuses instead on real elements of defense cooperation." Moreover, "as critical uncertainties about European security are resolved, and nations continue to evolve toward pluralistic, democratic states, then the question of expanded membership in NATO can be addressed."[58] Secretary Aspin then told reporters: "What we are proposing is a partnership that will expand interoperability—joint operations—between NATO as an organization and these countries as individual countries. From that, there will certainly be a certain amount of security comfort that will come from that."[59]

Approaching the Brussels summit in January 1994, the administration decided it was too early to enlarge NATO but was enthusiastic about the PfP initiative, which would expand military-to-military cooperation and exercises without alarming Russia. Though stopping short of enlargement for the time being, Secretary of State Christopher highlighted the benefits of more military-to-military cooperation: "There can be no better way to establish a new and secure Europe than to have soldiers from Russia, Ukraine, Poland, Hungary, and the other new democracies work with NATO to address their most pressing security problems. We believe NATO and our Eastern colleagues should establish joint planning and training, and joint exercises for peace-keeping. Such cooperation can help ensure that all European peace-keeping operations are conducted in accordance with UN and CSCE."[60] Clinton formally announced the PfP initiative at the summit, anticipating disappointment from Eastern European leaders desiring immediate NATO membership. When responding to reporters about what he would tell Poland, Hungary, Slovakia, and the Czech Republic about membership, he rejoined: "I think I'll be in a position to tell them, number one, the purpose of the Partnership for Peace is to open the possibility of NATO's enlargement as well as to give all the former Warsaw Pact countries and other non-NATO nations in Europe the chance to cooperate with us militarily."[61] Thus, senior officials in the Clinton administration sought to recruit potential NATO members and multinational partners by increasing military and security cooperation through the PfP program.

## Partnership for Peace Framework and Military Exercises

The PfP Framework document, signed in 1994 by twenty-three non-NATO countries, declares: "In joining the Partnership, the member States of the

North Atlantic Alliance and the other States subscribing to this Document recall that they are committed to the preservation of democratic societies, their freedom from coercion and intimidation, and the maintenance of the principles of international law."[62] The program was open to all OSCE members, which included all of Europe and the former Soviet Union.[63] Not only was the document signed by former Soviet states such as Kyrgyzstan and Uzbekistan (who also signed a separate collective security agreement with Russia), historically neutral states such as Switzerland and Ireland also joined later in 1996 and 1999, respectively.[64] The document delineated five main goals for participants: (1) facilitate transparency in national defense planning and budgeting processes; (2) ensure democratic control of armed forces; (3) maintain readiness to contribute to operations under UN mandate; (4) develop cooperative military relations with NATO for joint planning, training, and exercises in the fields of peacekeeping and humanitarian operations; and (5) develop forces better able to operate with NATO militaries.[65]

The first two tasks, budget transparency and civilian control of the military, were largely addressed through military and security cooperation at the upper echelons of defense ministries.[66] These objectives were also met through military-to-military exchange programs, such as the George C. Marshall Center for Security Studies in Garmisch, Germany, which offered seminars, workshops, and conferences to encourage senior post-communist military officers to adopt democratic reform.[67] The latter three tasks—readiness for UN missions, exercises to train for peacekeeping and humanitarian assistance, and interoperability—were the main focus of exercises. The stated purpose of these training events was to, "exercise and simulate common peacekeeping tasks from planning through deployment to improve the ability to work together in actual missions."[68] The funding for PfP exercises came largely from the United States through the Warsaw Initiative, launched in July 1994. The stated objectives of the initiative were to "(1) facilitate the participation of partner states in exercises and programs with NATO countries, (2) promote the ability of partner forces to operate with NATO, (3) support efforts to increase defense and military cooperation with Partnership partners, and (4) develop strong candidates for membership in NATO."[69]

The program was not without controversy, however. Some feared that military exercises would dominate the program, providing Eastern European military officers greater clout and preventing the transfer of democratic accountability to civilian leaders. Others feared that increasing military cooperation with former Soviet satellites would reignite mistrust between the West and East. In particular, Russian military officers perceived the PfP as a potential security threat and wanted to ensure Russia was provided a special status within the program to prevent loss of control over its region.[70] Despite these concerns, PfP was widely popular among the United States,

NATO, and former communist countries as a means to develop military cooperation, promote democracy, and address new threats to the volatile region.

## Exercises "Cooperative Bridge" and "Cooperative Nugget"

The first PfP exercise, "Cooperative Bridge," was held in Poland in September 1994 and involved thirteen countries, six of which were NATO members and the others were former communist states: the Czech Republic, Poland, Bulgaria, Slovakia, Lithuania, Romania, and Ukraine. During the exercise, US soldiers compared weapons, helicopters, and vehicles with previous enemies from the Warsaw Pact, attempting to understand how the unfamiliar equipment operates for future missions. The exercise allowed former adversaries to see each other at a more human level. One US lieutenant claimed his soldiers' opinion of the Polish Army and the Warsaw Pact in general was low; after the training event, however, "Now they realize they are soldiers who are quite capable and quite human, too."[71] He goes on to describe sharing a room with a Polish lieutenant whose wife was pregnant, which to him provided a more personal experience to build trust for future peacekeeping operations. After-hours socializing allowed the soldiers to see each other as friends and overcome the prejudices that Cold War hostilities encouraged. The desire to join NATO was present in some Eastern European soldiers, as one officer put it, "I think every officer in the Czech army would like to be in NATO because we see it as a chance to make our army better."[72] The training event allowed the United States, NATO, and partner militaries to practice for potential UN or NATO peacekeeping operations; for instance, humanitarian assistance was present in soldiers who escorted food convoys to hungry civilians, while a respect for human rights and international law was apparent in managing refugees escaping conflict and using checkpoints to monitor violence against civilians.

The training event did uncover problems of interoperability: not only did soldiers need a cadre of translators to communicate in person, the former communist militaries' low defense budgets precluded purchasing enough fuel for the exercise. Moreover, US officers noticed how the command structure of the former Warsaw Pact states reflected the heavily hierarchical Soviet system, which tended to suppress initiative, possessed a weak noncommissioned officer corps, and maintained a sharp distinction between officers and enlisted soldiers. US Army European Commander General David Maddox admitted, "There are clearly approaches or policies that are a result of operating for 45 years under one regime. We have to come to grips with that."[73] Yet attraction, not interoperability, was the focus: even for a skeptical Eastern European public. As one planner for NATO's PfP recalled:

At the outset, at the very outset, they were, to put it bluntly, public relations exercises and photo-op's. The first big PfP "exercise" in Poland was, I mean, you lined all the flags up, you had a photo-op, and then people stood around and said "oh well that's the way the magazine goes in your rifle, well this is how the magazine goes in my rifle." "Is that guy a sergeant? Well no, he's a [Polish rank] or something else." And there was no real substance to them; there were two big ones, one in Poland and one in the Netherlands. It was all sort of *acclimating the public to the notion that you could get all these disparate folks in one place at one time and they didn't perceive each other as enemies.* They perceived themselves as doing something in common. That was the early view of exercises.[74]

This sentiment is reiterated by another NATO military officer, who recalled that the political goal of these exercise were to ensure "that a maximum number of states send contributions to mark solidarity in a symbolic way (in NATO events, regional partner states are most welcome), all well turned out as for a formal parade."[75]

The first PfP exercise on US soil, coined "Cooperative Nugget," took place in August 1995 at Fort Polk, Louisiana. This exercise included the United States, the United Kingdom, Canada, and fourteen former communist and Soviet states including former Soviet republics Kyrgyzstan and Uzbekistan. Each country sent forty soldiers, roughly a platoon-sized element, to the exercise and NATO planners divided the units into six companies: four commanded by American captains, one by a British captain, and one by a Canadian. A British officer who chaired the NATO military committee responsible for the exercise said the goal of the exercise was, "to foster co-operation and understanding among the multinational units, as well as to learn more effective methods of conducting humanitarian and peacekeeping tasks."[76] Cooperative Nugget focused primarily on peacekeeping drills, such as protecting civilians in mock villages from violence while under fire from snipers and car bombs. The scenario was built around a ceasefire agreement that NATO was given mandate to enforce between ethnic rivalries in a fictitious country.

When asked about how NATO planners determined which peacekeeping tasks to train and evaluate at the exercise, the commander of the training center at Fort Polk, Brigadier General Michael Sherfield, admitted: "We went to many sources to develop the tasks for humanitarian and peacekeeping operations. Right now, NATO does not have a [sic] approved doctrine for peacekeeping or humanitarian operations, so we used the model based partly on the United Nations and our own Army's experiences in peacekeeping operations over the last couple of years."[77] In addition to traditional peacekeeping tasks, an emphasis on democratic practices were apparent in Cooperative Nugget. For instance, the exercise rehearsed interagency support from nongovernmental organizations (NGOs): soldiers swapped prisoners under the supervision of the American Red Cross. Additionally, a Slovak platoon provided protection to a dignitary addressing a crowd at a political rally; when he was "shot" by a simulated sniper, the medics addressed his injury and led him to safety.[78] Speaking to reporters about the success of the exercise, Marine Major General John Sheehan noted the symbolic importance of joining NATO and former communist states in a joint exercise: "From a political level, (success is) the ability to bring these nations together for the first time in the United States, to enhance interoperability from a political perspective."[79]

## Assessing the Effectiveness of NATO's PfP

After hundreds of exercises and other activities through the 1990s and early 2000s, what was the effect of NATO's shaping program? The logic of attraction relies on the ability to convince others to align closer to the major power; how did the PfP fare? Although conventional wisdom holds that leaders of aspirant states were desperate for inclusion in NATO, Alexandra Gheciu finds that conservative political parties in the Czech Republic and Romania—prominently communists and nationalists—were skeptical of joining the alliance and adopting liberal values. In fact, as late as 1997, Czech polls indicated that more than half of public opinion would say "no" to NATO accession.[80] A RAND report revealed that senior Polish officers were initially distrustful of the program because of PfP's insistence on changing doctrine, equipment, and the rejection of self-sufficiency in favor of reliance on allies. The same report also credits the PfP with softening the German public's views on building military relationships with the former communist East.[81] Conducting military training with former adversaries is challenging for soldiers; yet, as noted above, Poland's agreement to host the first PfP exercise allowed American, German, and Polish soldiers to view each other at a more human level in a country that NATO officers believed would be the frontlines of next world war.

In terms of the operational benefits to NATO, a Government Accountability Report credits the PfP program with preparing non-NATO partners for peacekeeping missions in the Balkans: troop contributions from 20 partners grew from 5,800 (in 1996) to 12,800 (in 1999) and many NATO leaders asserted that PfP exercises made this possible.[82] NATO also gained aircraft basing rights in the Czech Republic, Hungary, and Poland, as well as additional airspace rights in Romania and Bulgaria, during the alliance's air strikes against Serbia in 1999.[83] Because PfP was open to all OSCE members, even neutral states such as Sweden, Switzerland, and Austria joined the exercises to increase effectiveness and interoperability during peacekeeping missions.[84]

At the same time, NATO also attempted to use PfP exercises to stand up and train a few peacekeeping units that would never deploy, including the Central Asian Battalion (CENTRASBAT), which sometimes called into question the usefulness of these exercises.[85] Overall, however, there is evidence that NATO's use of shaping increased its ability to influence skeptical domestic actors to join NATO, as well as to prepare units for multilateral operations and achieve operational access for kinetic operations.

## CASE STUDY II: INDIA AND CHINA'S "HAND IN HAND" PROGRAM

One of the most prominent attraction exercise programs to emerge in Asia is known as "Hand-in-Hand", intended to reduce tensions between India and China. The border between these two growing powers has been a flashpoint historically: India and China fought a short war over their shared border in 1962 and tensions rose again in 1967 and 1987. There is no agreed upon boundary between the countries, referred to as the Line of Actual Control (LAC) in bilateral documents, which has resulted in each side claiming hundreds of border incursions by the other.[86] From 2006 to 2016, these states conducted eight ground-based cooperative exercises, six of which were part of the "Hand-in-Hand" program, and two between border guards along the LAC. The case study below reveals how Indian and Chinese military leaders attempted to reassure one another through cooperative training events.

### Indo-Chinese Relations during the Cold War

The relationship between the two nuclear powers has experienced periods of cooperation but also intense competition, especially since the Sino-Indian War of 1962. The two countries' shared border spans the vast Himalayan mountains and includes over 130,000 square kilometers of disputed territory, primarily involving Ladakh in the west and Arunachal Pradesh in the east. This immense border presents both rising powers with an intense security dilemma.[87] India lays claim to land within borders drawn primarily by British colonists—known as the McMahon Line—while China asserts that its sovereignty extends far south of this "obsolete" colonial boundary. Moreover, Tibet, a largely autonomous region until Chinese occupation in 1950, serves as a point of contention among the two powers. Though officially annexed by China in 1951, Tibet holds strong cultural and economic ties to India, which, since 1959, has hosted the religious leader Dalai Lama's government-in-exile. Tensions came to a head in 1962 when both states deployed troops to a deteriorating situation along the border after the Chinese repressed a rebellion in Tibet. In October 1962, the Chinese People's Liberation Army (PLA) invaded and defeated the Indian army at Arunachal Pradesh (formerly the Northeast Frontier Agency, or NEFA) and Ladakh within a month.[88] After peace negotiations failed in November, China ordered a unilateral ceasefire in December and withdrew 20 kilometers behind the LAC—the de facto territory occupied by both armies at the time. A decade-long diplomatic freeze ensued over differing interpretations of the boundary.[89] Though both states offered diplomatic overtures over the next forty years, progress was disrupted by militarized border standoffs in 1967 and 1987.

## Indo-Chinese Confidence-Building Measures since the End of the Cold War

After several smaller crises were settled during the Cold War, India and China signed an agreement in 1993 as a commitment to preventing military incursions over the 1962 LAC. Despite the ostensible goodwill, the document did not settle the border question and disagreements about the actual shape of the border remained.[90] In 1996, both countries reaffirmed their commitment to refrain from the use of military force against each other in a shared confidence-building document, even though the agreement recognized there was still no acceptable settlement to the "boundary question." The agreement included provisions to limit exercises along the LAC to 15,000 troops and required advanced notice of exercises involving more than 5,000 soldiers.[91] Despite the progress on CSBMs to improve relations on the border, India's second nuclear test in May 1998 drew sharp condemnation from the Chinese government, especially after Indian Defense Minister George Fernandes claimed in the same month, "China is potential threat number one."[92]

Two confidence-building agreements in the 2000s signaled cooperation toward using training to build a positive relationship. The 2003 *Declaration on Principles for Relations* attempted to transition from restrictions on purely military activities to an acknowledgement of more common political and economic interests, such as the shared goals of promoting trade, protecting the environment, eliminating poverty, and strengthening the UN. Both states also committed to working together toward countering terrorism, a growing threat after the September 11, 2001, attacks on the United States and December 2001 attacks on the Indian Parliament.[93] Indian and Chinese government officials announced that 2006 would mark a "Year of Friendship" in which the two sides would attempt new ways to forge closer ties and find a solution to the border dispute.[94] In May 2006, the defense ministers of both countries signed a "Memorandum of Understanding" that served as the first formal agreement between the two rivals to institutionalize multinational military exercises.[95] The document committed both countries to hold military officer exchanges, annual defense dialogues, and joint military training in the fields of "search and rescue, anti-piracy, counterterrorism, and other areas of mutual interest."[96]

## The Planning and Execution of Indo-Chinese Bilateral Exercises

Pursuant to the 2006 Memorandum, India and China conducted eight land-based multinational exercises from 2006 to 2016: six exercises entitled "Hand-in-Hand" and two humanitarian and disaster-relief exercises among border guards. "Hand-in-Hand" exercises usually included 100–150 troops from each side and focused on counterinsurgency and counterterrorism; these exercises were intended to be conducted annually but were interrupted between 2009 and 2012 through a series of crises between the two countries. Though the decision to hold exercises is made by political leaders, the actual planning is conducted months in advance by Indian and Chinese military officers; the execution of tasks is conducted at the lowest tactical levels involving soldiers and sergeants. In general, the military attaché teams from both countries meet together to choose the specific location and determine the training tasks, with the host country ultimately responsible for the general format and sequence. The planners (usually mid-grade officers) discuss possible objectives, such as hostage-rescue or counterterrorism, and choose an agreed-upon scenario. Multiple phases are planned into the exercise, such as familiarization of equipment, discussion of each other's doctrine, and execution of tasks in units mixed with soldiers from both countries.[97] In the case of India, military officers coordinate with their Chinese counterparts, keeping Ministry of Defense and Ministry of External Affairs officials abreast of developments.[98] Different units are chosen for each exercise based on operational requirements, which provides various units throughout both armies with exposure to their rival counterparts.

During training, soldiers from different countries maneuver together in basic tactics, which "don't need language" because they are considered standard to all armies.[99] Additionally, since China and India do not share a common conventional enemy, planners create a third-party threat that consists of insurgency and terrorism in their "Hand-in-Hand" scenarios; as former Indian director general of the Infantry, Lieutenant General JS Bajwa notes,

> When you are doing military exercises for conventional operations, then you have to identify an enemy. China and India don't have a common enemy, so there is no point in having exercises in conventional operations, because we are not going to be fighting together against an enemy; however, we wanted

to continue to have military-to-military cooperation, more to understand their military and not to take the Chinese as some "ten-foot-tall soldiers."[100]

Between training events, soldiers are encouraged "to live together, eat together, play games together" for several weeks in order to develop relation-ships and build camaraderie. During these interactions, officers hope that soldiers come to the undestarstanding that the other side is "represented by human beings" and not "animals," which is a common myth that soldiers acquire throughout their careers. Senior military officers believe personal contact with rival soldiers is viewed as a means to dispel these myths.[101] General Bajwa argues that since Indian units are deployed along the LAC, military cooperation such as exercises ensure that the situation "doesn't flare up" and both countries can "avoid hostilities"; he notes, "When two armies have been operating in this sense, like this, generally you do not intend to become very hostile and there is an element of restraint on both sides, par-ticularly along the Line of Actual Control."[102]

The two countries conducted their first cooperative exercise in the Chinese city of Kunming, a town near Arunachal Pradesh, in December 2007. The exercise named "Hand-in-Hand 2007" involved 100 troops from both coun-tries and focused on counterterrorism to provide opportunities for the armies to share lessons learned from past experience.[103] An anonymous Indian defense official noted: "This indicates that India's growing military ties with the US will not affect the process of confidence building with China—we can achieve a lot together . . . It's time to bury the ghosts of 1962."[104] Despite the exercise's military focus on counterterrorism, military officers encouraged their troops to socialize and get to know one another: in between training events, the soldiers would conduct trust-building activities and play sports such as tug-of-war, basketball, martial arts, and yoga. The soldiers would also intermix to dine and live side-by-side in the same building, learn phrases in each other's languages, and enjoy sightseeing in their off-time together. One reporter remarked about the exercise:

Although some military and diplomatic observers said that the joint training is more symbolic than substantial, many acknowledged that the point is not the scale of the joint training or what specific anti-terrorism skills are involved. The point is that the soldiers on both sides are moving toward each other in a friendly way.[105]

The two armies repeated the counterterror exercise in December 2008, held for the first time on Indian soil in the Belgaum District in Karnataka. The exercise opened with a ceremony that displayed performances of Chinese tai chi and Indian martial arts, as well as remarks by the Chinese officer in charge who explained that the aim of the exercise was to develop friendship, promote mutual understanding, and build trust.[106] Retired Indian Army Major General Dipankar Banerjee argues that these exercises are conducted so that "soldiers get to know each other, build trust and confidence in one another," by providing a "human face" that "removes a sense of enmity and remoteness." Moreover, he notes that these exercises are intended to humanize and prevent soldiers from "demonizing" one another.[107] About 137 Chinese PLA troops joined a similar number of Indian infantry soldiers to conduct attacks against a simulated enemy assisted by helicopters, supervised by a joint command post occupied by officers from both countries.[108] Despite the success of these two exercises, the relationship became strained once again in 2009 when border incursions resumed and China protested the official visit of the Dalai Lama to Arunachal Pradesh in November 2009.[109] Additionally, India canceled military officer exchanges in August 2010 after China refused to grant a visa to a Kashmir-stationed Indian general.[110] Though it is unclear whether exercises were canceled or never planned in the first place, no joint training occurred between 2009 and 2013.

Despite these cooperative exercises, tensions culminated in a crisis in April 2013—known as the "Depsang incident"—when a Chinese army platoon established an outpost in Ladakh, located in Jammu and Kashmir, ten kilometers into an area occupied and claimed by India.[111] The Indian army responded by moving a platoon of its own to about 500 meters from the Chinese position, waving flags to signal to the Chinese troops that they were intruding on Indian territory. During the standoff, the Indian media reported that China had engaged in over 600 incursions into Indian territory since 2010 and that meetings by high ranking military officials were going nowhere.[112] A group of Indian students at Jammu University protested the Chinese intrusion, carrying banners and shouting anti-Chinese rhetoric.[113] The three-week standoff did not escalate to war, but both countries' foreign ministers were forced to intervene and agreed to remove troops from the contested area.[114]

## India and China Restart Joint Exercises in 2013

Despite the numerous attempts to build confidence through high-level agreements since 1988, as well as two exercises in 2007 and 2008, the rival nuclear major powers still engaged in a military standoff that took three weeks to resolve. The ambiguous LAC and unwillingness by the two governments to clearly delineate boundaries is often cited as the cause of strained relations. Given the systematic disagreement over the shape of the border that dates back to 1962, as well as the fact that the two countries are some of the largest and most powerful in the world, the Sino-Indian relationship appeared bleak. However, in 2013 the two powers made substantial progress toward cooperation. First, in July 2013 India and China agreed to establish Border Meeting Points (BMPs) along the LAC for local army commanders to meet in times of crises. The Indian defence minister highlighted the practical role for local soldiers in diffusing cross-border tensions concurrently with high-level diplomatic talks: "The special representative-level talks will continue. But everybody knows it will take time. You cannot wait for it to solve immediate border problems."[115]

In October 2013, Chinese and Indian national leaders signed the Border Defense Cooperation Agreement (BDCA), which reiterated each side's commitment to the non-use of force, proposed meetings and a hotline between local military officers across the border, committed the countries to restart joint military exercises, and promised to combat non-state threats such as arms smuggling, natural disasters, and infectious disease.[116] The agreement was both lauded and derided by Chinese and Indian analysts, some arguing the measures were useless, others that it represented India's subtle surrender to China.[117] Commenting on the resolution of 2013 Depsang incident, one retired Indian army officer who worked on Chinese relations during his military career noted: "on most occasions, such incursions into each other's territory are settled at the local level and there is a mechanism of making announcements over microphone whenever such incursions are noticed." He continued that if these minor disputes cannot be settled by army units locally, sometimes they are handled at general/flag officer meetings or the diplomatic level.[118]

The first joint exercise since 2008 took place in China's Sichuan province in November 2013, though the decision to hold the exercise resulted from meetings between Indian and Chinese military officials several months before the official signing of the BDCA.[119] During Indian Defence Minister AK Antony's visit to China in early July, the two sides agreed to restart the exercises as a means to prevent a "Despang-like" incident from occurring in the future.[120] The exercise "Hand-in-Hand 2013" involved 144 soldiers from both countries and incorporated similar tactical training to the exercises in 2007 and 2008.[121] This exercise included a focus on interoperability, with soldiers from both sides learning hand signals and each other's doctrines on hostage rescue and detainee operations. To facilitate socialization, the officers organized troops into "mixed companies" which ensured interaction among unfamiliar soldiers (despite the language barrier). Indian Lieutenant General Ainil Jumar Ahuja told reporters: "This understanding at the level of the troops, at the level of the commanding officers, the company commanders, and the interaction that we have had at the level of generals, will definitely promote better understanding and a better appreciation of each other's concerns."[122]

In February 2014, military officers and government officials from India and China agreed to conduct the fourth iteration of "Hand-in-Hand" in November

2014, this time at the Aundh military camp in Pune, India.[123] The exercise again focused on counterterrorism, with 139 soldiers from each country practicing rappelling from helicopters, establishing a cordon and search, and attacking insurgent positions.[124] Military officers shared a joint command post to track the training and improve interoperability. Senior officers from both countries emphasized the importance of cooperating to defeat terrorism in all its forms. Additionally, Chinese PLA Lieutenant General Shi Xiangyuan remarked about the exercise:

> The demonstration by both sides shows how similar our nations and our civilizations are. This is the most convincing evidence that China and India have great similarities and we are among the oldest civilizations of the world. The joint training is a very important step towards a more conducive and complementary atmosphere between the two great armies.[125]

Despite the officer's remarks, not too far from the exercise location a standoff between the PLA and Indian border guards was underway. A few months prior to the start of the exercise, the Indian Border Security Force (BSF) reported that over 1,000 Chinese troops crossed the LAC in Ladakh; in Arunachal Pradesh, Indian Jawan border guards prevented Chinese troops from building roads through Indian-claimed land.[126] According to a reporter covering the exercise, an anonymous Indian army officer said, "We knew the exact situation at the LAC and we are aware of the BSF intelligence report as well. However, we have received special instructions from seniors regarding this exercise. Hence, we are ignoring these recent developments and are taking special care of the guests."[127] From the officer's comments, it appears that although the two countries were once again claiming border incursions by the other, senior military officers wanted the exercises to continue.

In September 2015, senior Chinese and Indian army officers met at a BMP in Chushul, Ladakh, along the LAC to discuss border incursions. According to a news report, the Chinese officers were asked about a watch tower that had allegedly been built 1.5 kilometers into Indian territory. Military officers from both sides resolved the issue and agreed to cease defense construction along the border.[128] A few weeks later, Chinese military officers invited the Indian army to participate in another iteration of "Hand-in-Hand" at the Kunming Military Academy in Yunnan Province, China in October 2015. One news agency reported an anonymous source as noting: "The fact that Burtse stand-off in Ladakh sector between the two countries was resolved in less than a week by the two Armies without any intervention by the [*sic*] Governments of the two countries early this month was an indicative of improving relations, which could further go up after 12 days long joint military exercises."[129]

The opening ceremony of "Hand-in-Hand 2015" involved performances from both nations, including demonstrations of traditional dance and martial arts. The Indian army selected its Naga army regiment to participate, including army officers from different states across the country, including Jammu and Kashmir along the LAC. In addition to counterterrorism tactics, the two armies also trained on tasks involving humanitarian aid and disaster relief. The exercise planners included events for the soldiers in between training, such as physical competitions, martial arts, mountain climbing, and tug-of-war organized into mixed-country teams.[130] According to a news report, Chinese Lieutenant General Zhou Xiaozhou asserted that "the joint exercise will play [*sic*] important role in deepening mutual cooperation and forging a closer development partnership."[131] An Indian military officer told reporters that the nations shared a common challenge in terrorism and may be forced to operate together in the future, for instance, as part of a UN-led force.[132]

In November 2016, China and India conducted their sixth iteration of "Hand-in-Hand," again held in Pune, India. A month before the beginning of the exercise, tensions rose when China blocked India's effort to obtain membership in the Nuclear Supplier's Group (NSG) and India's attempt to declare a Jaish-e-Mohammed chief a terrorist by the UN. Despite these tensions, the exercise went according to plan, with about 170 troops from each country participating.[133] A reporter covering the exercise for *India Today* observed, "This exercise has seen [the soldiers] coming closer than ever before. We've seen that different companies have Indian elements as well as Chinese operating together, so they're not essentially operating as two different armies, they're in fact operating as one composite force." An Indian colonel he interviewed noted, "there has been interaction at all levels: from soldier-to-soldier, from NCOs-to-NCOs, and officers to officers." After the end of the training day, soldiers from both sides enjoyed "laughter and camaraderie" together, practicing phrases in each other's languages. One Indian battalion was proud to report that it underwent three months of learning Chinese prior to the start of the exercise.[134]

## Assessing the Effectiveness of "Hand-in-Hand" Exercises

Some senior military officers from both sides of the rivalry agree that these trust-developing exercises are having a positive impact on Indo-Chinese relations. As one retired Indian general argues: "There can be no doubt that military CBMs have resulted in graduated and reciprocated reduction of tensions along the LAC with practically no incidents of cross-border firing in recent times. This has resulted in lowering of tensions despite periodic reports of intrusions and patrols straying across the Line of Actual Control."[135] Chinese Senior Colonel Wang Guifang argues in addition to increasing trust at higher diplomatic levels and developing mechanisms to prevent crises at the border, India and China should deepen military cooperation: "Joint military exercises at the tactical level of the army mark a good start, and should develop in the future."[136] Indian Army General K.T. Parnaik, chief of Northern Command, noted that the Depsang incident was settled between military units on the border along with higher-level diplomacy: "There was a simultaneous effort on the ground, at the tactical level by our formations, as well as the dialogue between the two countries at the foreign office level."[137] General Parnaik noted that because there is no mutually agreed-upon border, both armies patrol what they believe to be their territory and sometimes come in contact. When these standoffs take place, soldiers and leaders attempt to de-escalate at their level: "The entire process is peaceful. Whenever there is a face-off, we show manners to each other. We convince each other to de-escalate the situation. They go to their side and we return to our side."[138]

Yet others question the usefulness of these exercises and whether they are effective in reducing tensions during crises along the border.[139] In a 2014 Pew Research Center poll, only 30–31 percent of Indians and Chinese held favorable views of each other, while 72 percent of Indians were concerned about a territorial dispute with China.[140] Moreover, major standoffs along the LAC indicate that these exercises are not achieving the goal of de-escalation. In addition to the 2013 Depsang incident and the Doklam standoff in June 2017, troops from the two countries clashed in June 2020 resulting in 20 dead Indian soldiers from hand-to-hand combat along the border. India threatened to ban certain Chinese businesses in retaliation.[141] Given the ambiguous LAC, the fact that the two bordering major powers have not fought a war since 1962 or exchanged gunfire in decades is remarkable, yet the recent clash reveals the limits of military shaping between rival powers. Until Indian and Chinese government officials come to a political agreement on the border, standoffs and crises are likely to continue.

## SUMMARY

As major powers scan the horizon for partners and allies, they often look to the logic of attraction to draw states closer and manage their uncertain environments. By increasing interoperability and positive relationships between soldiers, as well as convincing reluctant government officials of the benefits of cooperation, major powers hope that neutrals can turn into allies and rivals can emerge as partners. Moreover, policymakers may view attraction as useful for driving a wedge between rivals and preventing an adversarial alliance from emerging in the future. The case studies above revealed attraction in practice. The United States and other NATO countries leveraged PfP exercises with former communist states to improve relationships, convince weary publics of the benefits of the alliance, and recruit and prepare partners for multinational peacekeeping. Through "Hand-in-Hand" exercises, Chinese and Indian officers attempted to prevent border crises from conflagrating into war by increasing personal contacts, emphasizing their similar cultural heritage, and convincing each other of a shared legitimate interest in security. The next chapter explores the second logic of shaping—socialization—which shares some overlap with attraction, especially when theories of alliances and international stability rely on the domestic characteristics of states.

# Chapter 5

# Socialization

## *Shaping to Transform Norms, Roles, and Practices*

Speaking to journalists about an ongoing Collective Security Treaty Organization (CSTO)-sponsored exercise called "Tsentr" ("Center"), Russian Chief of the General Staff General Nikolai Makarov explained to reporters how the training event would test the ability of the organization to react to mass uprisings, "like in North Africa and the Middle East."[1] The exercise was taking place in September 2011 and the Russian officer was referring to the nascent Arab Spring, which began as a massive protest against authoritarian rule in Tunisia and quickly spread to Libya, Egypt, Syria, Yemen, and Bahrain. Long-standing autocrats in Tunisia and Egypt were quickly ousted, while the other rulers were facing imminent threats of overthrow.[2] The CSTO, consisting mostly of authoritarian former Soviet states—Russia, Armenia, Belarus, Kazakhstan, Kyrgyzstan, Tajikistan, and formerly, Uzbekistan—felt the pressure of potential revolution: the security organization even publicly announced that its member states agreed to control social media in order to avoid repeats of the Arab revolutions.[3] Referring again to the Arab Spring, General Makarov told reporters that "Russia's military organization has to be prepared for the worst scenarios of the development of the situation" in Central Asia.[4] The possibility of democratic revolution along Russia's frontiers was unacceptable: Russia, through the CSTO, would ensure its contiguous former republics were capable of resisting rebellion.

This chapter explores the second logic of shaping: socialization. Major powers employ this logic to impart norms and practices, as well as to influence what type of "role" partner militaries will adopt, such as external defense, regime-support, or expeditionary peacekeeping. The mechanism by which major powers leverage socialization to reduce strategic uncertainty is by developing partner forces that better serve the major power's national interests. For some major powers, encouraging democratic practices increases the number of trustworthy partners abroad; for others, regime stability insures against overthrow and volatility in a major power's region. If major powers are successful, partner militaries become either more trustworthy, or more competent to prevent revolutions that generate regional instability.

With its emphasis on democracy promotion and NATO expansion, the US-led Partnership for Peace exercises (described in chapter 4) involved substantial socialization in addition to attraction. However, to demonstrate the ubiquitous use of socialization, this chapter explores this logic of shaping through non-Western, non-liberal powers, particularly China and Russia. Although there is significant debate about whether these states are diligently engaging in "autocracy promotion" abroad,[5] it is clear that the two main regional security organizations in Eurasia—the Shanghai Cooperation Organization (SCO) and the CSTO—embody the norms of state security, sovereignty, and noninterference by external actors.[6] The case of Russian-led military exercises with Central Asian countries in the CSTO, in particular, highlights the use of exercises to prevent democratic revolution in Russia's neighboring states. Russia viewed the "Color Revolutions" of the mid-2000s a major security threat and used shaping to maintain the current balance in its region by training units to embody the role of regime defense. Through exercise scenarios that included political overthrow, Russia leveraged military training to habituate practices of regime defense and encourage the norm of state security and sovereignty.

## SOCIALIZATION AND MILITARY TRAINING

Socialization through military statecraft is the use of military power to convince and teach other militaries to adopt a set of values or norms that are eventually 'taken for granted.'[7] Teaching often involves the repetition of certain tasks and the building of habits or practices, which are "competent performances" by actors that are socially developed through learning and training.[8] Major powers employ the socialization logic through persuasion, teaching, and training to influence other states to adopt certain values or practices they view as favorable. Carol Atkinson argues that because most militaries have a major influence on a state's domestic politics, these organizations are often the target of international socialization efforts through military-to-military engagement. Her studies reveal how US military education programs expose and impart liberal values on visiting foreign officers (which then affect the political identity of the officer's country)[9] and this logic can also apply to one of the most important routine activities of all armies; that is, training.

From the dawn of warfare, military training emphasized the repetition of tasks to a degree in which these skills become habitual. As Sun Tzu notes, training brings discipline: "If in training soldiers commands are habitually enforced, the army will be well-disciplined; if not, its discipline will be bad"; moreover, "Maneuvering with an army is advantageous, with an undisciplined multitude, most dangerous."[10] In the contemporary military environment, soldiers are trained at regular intervals to retain "battle drills": automatic individual and unit responses to certain combat scenarios, which are vital in units' ability to effectively respond to enemy maneuvers on the battlefield.[11] Through personal interaction and the careful design of exercise scenarios, military training can move beyond simple drills such as firing a weapon or ambushing an enemy.

As major powers seek partners that are benign or serve their national interests, they often look for opportunities to socialize partner militaries with certain values through joint training. For instance, democratic states may be viewed as more trustworthy or authoritarian states may be considered more stable. A military's values and practices are most visible in the military's identity or "role" that it serves for its society, as described by Edmunds et al. These authors argue that in addition to providing national security, a state's armed forces may fulfill several other roles: for instance, an opportunity to inculcate national values in citizens ("Nation Builder"), uphold the power of a particular set of political or party interests ("Regime Defense"), offer support to address internal emergencies ("Domestic Military Assistance"), or provide an instrument to promote values and build relationships abroad ("Military Diplomacy").[12] Major powers may encourage partners to adopt one or more of these roles during training. Within the role of national security-provider, militaries may train tasks that focus purely on national defense against an external aggressor; conversely, they sometimes emphasize a broadened definition of security through the practice of peacekeeping or humanitarian tasks. Although democracies often encourage democratic practices during training—such as focusing externally on threats, upholding international law, and defending human rights—they may also seek to strengthen an authoritarian regime against an uprising. For instance, during the Cold War the United States supported oppressive Central and South American militaries with training and military aid to prevent left-wing revolutions.[13]

The targets of socialization are primarily transitioning or consolidating states; that is, states that already enjoy a functioning military but are either experiencing a transition away from a particular regime-type, or states which are still maturing as a certain regime-type (for simplicity, either democratic or authoritarian). As states move from one regime-type to another, military exercises serve as an opportunity to socialize these norms. For instance, although NATO's PfP military exercises were primarily geared toward attraction, the explicit teaching of democratic norms—such as transparent budgets and civilian control of the military—took place at the ministerial level and the exercising of democratic practices during military training events served to prepare candidates for NATO membership.[14] Moreover, as states seek to consolidate their administrative capacity and develop mature regimes, major powers use socialization to strengthen central rule. Especially if a certain regime is struggling to resist political or social revolution, major powers may train that partner military to protect its regime's challenged grip on power.

Of the many functions that a military may perform, there are two primary roles that major powers seek to encourage through socialization: *regime defense* and what I label *democracy defense*. The latter role requires militaries to embody and defend democratic principles, such as establishing civilian control of the military, respecting political rights domestically, and defending international law externally. Democratic major powers promote both types of roles (depending on the nature of threat), while authoritarian powers largely promote regime defense; both role-forming efforts are explored below.

## DEMOCRACY PROMOTION AND AUTHORITARIAN CONSOLIDATION

First, major powers may encourage the role of democracy defense in transitioning partners to build more trustworthy states. War between democracies is rare in world politics and although there are opposing theories about what causes the democratic peace,[15] John Owen argues that liberal states share the idea that self-preservation and freedom from government oppression can only be achieved through peace. Because democracies express the collective interests of freedom-seeking individuals, liberals trust that other democracies share this desire for peace, prosperity, and liberty. Even if illiberal leaders are elected in a democracy, their ability to use force will be constrained through structural checks and balances. Conversely, he argues that non-democracies do not share this aspiration for liberty; they often seek conquest and are considered more untrustworthy in the eyes of democracies.[16] If major powers are able to build transitioning armies that protect political rights internally and respect international law externally, then major powers will more easily trust these emerging democracies. That is, as militaries in transition refrain from domestic oppression, avoid coups against their own government, and participate in UN-sanctioned peacekeeping missions, then democratic major powers will become more certain that they will pose little threat.

NATO's emphasis on democratic socialization was apparent both during the Cold War and after. For instance, John Pevehouse reveals how NATO membership helped guide Spain's transition to democracy after the death of authoritarian leader Francisco Franco. Following an attempted military coup in the emerging democracy in 1981, "the belief surfaced in government circles that entry to NATO would help secure the new democracy as it would modernize the Army through growing international contacts and direct its attention away from domestic politics."[17] He notes that a training focus on external security directed the Spanish military away from internal concerns: "Through joint maneuvers, modernization, and improvements in military technology, the Spanish military became oriented away from domestic politics."[18] After the Cold War, the US Clinton Administration strongly believed in the democratic peace and viewed both NATO expansion and the PfP program as means to promote democracy. Speaking to Congress in his 1994 State of the Union address, Clinton argued, "Ultimately the best strategy to insure our security and to build a durable peace is to support the advance of democracy elsewhere. Democracies don't attack each other; they make better trading partners and partners in diplomacy."[19] The consequence of this belief is that the more trustworthy democratic partners abroad, the fewer security threats in a democratic major power's strategic environment.

Second, major powers may shape a partner military to adopt the role of regime defense to protect the ruling party or leadership from internal revolution. Not only do the consequences of rebellion include instability, lack of capacity to prevent transnational crime, inability to secure borders, and often massive migration, overthrow may result in the installation of an unfriendly political system in a major power's environment. If a major power feels threatened by the possibility of overthrow in its neighboring states, it may provide support to "consolidate" rule in the partner country. Thomas Ambrosio argues that Russia actively encourages "authoritarian consolidation," or the solidification of autocratic rule in order to prevent democratic transition, in the former Soviet Union.[20] Nicole Jackson similarly notes that Russia supports autocratic Central Asian regimes by "actively countering democratization efforts, by providing legitimacy and political support, and by diversifying relations. This, in turn, at least in the short term, may increase regime stability and durability."[21] As previously mentioned, the United States assisted Central American regimes with military aid and training to prevent left-wing revolutions throughout the 1980s. By ensuring that a partner military is capable of suppressing rebellion, major powers that feel threatened by political revolution—either democratic or communist—train and influence partner militaries to defend the ruling regime.

# SOCIALIZATION AND THE ROLE OF SECURITY ORGANIZATIONS

The rise of regional security organizations offer major powers an opportunity to influence the role of partner militaries. NATO, for instance, has long provided the United States and the European major powers with a means to influence the roles of transitioning states. Despite its Cold War military mission to contain Soviet aggression, NATO's original political goal was to consolidate and protect the liberal democratic community, enshrined in the 1949 Washington Treaty. NATO's oft-referenced Article 5 commitment to defend allies in the case of an attack overshadows the other thirteen articles, including commitments to resolve conflicts peacefully (Art. 1), strengthen free institutions (Art. 2), and adhere to UN principles (Arts. 1, 7).[22] Although NATO has not published specific criteria for membership, an internal study in 1995 argued that enlargement would lure post-communist states to adopt democratic reforms, which in turn would provide European stability.[23] Since the early 2000s, Russia and China have also leveraged two regional security organizations to shape partner militaries in Central Asia; both institutions are described below.

## Socialization in Eurasian Security Organizations

Two Eurasian security organizations established in the early 2000s—the CSTO led by Russia and the SCO initiated by China—have sponsored multiple exercises almost every year since inception.[24] Although the roots of both organizations are located in diplomatic agreements to create stability and prevent conventional war in Eurasia after the collapse of the Soviet Union, the CSTO and the SCO in their contemporary forms were launched largely in response to the growing threat posed by violent non-state actors.[25] Specifically, both security organizations developed out of the fear of Islamic terrorism and political revolution: religious extremism beginning in the 1990s and the possibility of Western-sponsored democratic revolution throughout the 2000s. Militant religious groups, such as the Eastern Turkistan Islamic Movement (ETIM), the Islamic Movement of Uzbekistan (IMU), and Chechen rebels, threatened to overthrow local governments and establish caliphates throughout China, Russia, and Central Asia.[26] Political uprisings in the form of "Color Revolutions" threatened to replace autocratic regimes with democratic or pro-Western governments.

Despite these security concerns about transnational threats, the organizations emphasize noninterference in each member's internal affairs, which creates obstacles for major power military intervention during crises and even complicates efforts to produce joint operations.[27] Surprisingly, the

CSTO and SCO refrained from military intervention in Kyrgyzstan's political revolution in 2010, despite this state's membership in both organizations.[28] In fact, although government officials and military officers within the SCO and the CSTO consult and exercise regularly, neither security organization has publicly deployed joint units for any military mission—counterterrorism, peacekeeping, or humanitarian relief—either regional or UN-sponsored. Thus, CSTO and SCO exercises over the last fifteen years have trained forces that rarely (if ever) deploy together for actual operations.

## China, the SCO, and the "Three Evils"

The SCO originated in 1996 when five countries—China, Russia, Kazakhstan, Kyrgyzstan, and Tajikistan—met in Shanghai, China to negotiate their ambiguous shared borders, as well as develop confidence-building measures to reduce military forces and mutual mistrust between members. The breakup of the USSR not only resulted in border disputes, but also reduced the capacity for the emergent Central Asian states to exercise sovereignty over their new countries. Tajikistan collapsed into civil war from 1992 to 1994, with continued instability until 1997; war broke out again in 1998 when a former commander from the Tajik civil war attempted to establish his own government in the northern part of the country. In February 1999, the IMU detonated a bomb in the capital of Uzbekistan, nearly killing the president; the IMU also declared its intentions of taking control of the government. The IMU then waged an insurgency in the Fergana Valley later that summer with the intention of overthrowing regional governments and establishing an Islamic caliphate stretching from Muslim-majority Chechnya, Russia to Xinjiang, China.[29] Against the backdrop of increased terrorism in Central Asia, the "Shanghai Five" (along with Uzbekistan) met again in June 2001 to announce the creation of SCO as a means to address the growing problem of non-state violence in the region.

The SCO charter was signed in St. Petersburg, Russia in June 2002 and entered force in September 2003. The June 2001 declaration noted that the purpose of the organization was not to serve as a defense alliance, but instead to provide security against terrorism, separatism, and extremism, expressed as the "three evils" undermining regional stability.[30] Moreover, the group simultaneously released a joint document on the "The Shanghai Convention on Combating Terrorism, Separatism and Extremism" which further elucidated these threats to regional security, as well proscribed consultative measures in case of a crisis.[31] Three days after the September 11, 2001, attacks by Al Qaeda on the United States, the organization released a document which expressed empathy for the victims of the attacks, as well as measures to "accelerate the establishment of a regional anti-terrorist structure."[32] The CSTO (explored in detail in the case study below) was also established in 2002 largely in response to the growth of non-state threats, accelerated by US operations in Afghanistan.

## SCO and CSTO Military Exercises

The first SCO and CSTO multinational exercises took place in 2002 and 2003, respectively. The first SCO exercise—which also happened to be China's first-ever ground-based multinational exercise—occurred in October 2002 between China and Kyrgyzstan. The event kicked off with little media attention even though China had long preferred unilateral to multilateral training. Dennis Blasko argues that although, "Little also is known about the national-level decisionmaking [*sic*] process that led to the reversal of the decades-old policy of not training with foreign militaries," Chinese officials' concern about terrorism likely had a profound influence: "While the terrorist attacks of September 11, 2001, (9/11), probably added impetus to this decision, the Chinese government previously had been concerned about the threat of terrorism and other non-traditional security challenges."[33] The SCO hosts about one or two major multinational exercises per year and focuses mainly on transnational terrorism, ensuring partner forces are able to protect their countries' political and territorial sovereignty. Roughly half of SCO exercises include all members and consist of about 300–1,300 troops, while the annual "Peace Mission" exercises are much larger in scale—from 2,000 to 10,000 total soldiers—and on several occasions involved only Russia and China.

Although Russia conducted intermittent exercises with Commonwealth of Independent States (CIS) states throughout the 1990s, the first official CSTO training events were held in 2003, both of which simulated rapid reaction forces intervening in insurgent takeovers of Central Asian territory.[34] The CSTO conducts multiple multilateral training events per year, usually focusing on threats of terrorism or separatism—often portrayed to be sponsored by the West—and rotates the location through different member states. Most members are willing to hold exercises on their territory, while others—in particular, Belarus and (former member) Uzbekistan—resist Russian presence in their countries.[35] Exercises "Frontier" and "Interaction" are the most consistent counterterror exercise programs, consisting of troop levels between 600 and 12,000, while "Indestructible Brotherhood" was launched in 2012 as a training event for about 600–700 CSTO peacekeepers.[36] Each exercise with former Soviet states provides an opportunity for Russia and China to influence the role that partner militaries serve for their societies, namely regime defense. By shaping these partners through regional security organizations, Russia and China hope to eliminate the possibility of unstable or unfriendly governments along their borders.

## CASE STUDY: RUSSIAN-LED CSTO EXERCISES

As described above, China and Russia have expanded their use of socializing exercises throughout the 2000s and 2010s through two regional security organizations. As both institutions attempt to combat violent non-state threats, yet also emphasize noninterference in members' domestic politics, these training events serve as an opportunity for Russia and China to influence the norms and practices of Eurasian states without direct military intervention or multilateral deployments. Through training, both China and Russia encourage the role of regime defense in consolidating post-Soviet states. By strengthening the ability of these partner militaries to defend their regimes, China and Russia hope to reduce the risk of Islamic or democratic revolution along their borders. The case study below illustrates how Russia exploits the CSTO as a tool to encourage the role of regime defense in Caucasian and Central Asian states while honoring member states' sovereignty: as of this writing, the CSTO has never deployed soldiers to manage crises within its region or outside.[37] As with the other case studies, a brief assessment of the effectiveness of these programs will be offered at the end of the illustrative case.

### Russia, the Former Soviet Union, and the Origins of the CSTO

From the remnants of the precipitously dissolved Union of Soviet Socialist Republics (USSR) in December 1991 arose fifteen newly independent states. Russia, the most powerful country and successor to the Soviet Union, was now surrounded by troubled nations attempting to secure sovereignty and improve security. Russia itself was in need of order: by May 1992, the Russian defense ministry and armed forces were not yet officially established though the Federation was already in existence for five months.[38] Most of the countries that comprised Russia's "near abroad" signed an agreement that officially recognized their sovereign equality with Russia and formed a regional organization, the CIS.[39] Additionally, nine members of the CIS signed the Collective Security Treaty, known as the "Tashkent Treaty," between 1992 and 1993 to reaffirm individual sovereignty and the ability for each state to develop its own military, while also committing to peaceful resolution of conflicts between members.[40] The treaty prohibited its signatories from joining other alliances, engaging in treaties counter to the Tashkent agreement, and required that the use of force outside members' territory be "carried out only in the interests of the [*sic*] international security according to the UN Charter."[41]

*Russia Exerts Leadership in Its "Near Abroad"*

According to Roy Allison, Russia continued to exhibit primacy among the CIS in the 1990s, despite the loss of control with the breakup of the USSR. For instance, Russian leaders viewed the country's relationship with CIS members as largely hierarchical; President Boris Yeltsin claimed that Russia should be "first among equals" among the former Soviet republics.[42] In addition to security, ethnic Russians also inhabited the former Soviet republics, which provided an ethno-nationalist justification for Russian interest in its near abroad.[43] This leadership role was confirmed in Russia's multiple unilateral interventions—which Russia defended as peacekeeping—in CIS states' internal conflicts, such as in Moldova, South Ossetia, Tajikistan, and Abkhazia in 1992.[44] Russia's faith in its own leadership was further supported in its foreign policy concept of December 1992 and Yeltsin's February 1993 speech when he claimed that international organizations should, "grant Russia special powers as a guarantor of peace and stability in the former regions of the USSR."[45] Even after the collapse of the Soviet Union, Russia viewed a special role for itself in its near abroad, especially in regards to maintaining stability through unilateral peacekeeping.

Russian regional leadership was deemed even more vital in the shadow of US unipolarity. A senior Russian military officer warned in summer 1992 that growing conflict in the CIS could lead to direct intervention by NATO and the CIS Joint Forces Commander-in-Chief, Marshal Shaposhnikov, claimed that NATO had no right under the CSCE framework to use armed force to settle disputes in the CIS. Suspicions were confirmed when a leaked US State Department draft memo in August 1993 rejected a greater role for Russia to conduct peacekeeping in the CIS and that the United States should be ready to support UN operations in the troubled region, even in the face of Russian opposition.[46] Russia struggled to gain UN support for its unilateral peacekeeping missions in the former republics. Russian foreign minister Andrei Kozyrev asked for a UN mandate for its operations in the CIS, arguing that Chapter VIII of the UN Charter could be interpreted to allow the peacekeeping responsibility to be delegated to a regional organization with external monitors attached. UN secretary general Boutros Boutros Ghali largely opposed this idea, yet by 1994 he was willing to allow the CIS to conduct peacekeeping in its own region with the requirement that that the force be comprised of only 20–30 percent of Russian troops and solely under UN command. Given these restrictions, Moscow declared that its extra-territorial operations were fully legal and did not require a UN mandate. However, Russia finally conceded to UN monitoring in Abkhazia and Tajikistan to oversee ceasefires in mid-to-late 1994.[47]

Russia's concern for stability in its near abroad and suspicion of Western interference were described in its 2000 national security concept. The policy declares that major threats to security include the "outbreak and escalation of conflicts near the state border of the Russian Federation and the external borders of the member states of the Commonwealth of Independent States."[48] Additionally, Russia's suspicion of Western meddling is also apparent in the document, which cites NATO's eastward expansion, the appearance of foreign military bases by Russia's borders, and the striving of "particular states and intergovernmental organizations" to belittle the international security role of the UN and OSCE as other main threats to the country's security.[49]

## THE CSTO AS A RESPONSE TO TERRORISM AND WESTERN INFLUENCE

Russian attempts to maintain stability and primacy in the former Soviet Union were complicated by three factors in the early 2000s: the threat of Islamic terrorism, US strategic interest in Central Asia, and Western support for democratization through "Colored Revolutions." Islamic terrorism posed threats to Russia and Central Asia throughout the 1990s: Russia brutally repressed Chechen rebels in 1996 and 1999, while the IMU seized territory between Uzbekistan, Tajikistan, and Kyrgyzstan in 1999. Moreover, after the attacks on American soil by Al Qaeda in September 2001, the United States responded with NATO operations in Afghanistan to remove the Taliban regime and eliminate safe havens for Al Qaeda. To logistically support missions in the traditionally austere region, American military planners required access to Central Asia and consequently secured airbases in Kyrgyzstan, Tajikistan, and Uzbekistan from 2001 to 2002. American leaders also increased its security cooperation with Uzbekistan when US Secretary of State Colin Powell and Uzbekistani foreign minister Adulaziz Kamilov signed a Strategic Partnership and Cooperation Framework in 2002.[50] Intensified US involvement in Central Asia ran into existing Russian presence in the region, which viewed these former Soviet republics as buffers against terrorism and narcotics trafficking from Afghanistan.[51] Already in 2001, Russia had roughly 18,000 troops stationed in Tajikistan and in late 2002, developed a joint airbase in Kant, Kyrgyzstan. The purpose of the joint Kyrgyz-Russian airfield was ostensibly to provide a base to support the recently assembled Collective Rapid Deployment Forces (CRDF), one of the first major initiatives to emerge from the newly created CSTO.[52]

The CSTO, a security organization that was built on the principles of the Tashkent Treaty, was established in May 2002 by Russia, Armenia, Belarus,

Kazakhstan, Kyrgyzstan, and Tajikistan.[53] In addition to guarantees for mutual defense against external aggression, the CSTO's charter emphasizes the threat of violent non-state actors while respecting the sovereignty of each member state. The preamble establishes members' commitment to "continue and increase the close and all-round allied relations in foreign policy, military and technical areas, as well as in the sphere of counteraction to the transnational challenges and menaces to the safety of states and peoples."[54] Article 5 of the charter spells out the organization's insistence on respecting each participating country's independence, sovereignty, and equal rights, as well as asserting noninterference in member states. This focus on sovereign inviolability was important for the former Soviet republics as they often feared Russian intervention in their internal affairs.[55]

In addition to combating transnational threats, military cooperation within the CSTO allows Russia to maintain a clientelist relationship with former Soviet republics.[56] Former CSTO General Sectary Nikolai Bordyuzha noted in 2012 that the organization's two initial tasks were: national security from external enemies and the maintenance of peace in member states. Regarding the first task, he argued that member states such as Uzbekistan, Tajikistan, and Kyrgyzstan were afraid of spillover Islamic extremism from Afghanistan since the US invasion in 2001. Concerning the second, the desire for continued control was obvious when Bordyuzha noted how the, "Interests of Russia were confined to a wish not to lose influence in the former Soviet republics using historic, political and economic relations. Really it was planned to create a kind of post-Soviet counterpart of NATO in the best case and to preserve military bases on the territories of the neighboring republics in the worst case."[57] The CSTO thus provides Russia with a means to combat transnational threats, maintain a hegemonic or clientelist relationship with parts of the former Soviet Union, while adhering to principles of nonintervention within the organization.

Currently, the CSTO is comprised of four types of collective forces: regional group commands, peacekeepers, CRDP (for Central Asia), and the Collective Prompt Reaction Forces. Regional groups are joint commands signed through bilateral treaties and broken down into three regions: Eastern Europe (Belarus and Russia), Caucasus (Armenia and Russia), and Central Asia (not yet signed, though responsibility is delegated to the CRDP). The "Collective Rapid Deployment Forces for Central Asia" were created in 2001 to address scenarios similar to the IMU's infiltration into Batken, Kyrgyzstan, and are comprised of about 4,000 soldiers, special forces, and police units. "Collective Rapid Deployment Forces" were developed in 2009, are comprised of about 20,000 military and special forces, and conducted exercises in 2009 and 2011. Some of the tasks assigned to the rapid deployment forces are settling local and boundary conflicts, prevent drug trafficking, and countering terrorism.[58]

## The CSTO and Threats of Democratic Revolution

*Revolutions in Georgia, Ukraine, and Kyrgyzstan*

Beginning in 2003, the most salient threat to autocratic leadership that emerged in the former Soviet Union was democratic revolution. The region had experienced three regimes overthrown by democracy supporters in "Color Revolutions" by 2005: the Rose Revolution in Georgia (2003), Orange Revolution in Ukraine (2004), and the Tulip Revolution in Kyrgyzstan (2005). In the aftermath of the revolutions, the newly elected Ukrainian and Georgian presidents were unambiguously pro-West, while the Kyrgyzstani government would continue to be plagued with internal strife and draw closer to Moscow. Despite the lack of direct military involvement by either the United States or Russia during the political turmoil, Russia under President Vladimir Putin believed that these revolutions were fomented by the West, particularly the United States, presenting a direct threat to Russian interests.[59] One Russian official believed, "The 'revolutions' themselves are a combination of peaceful and violent methods designed to topple regimes disagreeable to the United States" and "Washington maintains that 'color revolutions' cost less than the toppling of regimes through military intervention," citing the US overthrow of the Iraq's Saddam Hussein autocratic government in 2003 as an example. For this official, American diplomats stationed inside the country and organizations such as the Soros Foundations develop and fund networks of opposition leaders to topple the existing regime.[60] Russian Defense Minister Sergei Ivanov asserted that Russia would react harshly "to exports of revolution to the CIS states, no matter [where] and what colour-pink, blue, you name it."[61] Russia's suspicions of US efforts to promote democratization were confirmed when Secretary of State Condoleezza Rice visited Belarusian opposition leaders in April 2005 and urged them to oppose the autocratic government. Foreign Minister Sergei Lavrov responded to the visit: "We think the democratic process, the process of reform cannot be imposed from outside."[62]

*Mass Protests and Government Responses in*
*Armenia, Uzbekistan, Belarus, and Kyrgyzstan*

Even during the 1990s, former Soviet states within the CSTO felt the force of democratic revolution and deployed their security forces to quell rebellion. As early as 1996, Armenia's presidential election faced demonstrations from protestors who claimed that the process was rigged. The military and police suppressed the protests by sealing off the capital, shutting down the offices of opposition parties, and arresting 250 opposition leaders. After the 2003 presidential and parliamentary elections were also alleged to be marred with intimidation, media bias, and ballot-box stuffing, thousands of protestors mobilized in the streets to oppose the unfair elections. Armenian security forces (including the military) quelled the protest movement and arrested hundreds of opposition leaders.[63] The protests were reignited in 2004 when opposition forces organized demonstrations of over 25,000, seeking to reproduce the results of Georgia's Rose Revolution. During this protest, security forces blocked demonstrators from entering the capital, ransacked opposition headquarters, and arrested hundreds of activists across the country.[64]

In May 2005, the Uzbek government deployed security and military forces to violently repress protests in Andijan, Uzbekistan. Thousands of demonstrators gathered in Bobur square to protest the unfair detention and trial of twenty-three businessmen accused of being Islamic extremists; however, a group of armed opposition supporters stormed military and police barracks, stole weapons, freed the businessmen, and took hostages in government offices. The protestors hoped that President Islam Karimov would address the perceived injustice and calm tensions; instead, he sent police, as well as military troops, who fired on the protestors. Human Rights Watch claims that the military sealed off streets, prevented people from leaving, and, in cooperation with internal security forces, killed hundreds in the massacre.[65]

In the wake of the Orange Revolution and in preparation for Belarus' 2006 presidential election, President Alexander Lukashenko initiated preemptive measures against democratization efforts. In addition to arresting opposition leaders for organizing protests, the regime began amending laws to allow security forces to fight demonstrators with firearms or "in other cases determined by the president."[66] After an uprising in Osh, Kyrgyzstan, in 2011, the Kyrgyz Defense Minister Abibilla Kudayberdiyev was asked about the Kyrgyz constitution's ban on the military's involvement in internal conflicts. Kudayberdiyev responded:

> Indeed, Article 14 of the constitution bans the use of armed forces for internal political goals. But Article 18 of the constitutional law on emergency situations says that 'military units can be used for handling the aftermath of emergency situations and ensuring citizens' security . . . Article 22 of the same law defines what extraordinary measures can be taken in case of an emergency and says that military units can be used to ensure public order and protect various facilities.[67]

He goes on to note, "And I disagree with statements that during the June unrest the army failed. On the contrary it played a big role in stabilizing the situation. The military patrolled the streets and manned check points around the clock for five months."[68] Throughout the decades since Soviet collapse, CSTO member leaders required the ability to counter democratic revolution; security forces, including the military, often served as the best option.

### *"Sovereign Democracy" and Regime Security*

As the CSTO evolved against the backdrop of democratic revolutions throughout the former Soviet space in the mid-2000s, Russian officials began formulating policies to counteract these non-state threats. In 2006, during President Vladimir Putin's second term, Russian officials began promoting a concept known as "sovereign democracy," an idea that resonated with post-Soviet authoritarian leaders who feared foreign meddling in their internal affairs. The term "sovereign democracy" was first publicly articulated by Vladislov Surkov, deputy chief of the Russian presidential administration, at a speech in June 2006. He later spoke to American reporters to clarify the term and downplayed its significance: "And we want to be a free nation among other free nations and to cooperate with them proceeding from fair principles, we don't want to be managed from abroad. That's it." As opposed to "managed democracy," in which a state is directed by an external regime, Russia promoted sovereign democracy: an attempt to implement policies independent of foreign interference.[69]

Fearing the consequences of revolution in its near abroad for its influence in the CIS, let alone the possibility of revolution inside its own borders, Russian leaders enacted concrete steps toward preventing western interference and democratic revolt. Allison argues that Central Asian leaders engaged in opposition to democratic reform through a regional system of "protective integration" with Russia and fellow authoritarian states. Regime security, he argues, is the top priority for these leaders and the only way to prevent mutual suspicion of external sponsoring of domestic overthrow is to commit to a regional security organization with Russia and former Soviet republics.[70] When Russia was concerned about the increasing westernization of neighboring states, the country sometimes intervened militarily (as in the case of non-CSTO members, Georgia in 2008 and Ukraine in 2014). However, given the Putin administration's putative support for "sovereign democracy" in the region, as well as the statutory assurances of noninterference in fellow CSTO states, Russia needed a means to prevent democratic revolution short of intervention. The CSTO, as a security organization, would serve as Russia's instrument to oppose democratization by bolstering autocratic regimes in the former Soviet Union.

## CSTO Military Exercises to Consolidate Authoritarian Rule

One practical means by which Russia supports CSTO member states to consolidate rule is through military training. Exercises "Frontier" and "Indestructible Brotherhood" were designed to train CSTO soldiers how to combat the threat of violent non-state actors; the former trained counterterrorism tasks while the latter emphasized peacekeeping. The exercises were developed around scenarios in which an insurgent group—either politically or religiously motivated and sometimes funded by an outside source—would attempt to overthrow the regime or seize territory and create a secessionist government. Individual CSTO member units and collective reaction forces would then practice intervention to expel the terrorists from sovereign territory. Sometimes CSTO planners designed the exercise adversary to be explicitly an extremist Islamic insurgent group; other times the exercise enemy resembled the armed democratic protestors that seized government buildings during Color Revolutions. Below are explorations of three of these exercises: two from *Frontier* and one from the *Indestructible Brotherhood* program.

### *Exercise Frontier: Preventing Western-Supported Regime Change*

In March 2005, the CSTO planned to conduct an anti-terror exercise in Kyrgyzstan known as "Rubezh," or in English, "Frontier". However, following democratic protests against alleged unfair parliamentary elections and the seizure of public buildings by the opposition during the Tulip Revolution in Kyrgyzstan, the exercises were urgently moved to Tajikistan in order to avoid the impression of intervention by external actors.[71] During the revolution, Kyrgyz President Askar Akayev was ousted by armed insurgents, who captured government buildings unopposed by weak state security forces. The CSTO exercise was moved to early April, one week after the initial stages of the democratic revolt, and involved roughly 1,000 troops from all CSTO states.[72] The scenario of the training event was strikingly similar to the situation in Kyrgyzstan: one group, wearing blue shirts, was tasked with attempting to overthrow the local government due to discontent with the previous election, while the other team, wearing red shirts, protected the sovereignty and territorial integrity of the regime.[73] Erica Marat argues, "The implication of this division into red and blue camps during the drills emphasizes the blue team's ties with destructive foreign powers, be they terrorist organizations . . . or international NGOs, as in Kyrgyzstan's regime change."[74]

"Rubezh 2006," this time held in Aktau, Kazakhstan, along the Caspian coastline, resembled a similar scenario to its 2005 predecessor, though this exercise involved more troops (over 2,500) and integrated the recently created CRDP.[75] Russia, Kazakhstan, Kyrgyzstan, and Tajikistan participated in this exercise, while Armenia and Belarus did not (Uzbekistan sent observers). The exercise was divided into three phases, the last of which involved joint maneuvers with land, air, and naval forces.[76] Also joining the training were elements from Kyrgyzstan's special forces unit, known as the "scorpion brigade," a unit that is alleged to have taken part in countering protests in the 2005 Tulip Revolution.[77] The tactical portion of this iteration also focused on terrorists objecting to the results of an election and attempting to overthrow the government, though the adversary to the regime was an Islamic movement striving to establish a caliphate. One news story reported that a goal of the exercise was to practice, "a joint operation for stabilization of the situation in the aforementioned region of Kazakhstan."[78] The scenario again incorporated "red" (CSTO members) vs. "blue" (armed Islamic terrorists) combat, but included a third "brown" team which represented "countries that wish to exploit the situation so as to strengthen their influence in this part of the world."[79] Another story, entitled, "The 'Red' Will Suppress the Mutiny of the 'Blue'; Russia and its Allies Learn to Defend Central Asian Regimes," reported the Russian defense ministry's confirmation that "the scenario of the exercise is based on a conflict in Central Asia." The reporters speculate that the "brown" team was, "not ODKB [CSTO] members in which it is easy to guess Afghanistan and the contingent of NATO and US forces staying there."[80] Russian TV showed images of the exercise and an anchor reported, "The Blues are operating with the clear sympathy of, and secret assistance from, the Browns – the countries interested in destabilizing the situation in the region."[81] The plan also called for a simulated mobilization of larger multinational military units in the case of external actors seeking to intervene militarily.[82]

The concern about Islamic terrorism was ostensibly to address the Andijan massacre in May 2005, when Uzbek soldiers fired on a crowd of protestors who supported twenty-three men on trial accused of being Islamic extremists.[83] By construing the exercise scenario as a fight against Islamic terrorism, CSTO planners painted Uzbekistan's actions as "anti-terror" as opposed to repressive against democratic demonstrators.[84] However, given the exercise scenario's focus on combating the ability of external supporters to influence the conflict or conduct independent attacks, Islamic terrorism seemed a lesser concern than the threat posed by democratization backed by the United States. Moreover, during the exercise there was speculation that the maneuvers were conducted to prepare for Tajikistan's upcoming presidential election in November 2006 or potential instability created by Kyrgyzstan's constitutional reform efforts.[85] Regardless, it is clear that in both *Frontier* exercises, Russia, through the CSTO, hoped to train former Soviet militaries to fulfill the role of regime defense.

*Exercise Indestructible Brotherhood: Peacekeeping*
*to Prevent Mass Disorder*

In addition to annual *Rubezh* exercises, the CSTO conducted "Nerushimoye Bratstvo" ("Indestructible Brotherhood") exercises to train its standing peace-keeping force. In the first of such exercises conducted in October 2012, also held in Kazakhstan, the training involved all member states of the CSTO. According to official statements, the exercise was intended to prepare for the conduct of peacekeeping operations within the CSTO region, as well as possible operations with a mandate from the UN. One news report suggested that peacekeepers may be deployed in scenarios like the ethnic conflict in Kyrgyzstan in 2010, even though the CSTO denied this request and provided no forces. The report also cautions that CSTO states cannot rule out "the probability of appearance of big-scale uncontrolled conflicts similar to those that have happened recently in some Arab countries."[86] Familiar peacekeep-ing tasks such as separating conflicting parties, escorting humanitarian car-goes, and guarding vital facilities were present in the plan. However, there was a larger focus on protecting vital facilities and "preventing mass disor-ders."[87] Journalist Joshua Kucera claimed that "According to the scenario, a crisis situation arises connected with the activity of international extremists and terrorist organizations and conflict between ethnic groups living in the country."[88] The concern about revolution, whether democratic or Islamic, was obvious in other CSTO exercises as well. Though not historically a peace-keeping-style or anti-terror exercise, the CSTO's "Center" exercise in 2011 was tailored to address situations that reflected the Arab Spring revolutions, as mentioned in the introduction. Exercises such as *Center* and *Indestructible Brotherhood* were geared toward managing protests and revolts after auto-cratic Arab regimes began falling to democratic revolutions in 2011 and 2012.

*Assessing the Effectiveness of CSTO Exercises*

Although the case study above reveals Russia's efforts to socialize the role of regime defense in CSTO member states, was the major power success-ful in protecting certain regimes against overthrow through exercises? There are countless reasons why an overthrow may or may not be successful, and a handful of exercises per year seems minor compared to other explana-tions.[89] However, authoritarian survivability often rests on the loyalty and effectiveness the regime's coercive capacity.[90] If Russian-led training is one potential influence, the results seem mixed. Although autocratic leaders (and their appointed successors) have retained power in Belarus, Kazakhstan, and Tajikistan, other regimes have not fared as well. Armenia's Serzh Sargsyan and Kazakhstan's Kurmanbek Bakiyev resigned in 2010 and 2018, respec-tively, amid democratic protests.[91] Interestingly, however, Lucan Way argues that Russia favored political turnover in Kyrgyzstan because Bakiyev started to draw closer to Western interests, primarily by allowing the United States to build and continue to operate Manas Air Force Base.[92] Thus, although Russia attempts to encourage regime stability in CSTO member states, it is difficult to determine with high certainty the effectiveness of its efforts given the multitude of alternative factors at play.

## SUMMARY

As one of the most vital routine tasks for preparing warriors for the rigors of battle, military training also provides the opportunity to socialize soldiers with different norms, roles, and practices. As major powers attempt to shape other militaries to become more favorable to their interests, they often turn to multinational exercises to teach and habituate certain practices that they view as useful. Some major powers attempt to increase the odds of democratization through the teaching of liberal values, such as respect for civilian control of the military and international law, while others seek stable partners that are prepared to repress political revolution that would overthrow the current regime. Regional security organizations—such as NATO, SCO, and CSTO—provide an opportunity for major powers to host iterative training events and determine the scenario in which the soldiers participate. The case study above reveals how Russia leveraged CSTO exercises to practice the ability for Central Asian states to prevent democratic revolution along its near abroad. The next chapter explores the third logic of shaping—delegation—which is similar to socialization in that major powers use these exercises to alter the character of partner militaries, yet delegation attempts to build the coercive capacity of weaker states, which may or may not involve the socialization of values.

## Chapter 6

# Delegation

## Shaping to Pass the Burden

In February 2017, the US Army announced that it was creating six new brigades specifically tailored to one type of mission: advising and assisting foreign militaries. These "Security Force Assistance" brigades would be comprised of only the leaders from a typical combat formation and become the first permanent US Army units solely dedicated to security cooperation.[1] Though critics were quick to point out that this mission had long been the domain of Special Forces, the creation of specialized advisory units signaled the acceptance by the US military of the permanent need for this capability, which was already in high demand for over a decade in the ongoing wars in Iraq and Afghanistan. As a political settlement or exit strategy after years of counterinsurgency seemed elusive, the US Army began employing a doctrine of "Building Partner Capacity" to manage the insurgencies challenging state control in these post-war, fragile countries. When asked about America's role in Iraq in October 2015, US Army Chief of Staff General Mark Milley responded, "Well, that means our job right now, and I think appropriately, is to continue to build partner capacity, to continue to train, advise and assist the Iraqi government. We cannot, and I do not think we should, do it for them because that will not be sustainable over time."[2] General Milley's insistence that the US Army should assist the Iraqis, but not do it *for them*, succinctly illuminates the logic of delegation.

The US Army's force structure change reflects the growing importance of delegation for major powers in the current threat environment. Delegation is the attempt to assist other militaries in increasing their military strength and/or government capacity against state or not-state actors. Against peer adversaries, major powers may provide weapons, training, or financial assistance to third-party states to shift responsibility for deterring the adversary, often referred to as "passing the buck." For weak and fragile states, major powers employ the logic of delegation by strengthening the ability for these countries to provide

103

for their own security in the long-term, primarily against insurgents and rebels, or to participate in other multilateral missions. Major powers hope that by delegating this responsibility for security, their own forces will not be required to intervene or serve as peacekeepers in the future. The mechanism by which they delegate this security responsibility is through training local forces to become sustainable and professional units, often in the image of the major power's military organization. By combating non-state threats and obviating the need to deploy their own forces, major powers seek to reduce another source of uncertainty in their strategic environments. Though the terms "Building Partner Capacity" (BPC) and "security cooperation" are often applied to the American military's use of this logic, the British and French armies have also led programs designed to reinforce fledgling partners.[3] This chapter will apply an illustrative case study of British military training programs in Sierra Leone from 2000 to 2016 to reveal how a former colonial power attempted to create professional and sustainable forces and prevent the need for future intervention.

## DELEGATION AND AVOIDING THE COSTS OF WAR

The logic of delegation is bred from a major power's desire to accomplish a strategic objective at the lowest cost to itself. As noted in chapter 3, war is a costly business and major powers often seek ways to reduce losses in terms of soldier lives and state wealth. Sun Tzu warned about the economic consequences of long, drawn-out wars that require immense resources and expenditures: the people will suffer, inflation will rise, and the kingdom will become impoverished.[4] Awareness of costs is especially acute in in contemporary democracies, as an increase in media exposure allows citizens to receive updates on the number of casualties during the nightly news. Gelpi, Feaver, and Reifler find that the public is more willing to bear the human costs of war when they have high expectations that military operations will be successful.[5] However, wars against rebels are notoriously difficult for major powers to win. One study found that although counterinsurgents defeated insurgents in 81 percent of pre-World War I cases, that number dropped to only 40 percent after 1919: these authors attribute this lack of success to the restraining effects of mechanized vehicles on the ability for counterinsurgents to collect information and accurately discriminate insurgents from the rest of the population.[6] Paul McDonald instead argues that a change in the character of the international system is responsible for this growing failure of counterinsurgency. While in the nineteenth-century colonialism and domination of local politics were considered legitimate by major powers, in the twentieth-century norms of colonial authority were challenged as publics grew skeptical of colonial excess, sapping the resources and support for effective counterinsurgency doctrines to be effective.[7] What these studies reveal is that in the current era of mechanized warfare and norms against intervention in weaker states, major powers seek opportunities to avoid war with rebels and reduce their footprint abroad.

Even against other peer competitors, leaders often look for ways to pass the burden of preventing others from upsetting the balance of power. As opposed to committing to defend an ally against an aggressor, buck-passing is a strategy in which major powers attempt to induce another state to check the aggressor while the buck-passer "remain[s] on the sidelines."[8] According to John Mearsheimer, major powers prefer this strategy to balancing because they avoid the losses if competition leads to all-out war. He argues that most buck-passing strategies involve little diplomatic engagement with the buck-catcher, except for at least one: to allow or facilitate the growth of another power to oppose that of the rival. Britain's attempts to limit casualties by free-riding on French and Russian efforts during World War I, as well as the US reliance on Soviet casualties on the Eastern front of World War II, are demonstrative of this logic.[9] B.H. Liddell Hart argued—though controversially—that limiting alliance commitments was *the* "British Way in Warfare" prior to its disastrous decision to offer a commitment to France in 1914. Without this promise of aid, he claimed, France would have felt compelled to increase its own power and adopt a prudent defensive doctrine rather than its ill-fated offensive strategy against Imperial Germany.[10]

Although Mearsheimer labels buck-passing a rational strategy, this logic is elsewhere characterized as a "pathology" and inefficient because two would-be allies refuse to extend security guarantees and thereby fail to properly deter an aggressor. This situation is exemplified by the case of French and British diplomatic behavior in the 1930s against an increasing powerful and expansionist Germany.[11] Prior to the German invasion of Poland in 1939, British military cooperation with the French was limited to mere staff talks and the use of attachés to determine the size and quality of the French Army against a potential German attack, rather than joint maneuvers or promises of security guarantees.[12] However, other buck-passing attempts could be more active. US security assistance during the interwar period—through the sale of bombers to France and the leasing of military equipment to Britain—to deter additional German aggression reveals how an offshore major power attempted to shape while remaining neutral.[13]

## DELEGATION THROUGH "BUILDING PARTNER CAPACITY"

As described at the end of chapter 2, the consequences of contemporary globalization and collapse of the Soviet Union resulted in weakened state rule and increased capabilities for violent non-state actors. The post-Cold War lack of incentives for the United States or Russia to bolster client states as a buffer against each other's sphere of influence produced significant effects. Kalyvas and Balcells argue that although the number of civil war onsets declined after 1991, the end of the Cold War changed the relationship between the two great powers and their clients: without the need to counter each other's influence, both the United States and Russia limited or withdrew their funding in peripheral regions, causing further state weakness. Additionally, the proliferation of sovereign states from the remnants of Yugoslavia and the former Soviet Union created more political units with advanced conventional weaponry and motives for conflict against one another or to suppress rebellion.[14] Thus, although civil wars in the aggregate declined after 1991, major power militaries (especially the United States and Russia) were faced with the prospect of failed states and spillover from civil war.

## Major Powers and the Threat of Failing States

One approach to preventing state collapse and ending civil wars was through direct, large-scale intervention. Throughout the 1990s, the UN, NATO, and other regional organizations deployed tens of thousands of peacekeepers to conflict hotspots such as Somalia, Liberia, Bosnia, Rwanda, and Kosovo.[15] US intervention in Afghanistan and Iraq in the early 2000s also involved large troop presence after initial major combat operations, involving up to 160,000 and 100,000 troops, respectively.[16] Yet years of war, mounting casualties, and soaring budget deficits forced American policymakers to consider other approaches to reduce these negative aspects of large-scale combat. US Defense Secretary Robert Gates recalls a debate within the President Barack Obama administration concerning how many troops would be necessary to stabilize Afghanistan in 2009: "The president kept returning also to the matter of costs . . . He said that if the war continued 'another eight to ten years, it would cost $800 billion,' and the nation could not afford that given needs at home. His argument was hard to disagree with. The costs of war were staggering."[17] The administration entertained different alternatives to a large-scale counterinsurgency, to include a "Counterterrorism Plus" (CT+) option supported by Vice President Joseph Biden, which would require fewer troops with a limited focus on raids against high-level targets and training the Afghan forces.[18] As Stephen Biddle et al. notes, such delegation logics are essentially "cost-saving strategies" intended to limit the number of soldiers and amount of money required for success.[19]

In May 2010, Secretary Gates explained the necessity for a delegation-approach in an opinion essay entitled "Helping Others Defend Themselves:

The Future of U.S. Security Assistance." Gates described the dangerous contemporary environment: "The global security environment has changed radically since [the Cold War], and today is more complex, more unpredictable, and even without a superpower adversary, in many ways more dangerous."[20] Gates was concerned about the threat of non-state actors with the ability to target the US homeland from the sanctuary of weak states; he argued that in the coming decades, "the most lethal threats to the United States' safety and security—a city poisoned or reduce to rubble by a terrorist attack—are likely to emanate from states that cannot adequately govern themselves or secure their own territory. Dealing with such fractured or failing states is, in many ways, the main security challenge of our time."[21] He noted that organizational strain caused by the ongoing wars in Iraq and Afghanistan required that the United States move to a strategy that forced local partners to take up the burden of war and security with US assistance.[22] The US Secretary of Defense's fear of another major terrorist attack, as well as his desire to lessen the US "burden" of security responsibility for other states, led him to promote the logic of delegation to stabilize weaker states which became known as "BPC" in defense circles.

## Building Capacity through Sponsorship

Although the term BPC has often been applied ambiguously, BPC can be generally understood as military efforts employed for "enhancing the security capabilities of partners in less capable, weak, and/or failing states" in order to advance national security interests.[23] The term BPC was first formally used in the 2006 US Quadrennial Defense Review (QDR), which highlighted the need for US forces to develop the means to assist fragile states in defeating insurgencies and terrorist cells. Although the United States consistently employed BPC activities to strengthen weaker Cold War allies against communist influence—Greece and South Korea, for instance—after 9/11 US forces began targeting weak non-allies in regions in which terrorist units could plan and operate without fear of interference from local governments.[24] The 2010 QDR delineated a distinction between traditional security cooperation (conducted with allies) and this newer concept of BPC (with non-allies): "Rather than using 'traditional' security cooperation programs exclusively to help its allies, the United States would help weaker states, thereby preventing conflicts stemming from non-state actors from becoming serious or even beginning in the first place. This approach could be seen as using BPC as a state-building tool for partner countries."[25] Thus, BPC efforts are aimed primarily at strengthening the ability for weak or failing partners to combat insurgents and prevent the onset of conflict.

BPC can be understood as a strategy of "sponsorship" in which major powers delegate security responsibility to local armies in order to preclude the need to deploy their own forces. Conceptualized by Dombrowski and Reich, sponsorship strategies allow major powers to "bolster and subsidize allies who share America's interests and are motivated to implement them."[26] They argue, "Sponsorship strategies have the advantage of conserving both blood and treasure while clearly supporting American friends and allies."[27] The authors cite recent US actions, such as supporting the Iraqi government against ISIS or the Kenyan military against the Lord's Resistance Army, as prime examples of sponsorship. Though providing trainers and material to troubled states do carry risks, the benefits of sponsorship include conservation in blood and treasure, ability to support allies with limited resources, and the retention of exit-strategy options.

To achieve the goals of BPC, major powers leverage military training, equipment, and financial assistance in an attempt to build a professional and sustainable local force. That is, major powers deploy military trainers and advisors to develop individual soldiers and units to become *professional*—competent in the ways of coercion to protect the population and, at least in the case of democracies, apolitical and deferential to civilian control—and *sustainable*—able to not only tactically defeat adversaries but also institutionally and logistically support themselves in the future.[28] By training soldiers and units to be both professional and sustainable, major powers hope that these partner forces can protect their own citizens or participate in security cooperation in regional peacekeeping or humanitarian missions. Since major power militaries view themselves as professional organizations, the template for creating and evaluating partner forces is generally in their own image. For instance, major powers will often guide partner forces to develop rank structures and organizational hierarchies like their own; moreover, they commonly evaluate partner forces based on their own standards for training.

## Major Power Delegation in Africa

According to a Government Accountability Office Report, the United States carried out 194 separate security cooperation and security assistance programs intended to build partner capacity around the world in fiscal year 2016.[29] In Africa alone, the US Army deployed conventional military units to at least thirteen African countries to conduct training missions, which is in addition to any covert activities.[30] As Balcells and Kalyvas note, although during the Cold War most civil wars took place in Asia, by 1993 most internal wars were occurring in sub-Sahara Africa.[31] In addition to holding the majority of former European colonies, the African continent also became a potential hotspot for terrorism as the number of fragile and failed states climbed in the 1990s.[32] Thus, BPC became an attractive option for other Western powers in addition to the United States. In the mid-1990s France's Reinforcement of African Peace-Keeping Capacities (RECAMP) program trained African soldiers for peacekeeping missions, to which "Some 30 African countries have sent military contingents to participate in these training events."[33] As of mid-2014, the French army stationed approximately 7,500 soldiers in Senegal, Gabon, Cote d'Ivoire, Djibouti, and the Central African Republic in addition to the 3,500 troops deployed in 2015–2016 to Mauritania, Mali, Niger, Chad, and Burkina Faso to fight the growing threat of Islamic terrorism in the Sahel. Some of these troops protect the 240,000 French nationals living in Africa or engage in direct combat, while others serve as trainers for local forces.[34]

The United Kingdom engaged in extensive BPC activities, most notably in Africa, after the end of the Cold War. The British have deployed military trainers to Sierra Leone, Ghana, South Africa, and Nigeria and have four permanently stationed advisor teams in Kenya, South Africa, Nigeria, and Ethiopia. The British also helped staff the Kofi Annan International Peacekeeping Training Centre in Ghana, which trained 2,500 personnel in about 70 courses in its first year (2004).[35] As one British military officer who served on several training teams remarks: "Ultimately, if you wish to have an influence as a nation, there are different ways of doing it . . . Training teams—going into a country with a small footprint—and sending what we nowadays might call a Short Term Training Team (or a Training Team) to capacity-build is something which the British military have been involved in for years and continue to be. If you target it right, you get a lot of positive outcomes for an, arguably, small footprint."[36] In 2013, British Chief of the General Staff General Peter Wall articulated the benefits of what he labelled Defence Engagement "In concept, upstream engagement and overseas capacity building, if properly targeted and resourced, should deliver benefits to us and they should help our role in global stability by reducing—but probably not removing—the need for us to deploy in future on much more costly intervention and prevention operations."[37] The use of BPC programs by the United States, France, and especially the United Kingdom provides a means for these major powers to reduce one source of uncertainty without the need for large-scale intervention and combat.

## CASE STUDY: BRITAIN'S CAPACITY-BUILDING IN SIERRA LEONE

As mentioned in the introduction, although American BPC efforts are most publicized in the news, the British military has also invested heavily in

developing partners—especially its former colonies. The 2000 British intervention in the Sierra Leonean civil war is one of the most prominent, and
arguably successful, European-led military interventions in the post-Cold
War era. What is less known is the British Army's commitment to developing
the Sierra Leonean forces both before and after major fighting commenced
in 2000 and ended in 2002. The United Kingdom and Sierra Leone share a
long colonial history, dating back to 1787 when the capital Freetown was
established as a British settlement.[38] The country served as a port for British
antislavery naval patrols until the 1860s and continued to provide a regional
base for the British-led West Africa Regiment (WAR) and West Africa
Frontier Forces (WAFF) until independence in 1961.[39] A military coup in
1967 resulted in decades of political turmoil, culminating in civil war in
1991. When British troops intervened on behalf of the Sierra Leonean government in the country's civil war in May 2000, the *Economist* claimed that
the country's capital symbolized "failure and despair" and manifested "all the
continent's worst characteristics."[40] After a decade of intrastate war, as well
ranking last on the United Nation's Human Development Index, Sierra Leone
appeared to be on the brink of collapse.[41]

However, after British intervention and a 17,000-strong UN peacekeeping mission until 2006, Sierra Leone's stability began to materialize and
the country's army increased its contribution to regional security. In 2012,
the country conducted its third peaceful democratic transfer of power and,
impressively, deployed 850 peacekeepers to the UN mission in Somalia.[42] In
the background of this turnaround was the role of the British military trainers
who continue to conduct joint military exercises with Sierra Leonean forces
under the International Security Assistance Team (ISAT) mission.[43] The following study illustrates a successful case of how a major power leveraged
capacity-building training to develop a sustainable, professional local force
intended to provide for its own security, contribute to regional peacekeeping operations, and to obviate the need for future major power intervention
at a relatively low cost.[44] Yet, the conclusion provides a cautionary tale: the
British success in Sierra Leone is relatively rare and the overall, delegation
by major powers has experienced mixed results, at best.

## The Sierra Leonean Civil War and the
## Origins of British Military Assistance

After decades of patrimonialism and perceived corruption in the Sierra
Leonean government, a rebel group known as the Revolutionary United Front
(RUF), supported by Liberia under Charles Taylor, crossed into Sierra Leone
and began waging an insurgency in March 1991. Instability and dissatisfac-
tion with the government's response led to military coups in 1992, 1996, and

1997; after the last takeover, the leader of the military junta invited the RUF to join the government to engage in combat against ECOMOG (Economic Community of West African States Monitoring Group) forces, led by Nigeria. The two warring factions signed a ceasefire agreement known as the Lomé Accord in July 1999 to freeze the civil war, whereby ousted President Ahmad Kabbah was restored to power. The agreement also struck a power-sharing arrangement between Kabbah's government and the RUF: the latter was given control of the government's natural resources as well as immunity from prosecution.[45]

## Security Sector Reform to Prevent Sierra Leone's Collapse

The Sierra Leonean government under Kabbah maintained a consistent relationship with the British government, which struggled to determine the best way to aid its former colony. The growing instability leading up to the Lomé accord set into motion two initiatives from the UK's Department for International Development (DfID): the Sierra Leone Security Sector Reform Programme (SILSEP) and the International Military Advisory and Training Team (IMATT). These two programs were joint initiatives planned and executed by military and civilian planners in the Ministry of Defence (MoD), Foreign & Commonwealth Office, and DfID.[46] SILSEP was developed first in June 1999 as a "whole-of-government" approach to reforming Sierra Leone's security sector. During initial planning for this approach to improving security, a military officer within DfID identified the need for military trainers as "key to the sustainable implementation of SILSEP reforms."[47] Peter Albrecht and Paul Jackson, academic-practitioners with practical involvement in Sierra Leone's reform process, note: "It was the MoD [Ministry of Defence] Advisory Team within SILSEP— Colonel Mike Dent and Robert Foot, a UK civil servant—that identified the need for a British Military Advisory and Training Team (BMATT)."[48] In June 1999, the MODAT—comprised of one active military officer, one contracted retired officer, and a civil servant—deployed to Freetown to assess the rising instability in the country and to determine the best means for the British to assist the fledgling government. The team determined that the rule of law had broken down, there were only three personnel assigned to the MoD, and "In essence there was no proper functioning RSLAF [Republic of Sierra Leonean Armed Forces]."[49] The MODAT completed a mini Strategic Defense Review in October 1999 which determined the need for a complete restructuring of both the Sierra Leonean MoD and armed forces. Concurrently, the British government agreed to send a small number of military trainers and equipment for new Sierra Leonean Army (SLA) recruits under the program *Operation Basilica*.[50]

After this dire assessment, the MODAT recognized the need for more military trainers and advisors. Other UK government officials noticed that not only would the British military advise, assist, and train the SLA, but would also be engaged in broader institution-building in the failed state. Due to the greater political role the British military would serve, as well as the potentially negative impression that the British were unilaterally involved in its former colony, the British MoD and DfID decided to extend the mission to include multinational partners by creating an international advisory team ("IMATT"). Officials from the British Defence Ministry hosted a conference in London in January 2000 to encourage military officers from the Commonwealth to participate in the mission: officers from Australia, Canada, and the United States agreed to join. After military officers volunteered to fill command and staff positions for the advisory mission, one senior British officer remarked "we are now stable, let's think longer term."[51] In February 2000, the MODAT consolidated a defense white paper and developed a system for determining the type of units and appropriate ranks for the SLAF based on the findings of the mini Strategic Defence Review. With the help of additional British Army, Navy, and Air Force advisors, the envisioned unit composition consisted of land, maritime, and air components as the future organization of the Sierra Leonean armed forces. Because Sierra Leone was once a British colony, much of their rank and command structure was already established on the British model. Planners decided to keep a similar structure for the future SLAF but also split the major commands to prevent one command from dominating all soldiers and equipment (and thus, prevent a possible coup).[52]

## British Intervention and the Fear of Endless War

The situation in Sierra Leone began to deteriorate after infighting within the power-sharing government reached new heights; consequently, the British government considered new options for how to support its fledgling former colony. After ECOMOG transitioned authority for peacekeeping to the UN Mission in Sierra Leone (UNAMSIL) in early 2000, RUF officers refused to demobilize, abducted hundreds of UN peacekeepers, and threatened to take Freetown. The British government accelerated its involvement by deploying a reconnaissance team on May 6, 2000, under Brigadier David Richards to prepare to evacuate British citizens in a Noncombatant Evacuation Operation; two days later, British Army units secured a vital airport and the capital of Freetown. During this mission, known as *Operation Palliser,* the British government afforded Brigadier Richards "'full political and military decision-making powers' concerning the [operation] and any assistance given to UNAMSIL and the local government."[53] The British military then deployed the 1st Parachute Regiment, an Amphibious Readiness Group from the Royal

Marines 42 Commando, and other special units to repel RUF attacks on the capital and bolster the UN peacekeeping presence.

When British troops arrived to support the fledgling SLA, they immediately noticed a lack of professionalism in the local soldiers. An intelligence officer from 42 Commando remarked about initial training efforts with Sierra Leonean troops:

> The main issue was a lack of confidence and lack of moral authority, and we were obviously trying to build that up at all times. And a lot of it was their authority because of the nature of the operation effectively being sort of an insurgency in which they were dealing with. It was the authority of the government troops in the eyes of the people who they were operating amongst that was at an all-time low. So we were trying to build that up all the time: put them on a pedestal and make sure that they looked the part, they went into those contacts with the local population looking as though they were trained soldiers. And a clear differentiation between the rag-tag appearance of the multitude of rebel groups that were operating around there at the time. Things like that: military discipline, bearing, was at the uppermost of what we were trying to do.[54]

The increase in Britain's military involvement raised political questions about the goals of the intervention. By mid-May, the media decried the lack of clear military objectives.[55] Members of Parliament criticized Prime Minister Tony Blair's administration for getting pulled into a conflict without establishing well-defined tasks for the units on the ground, especially after troops remained in-country following the successful evacuation of British citizens.[56] In response to these calls for clarity and an end state for British forces, secretary of state for Defence Geoffrey Hoon announced to other members during a House of Commons debate on May 23 that a "UK-led international military assistance training team" was arriving in Freetown to transition from major combat operations to a more sustainable solution: training and advising local forces. Secretary Hoon argued that "Creating new, democratically accountable armed forces in Sierra Leone is vital to the long-term restoration of peace and security in that country."[57] After several politicians focused on British military achievements in Sierra Leone, one Member asked Secretary Hoon, "Is it not our duty not merely to pay tribute in the House to the skill at arms of our forces—the Paras and 42 Commando—but to ensure that their achievement is lasting so that they do not have to go back and do it again?" Secretary Hoon agreed that a lasting solution was necessary to preclude the need for British troops in the future; thus, he responded, "That is why I consciously linked the timetable for withdrawal to the prospect of an effective training team."[58] The Blair administration believed military training teams were the best hope for long-term stability without the need for future intervention.

## Training, Equipping, and Professionalizing
## the Sierra Leonean Forces

On June 1, the British military in Freetown announced that the reconnaissance team determined the need for a team consisting of about 100–150 trainers.[59] After *Operation Palliser* came to end in mid-June 2000 and the UK Chief of Defence Staff, as well as the Foreign Secretary, visited President Kabbah in Freetown, the UK government pledged £21.27 million to reequip the SLA and deploy a British infantry battalion to serve as a training team. In mid-June, the initial entry force was replaced with 250 officers and soldiers drawn primarily from the 2nd Royal Anglian Regiment as part of a Short-Term Training Team (STTT) led by Brigadier Gordon Hughes. The team led six weeks of training and provided British-issued uniforms and rifles for 1,000 SLA recruits, producing two new battalions for the SLA.[60] Commenting on the training, British Lieutenant Colonel Aladsair Wild remarked, "We did have some Sierra Leonian [*sic*] instructors turn up drunk and they were swiftly dealt with. Overall, the training has gone far better than one could expect. They are good soldiers. All they need is proper support, equipment and regular rations and payment."[61] Asked by a British reporter about the British-led training, one SLA sergeant was confident in his army's competence: "We've learnt many things—tactics, fieldcraft. We've learnt how if we fall into an ambush, how to combat it and then how to counterattack. We know how to capture a base, now. We are ready to prove ourselves: we can finish this war in six months because we are now professional British soldiers."[62] As one officer recalls, despite the expediency of STTTs, the British military understood the need to develop the SLA over a longer period: "According to the planners at the time, and it started off with the Royal Anglians, it wasn't the case of 'we're going to do a six-month training team and we're outta here.' I think there was very much a long-term view. As we set sail to head back to the UK, our thoughts at the time were, 'Well, they're going to be there for at least five years.'"[63]

As restoring and building security became the focus of the intervention, it became clear that the British military would direct the government's efforts, even shaping the SLA to mirror British forces in organization and practice. In November 2000, *Operation Silkman* launched a larger contingent of British leaders and advisors "to command the overall UK effort and to provide high-level operational advice" to the SLA.[64] The British IMATT funded the training program and built training facilities, as well as a mentoring program for SLA soldiers and MoD officials.[65] As UK advisors began aiding the SLA and MoD in restructuring their organizations, British Wing Commander Richard Woodward noted:

> I didn't know what to expect . . . the only thing that was helpful was that the
> organisation and the structure [of Sierra Leone's defense sector] was similar to

the UK armed forces, in terms of having a MoD, a Joint Force Command—rank structures, organisation from section, to platoon to companies to platoons. It was very much a British structure.[66]

To restore stability during the chaos brought by the civil war, British advisors had shaped a Sierra Leonean military structure that resembled their own. Woodward emphasized the central decision-making role of the British military in rebuilding the Sierra Leonean armed forces during the civil war: "Following David Richards' intervention we put a military organisation on top of it [IMATT], and threw resources, human and financial, into it, reintegrating the armed forces into society."[67] At first, British officers essentially took over the SLA, as former IMATT commander Barry Le Grys notes: "In 2001 the SLA was effectively led by UK officers. While there were some courageous and capable SLA officers at battalion level and below, they were in the minority. UK officers were formally embedded in command positions . . . Without UK spine, the SLA would have continued to fall into chaos and disrepute."[68] Given the need for structure, British military advisors directed changes for the Sierra Leonean government, which understood and was receptive to the support during the chaotic civil war.[69]

*End of Civil War and the Improvement of Military Training*

In January 2002, the British announced an official end to the civil war in Sierra Leone. The SLA was renamed Republic of Sierra Leonean Armed Forces (RSLAF) after officials from UK DfID and MoD helped reintegrate roughly 2,000 fighters from outside the military, bringing the total armed forces to about 12,000. Both joint headquarters, the MoD, and the Chief of the Defence Staff were subordinated to the command of the IMATT, "whose objective was to steer initial development and help to build capacity."[70] By March, the British had trained roughly 9,000 SLA soldiers, to include former rebels, at the Benguema training camp. British trainers applied the UK model for SLA recruits, as former IMATT commander Colonel Mike Dent recalls: "Basically, the UK took over training and utilized the UK basic recruit training and infantry training programmes used in the UK system, but with a reduced course length the maximize throughput."[71]

The training program had increased to nine weeks and included instruction not only on tactics, but also on appropriate behavior for professional soldiers, such as refusing to abduct children to serve as combatants. Overseeing the training, British Major Peter Hill told reporters: "We don't just train them to be deadly killers. A critical part of the training is the moral component of being a soldier. . . By the time they leave, they will be aware that some actions they have conducted previously are not acceptable."[72]

One former RUF fighter admitted this transformation of his understanding of warfare: "In the jungle, I did not know the difference between soldiers and civilians." Though Major Hill's training team sought to transform the SLA into a force that protected human rights, he was surprised to see how well the former rebels were able to integrate into the government's military: "They get on fine. It is a real asset of these people that they have a capacity to ignore possible gripes on things that we in the West would consider quite major."[73]

## *The Challenges of Delegating Security: Disagreements and Deadlines*

In March 2002, after a directive from the UK MoD, the IMATT conducted another defense review in anticipation of an imminent UK military drawdown. The defense review noted that the UK's "strategic end state" for IMATT's presence and planning should be: "A self-sustaining, democratically accountable and affordable armed forces, capable of meeting Sierra Leone's defense missions and tasks, assisted as necessary by an appropriate regional peace support organization, but without a UK military presence."[74] The IMATT's focus on building a sustainable, professional force that could provide its own national and regional security without the need for UK forces was present in the defense review's "end state."

The leading role assumed by British military and civilian advisors was welcomed by the Sierra Leonean MoD's director of policy, Al-Hassan Kondeh. At the same time, however, he feared too much involvement at the cost of domestic support by Sierra Leoneans who, "had not been involved or informed about reforms of Sierra Leone's military structures." Thus, the British advisors agreed to allow Sierra Leonean officers and officials to lead the effort to develop a sustainable military structure that could, in the future, be run independent of British oversight, published in the 2003 Defence White Paper. Although this review process did not fundamentally alter the structure of the MoD and RSLAF, it was seen as a natural move away from the original British model. Albrecht and Jackson note:

> The UK blueprint that had been its original point of departure had never been fully implemented; it was also inappropriate in terms of the historical and cultural context in Sierra Leone . . . .For example, in Sierra Leone there was no established culture of military and civilians working together, particularly given the historical attitude of the military towards civilians and the documented history of human-rights abuses. For a civilian even to sit next to an officer required a degree of "cultural adjustment," let alone for a civilian to disagree with or give instructions to military personnel.[75]

One British officer who worked as a member of IMATT in 2003 recognized the pitfalls of this type of approach:

> You design an MoD on the basis that you've got fifty British officers running it, and then the next week there is going to be four British officers. And you say: what? They haven't got the capacity for that . . . So you have to be careful not to take the blueprint that was written in London, change the date and time and reproduce the model. You've actually got to design the model for what they require, and we had an MoD where we made exactly that mistake.[76]

Kondeh articulated some of the frustrations in working with IMATT advisors, who he felt oftentimes disregarded the input by MoD civilians or used intimidating tactics to "prevent officers from making objective contributions that could lead to outcomes unexpected or unwanted by IMATT."[77]

In 2004, the commander of IMATT Brigadier Simon Porter oversaw an initiative to develop a long-term plan to hand-off security and military responsibility to the Sierra Leoneans, labelled Plan 2010. This initiative envisioned British assistance to help the RSLAF to eventually "run itself" and build "the capacity of the force, individually, collectively, intellectually, and physically, to allow it to fulfill the missions and tasks asked of it by the government."[78] Brigadier Porter also viewed increasing progress as an opportunity to turn training over to the RSLAF instead of relying on expensive British STTTs. Capacity-building by British mentors became more structured in 2004 with unit-level training as well as senior-officer schooling. IMATT officers conducted courses for senior RSLAF officers at the IMATT-funded Horton Academy, which was built in the image of the Defence Academy of the United Kingdom. Instruction for younger officers was conducted at the Armed Forces Training Centre (AFTC) which was modeled after Catterick's Infantry Training Centre and the Royal Military Academy at Sandhurst, the British officer training school.[79] The AFTC was designed to "train officers and other service personnel in basic military skills and to generate understanding of concepts such as neutrality and democratic accountability."[80] These training centers, built in the image of British military schools and professional standards, were crucial in RSLAF officer and soldier development.

## Beyond Internal Capacity: Building the RSLAF for Regional Peacekeeping

During and in the immediate period following 2000 civil war, the SLA had been largely incapable, or unwilling, to protect the population against internal or external threats. Thus, "The task following the war was therefore to construct an army that could be effective against any future rebellion, protect the territorial integrity of Sierra Leone and also, perhaps, act as peacekeepers elsewhere."[81] British advisors sought to separate the roles and responsibilities of the RSLAF from the Sierra Leonean Police (SLP) by granting a domestic focus to the latter and an external national defense focus to the former. This model of separation of police from military, as well as civilian control over the military, is common among Western democracies but unfamiliar to Sierra Leone. As former IMATT commander Barry Le Grys argued: "While this subordination of military forces to the police in internal security situations is not the norm for an army in West Africa, the SLP and RSLAF have overcome their traditional rivalry; their relationship is much improved."[82] In helping the RSLAF define its role vis-à-vis the national police force, the IMATT considered preparing the RSLAF to contribute to regional commands such as the ECOWAS Standby Force (ESF) in addition to UN or African Union peacekeeping missions. However, the IMATT understood the challenges of building a force not only with a national pride and sense of purpose in defending its own people, but now also willing to conduct peacekeeping abroad when it stated in a 2006 report: "Rather like the difficulty of conveying the concept of community policing to the SLP, a shift from conventional to PSO [peace support operations] activities will need much close involvement at the tactical level."[83]

The British encouraged the RSLAF to adopt a peacekeeping role and in February 2007, the Sierra Leonean government committed to the ESF and signed an agreement with the UN to contribute peacekeeping forces. This "external focus" for the RSLAF was seen by both the British advisors and the Sierra Leonean soldiers as an important step in capacity-building: "Apart from providing the RSLAF with a positively defined role for the foreseeable future, this was also considered to reinforce the UK's success in transforming Sierra Leone's armed forces through IMATT . . . To the RSLAF and IMATT alike, this development was considered an unqualified indication of success and the reflection of an army coming of age."[84] In fulfilling this role, the RSLAF contributed observers and staff officers to UN peacekeeping missions beginning in 2007 and deployed an entire reconnaissance company to Darfur, Sudan in 2009. Before the RSLAF committed units to UN missions, British advisors ensured the troops met certain standards of readiness. IMATT Commander Hugh Blackman (from August 2008 to February 2011) recalled:

> Over the years, we'd trained infantrymen in core combat skills (attack, defence, patrolling, etc.); also medics, intelligence, Military Police, logisticians, administration and mechanics. All of these were trained and prepared to a standard

that we would have considered an appropriate "start-state" before launching on mission-specific training, i.e., for Darfur specifically.[85]

As Blackman notes, British military advisors viewed their role in maintaining standards in RSLAF officers and soldiers as vital to their mission. Le Grys noted in 2007: "However, battalion commanders are not confident enough of their standing to wish IMATT farewell yet. They still feel that without IMATT on hand to monitor standards, old habits in the chain of command might overwhelm their good deeds."[86] In this view, British military advisors feared that RSLAF officers would fail to adopt the standards and habits encouraged by their counterparts and slip back into their pre-transformation routines.

## Reduction of the British Role in Sierra Leone

In mid-2007, after the first peaceful change of power during a general election since the civil war, the UK government decided to terminate the DfID-funded SILSEP program and transferred some of its responsibilities to IMATT. During this time IMATT began to relinquish some of his executive roles to Sierra Leonean military officers and officials and developed more of an advisory role. IMATT commander Brigadier Powe recalled how he made decisions during the transitional period:

> The focus of funding had switched away from West Africa to East Africa, and the [UK MoD] had to a certain extent lost interest [in the former]. There were bigger fish to fry [in Afghanistan and Iraq]. So we were working it out on our own, based on the resources we had available. We had a standard set of tasks that we were given [set out in Plan 2010]. I had a set of tasks, reasonably open, and after that it was up to me to decide, alongside the head of FCO and DFID [in-country], what the best way to use the resources was.[87]

By 2012, IMATT staff numbers went from 90 to 25 and began focusing more on training the RSLAF for peacekeeping operations and training senior leaders at the Horton academy. The rank of the IMATT commander was reduced from brigadier general to colonel, a symbolic signal of British withdrawal that was not well received by the RSLAF and MoD.[88] However, STTTs began taking more of a role in training the RSLAF, notably in the form of Brigade Advisory and Support Teams (BASTs).

The British Army published a story about the RSLAF's progress in April 2011 after a reporter observed training and interviewed British advisors at one of the training camps. The journalist noted: "Dressed in British camouflage and speaking English, the future soldiers at Benguema's Armed

Forces Training Centre (AFTC) would not have looked out of place on a UK exercise ground." Colour Sergeant Mark Beaton highlighted the developing hands-off approach:

> We let Sierra Leonean instructors run things on their own and we speak to them at the end of the lesson to advise and mentor . . . For example rather than simply take over or tell a RSLAF instructor what to do, I might suggest that he projects his voice to the whole group and makes sure he wears his headdress, uniform and webbing correctly while teaching.[89]

The reporter goes on to note how the "the troops train and operate in the same manner as their British tutors" and operate the same machine guns and rifles that the British used before the introduction of newer equipment.[90] By 2011, RSLAF leaders had graduated from understanding British tactics to embracing the proper appearance and conduct for professional soldiers, modeled on their British advisors.

## From Delegation to Partnered Operations

In about a decade, Sierra Leone's armed forces went from being a fledgling organization to a competent military. In 2013, the British government transitioned authority for security reform from IMATT to an ISAT. This new team was now led by a civil servant, not a military officer, who exercises a much broader view of security. After receiving an invitation from the RSLAF, the British Army conducted its first joint training event alongside SLA units in November 2016. The exercise was conducted at the RSLAF's Jungle Warfare School, intended in the future to be used for training Sierra Leonean as well as other soldiers. From reports of the exercise, it appears that the British Army began to see the RSLAF as equal partners rather than trainees in need of advice and assistance: "The joint exercise, taking place in the Guma Valley, will improve both militaries in parallel as they will be learning from each other and forging enduring ties."[91] Major Ollie Braithwaite, commander of the participating British unit, noted: "This was the first time members of the RSLAF had been integrated into our force on an exercise rather than being taught by us. It was a significant step forward and is a clear demonstration of the strong defence relationship the regiment has with the RSLAF as a result of the military skills training we have been delivering." One British soldier remarked about the experience: "I really enjoyed it. We learnt a lot from the RSLAF. It was an eye opener to see what they can do with the little equipment they have; quite remarkable really. How they survive off the land is incredible."[92] After fifteen years of instruction by British advisors, RSLAF officers and soldiers had finally become the trainers.

## Assessing the Effectiveness of British
## Military Training in Sierra Leone

The case study illustrates how a major power applied the logic of delegation to improve security in a fragile state by creating a professional, sustainable force while limiting long-term presence and the need for future large-scale intervention. From the early years of the program, IMATT advisors consistently noted the importance of building a future force that could provide for its own security and attempted to train and advise with this goal in mind. The number of IMATT advisors diminished as the RSLAF became more competent over time. Professionally, British advisors and trainers often applied their own understanding of military training and organization (the "British model") to advise, assist, and train RSLAF soldiers. For instance, the British military supplied the RSLAF with British uniforms and weapons, created units and command structures modeled after the British Army, trained and evaluated new recruits based on British practices, and built training centers modeled on three of its own military training centers. British Army advisors also developed Sierra Leonean soldiers to adopt their values, revealing overlap with the logic of socialization: RSLAF soldiers were instructed not only on uniform and appearance, but also on democratic accountability and protection of human rights. Moreover, the training and deployment of RSLAF to the peacekeeping mission in Somalia reveals the changing focus of the military from internal to regional multilateralism, viewed as a positive step toward a well-respected and internationally legitimate force.

Though the RSLAF is still evolving as an effective national military and ISAT advisors remain in Freetown to this day, progress has been impressive. In just over a decade, the British military advisory mission in Sierra Leone, in the form of BMATT, IMATT, ISAT, as well as other small training teams, helped the RSLAF develop from an organization in shambles into a force capable of deploying in support of UN operations. Friction existed between British officers and Sierra Leonean officials about how the new government should be organized and when the hand-over for security would occur, yet the RSLAF's progress was remarkable. Albrecht and Jackson note: "In stark contrast to historical popular perception, by March 2012 the RSLAF had become one of the better-respected organisations in Sierra Leone—a success largely attributed to UK support."[93] In an analysis of the British military reintegration program, Mimmi Söderberg Kovacs argues:

There can be no doubt as to the importance of IMATT in all aspects of the reform process, from the training provided in the MRP [Military Reintegration

Programme] to the strategic placement of advisers high up in the hierarchy of the completely reorganized MoD [Ministry of Defence]. The commitment of the British government to the Sierra Leonean peace process, particularly in the area of security-sector reform, has been both remarkably extensive and unusually long-term.[94]

## SUMMARY

Delegation is a shaping logic designed to pass the burden of security to other states and limit the costs associated with preparing for and waging war. Major powers look to shaping as a way to check the rise of emerging adversarial powers, as well as to increase the military effectiveness and coercive capacity of weak states. This chapter focused on the latter, particularly through the rise of "Building Partner Capacity" to bolster weak militaries in the wake of 9/11 while limiting the need for large troop presence. Capacity-building involves developing professional and sustainable forces that are competent enough to provide security for their own citizens and contribute to peacekeeping in the region. This chapter also explained why major powers view BPC activities as a low cost means to reduce strategic uncertainty by preventing threats from emerging in fragile states. Although the term BPC is commonly attributed to the US military, France and the United Kingdom also have invested in these types of programs in Africa and the Middle East. Capacity-building exercises were illustrated using the British military's experience in Sierra Leone from 2000 to 2016.

Despite the British success, major powers have often found it difficult to achieve their goals through this "light-footprint approach." Biddle, MacDonald, and Baker argue that unless a major power is willing to obtrusively monitor and force compliance on the partner state, delegation generally fails to improve the partner's military effectiveness. The disparity between the major power's interest in security against external (or non-state) threats and the partner state's interest in its own regime's survival often prevents the major power from achieving its goals. The authors cite multiple examples of US delegation failures, to include Afghanistan, Vietnam, Mali, Nigeria, Yemen, and Pakistan. Even the case study above revealed the discord over how forces would be organized and to what extent the British should direct Sierra Leone's future. Yet the authors also admit that even a "weak option may be better than available alternatives," which is a subtle nod to the attractiveness of the low-cost, low-risk logic in an uncertain international system.[95] One of the few successful cases examined in this study was the American effort to build capacity in South Korea, which went from a nominal force in 1950 to a substantial fighting machine in 1953. Yet what is interesting about the South Korean case was the American interest in extending a security guarantee to the country in 1953. Not only would this allow the United States to continue to deter North Korea from invading, but also deter *its own ally* from misbehaving. This paradoxical logic of assurance will be explored in the following chapter.

# Chapter 7

# Assurance

## *Shaping to Reduce an Ally's Insecurity and Manage its Behavior*

America's vast alliance system developed during the early years of the Cold War, with the North Atlantic Treaty Organization (NATO) as the flagship institution, is often described as a network of security guarantees intended to deter rivals, most notably the Soviet Union. Yet, Lord Hastings Ismay, the first secretary general of NATO, is rumored to have explained the purpose of the alliance in a three-part, simple logic: "To keep the Russians out, the Americans in, and the Germans down." According to Timothy Sayle, although in reality there is no written record of this famous statement, he asserts "No matter: it is the best explanation of NATO's function."[1] What is remarkable about this triangular function is not only that the external threat is only one-third of the focus, but also that one leg of the triad is openly concerned with controlling one of the alliance's *own* members. The other component of the strategy that brings it all together—the inclusion of the United States as the guarantor of European security, from threats both inside and out—is at the heart of assurance.

Assurance is a shaping logic intended to reduce an ally's insecurity by promising protection against a future attack by a third party. Although offering a security guarantee to another state is often motivated by the desire to deter an adversary—after all, another term for assurance is extended deterrence—this shaping logic parts ways from traditional conceptions of coercion since the target is the *ally* rather than the *rival*. However, as Brian Blankenship points out, the bulk of scholarly literature is concerned with how assurance deters rivals rather than how assurance serves a major power's other interests.[2] As the anecdote above reveals, major powers often look for ways to ensure that other states, including allies and partners, serve their interests. Some of these goals include preventing undesirable behaviors by allies such as acting aggressively toward others, developing an independent foreign policy, building their own nuclear arsenal, or accommodating a rival power. To achieve these interests, major powers use assurance to reduce an intense security dilemma or affect the domestic politics of the target state. When security dilemmas are intense, allies may escalate crises, launch preventive wars, or develop nuclear weapons to protect themselves against future threats, causing the major power to become enmeshed in a dangerous environment. Moreover, public opinion in allied states may result in undesirable outcomes, such as hawkish policies toward friends and dovish ones toward adversaries.

By reducing fears of abandonment through security commitments or placing troops in allied territory, major powers attempt to proactively construct and stabilize an environment rather than react after a crisis escalates. In this respect, assurance is nearly the opposite of delegation: instead of passing the burden of security to another state, the major power assumes the responsibility in the hope of managing the ally's behavior. Although this type of shaping logic differs from coercion, assurance also differs from the engagement logics given its greater reliance on hard power and coercion. Though the purpose of assurance is to convince state leaders and their publics of the major power's protection, anxieties are assuaged because only hard power can protect.

This chapter further explains why major powers offer promises of protection to weaker states and how a fear of undesirable ally behavior drives this logic. By creating a defense treaty or positioning troops on a partner's territory, another benefit emerges: the ability to secure operational access and gather intelligence if shaping and deterrence fail and war becomes necessary. As the major power with by far the most security commitments in the world—by one count, at least sixty-six other states—the United States is the hallmark example throughout the chapter.[3] The logic of assurance is illustrated through a recent military exercise that was clearly designed to assuage a weary public by demonstrating American presence: the US-led Operation "Dragoon Ride" through Eastern Europe in 2015 following Russia's invasion of Ukraine. The chapter concludes with a brief note on the relative success of US assurance over time.

## ASSURANCE AND CONSTRAINING ALLY BEHAVIOR

### Promising Security to Manage Ally Actions and Options

In one of the most comprehensive accounts of the concept, Jeffrey Knopf defines assurance as the attempt to influence another's state behavior by increasing its sense of security or decreasing its perception of insecurity. Because of the broad and sometimes contradictory use of the term, he creates four sub-types to better explicate the purposes of the logic: an alliance commitment, an effort at nonproliferation, a component of deterrence, or as reassurance toward rivals.[4] The first two definitions are generally directed toward allies and partners, while the latter two are aimed at adversaries. There is clearly overlap between the logics of deterrence and assurance, especially for the first, third, and fourth logics.[5] For instance, since an alliance commitment is the promise by one state to come to the aid of another in the case of an attack by a third party, this pledge assuages the partner's insecurity because it warns would-be attackers of the consequences.[6] This is why another term for this type of assurance is "extended deterrence": that is, expanding the umbrella of protection to cover a protégé so that would-be attackers understand that invading this partner would be costly.[7] Yet assurance, as a logic of shaping, is more concerned with ensuring the ally is restrained in its behavior and options as much as the rival.

Since defense-pact alliances are promises to protect one another in the future, an "alliance security dilemma" often emerges when allies are attempting to predict one another's uncertain future behavior. That is, since one ally can never be certain whether the other will live up to its commitment and intervene in the case of an armed attack, the fear of abandonment is ever present. Assurance is the attempt to reduce this fear of abandonment by providing verbal promises of support, treaties, arms transfers, or stationing troops on the ally's territory.[8] However, another unfortunate outcome of this alliance dilemma is the opposite risk of entrapment if an ally drags the patron into an otherwise unwanted conflict.[9] If one ally expects a strong commitment from the other ally, the latter may become emboldened to engage in aggressive action since it feels it can act with impunity. Major powers thus need to carefully manage these dual risks when they commit to defend other states against aggressors.

As Blankenship explains, there are two principle reasons why major powers would offer assurances given the risk of entrapment described above. First, protégés may seek more independent foreign policies that are nondeferential to the major power's desires. This becomes more important if the partner chooses a policy of "self-reliance," such as developing its own nuclear weapons program. Francis Gavin reveals how the United States went to great lengths during and after the Cold War to limit the spread of nuclear weapons, even among its allies. One of these "strategies of inhibition" includes extending the nuclear guarantee over nonnuclear allies, such as Japan and Germany.[10] Second, allies could draw closer to third-party states or submit to concessions from the major power's rival.[11] In the 1950s, the Japanese government publicly expressed an interest in pursuing an independent foreign policy from the United States, as well as a desire to normalize relations with the Soviet Union.[12] NATO's fear of communist influence in

Europe and Soviet demands on Norway in the early years of the Cold War, described below, is also illustrative of this concern.

## Managing Ally Behavior: Dampening Security Dilemmas and Influencing Domestic Politics

As noted above, security guarantees help bolster deterrence against an adversary by improving the capabilities of the allies and signaling resolve to stand firm in a crisis. But assurance often involves what US policymakers have deemed "dual deterrence" or "dual containment": that is, efforts to control both the rival and the ally.[13] The use of defense pacts to direct allies is historically common: after a review of treaty alliances from 1815 to 1965, historian Paul Schroeder contends, "All alliances in some measure functioned as pacts of restraint . . . restraining or controlling the actions of the partners in the alliance themselves."[14] Even the four great power victors of the Napoleonic wars invited the war's main belligerent France into its Quadruple Alliance in 1818 in order to prevent its resurgence.[15] Although alliances are often viewed as an unfortunate trade-off between security and autonomy (i.e., freedom of action to change the status quo), James Morrow notes that alliances may increase autonomy benefits for stronger states. For instance, in exchange for security, major powers may force allies to change their internal policies or provide military bases to allow the projection of military power in the region.[16]

Through these types of asymmetric alliances, major powers attempt to constrain an ally's policy or behavior through two mechanisms: reducing the security dilemma between the ally and its rival or influencing the partner's domestic politics. As mentioned in chapter 2, a security dilemma results when one state's attempt to protect itself may appear threatening to others. For instance, even the deployment of air defense weapons (with the word *defense* in the equipment's title) could create fear among rivals uncertain about how this weapon system could be used.[17] Intense security dilemmas result in arms races, shortened windows for diplomacy, and incentives to impose the first strike against an adversary that is trying to do the same.[18] By providing security guarantees, major powers seek to remove the ally's need to increase the number of weapon systems and military units ready to invade, which would consequently reduce the adversary's fear of imminent attack. In this respect, the major power serves as a pacifying force or "regional buffer" to dampen otherwise fierce contests between regional competitors.[19] As Brooks and Wohlforth argue in favor of US alliance commitments: "US assurance thus makes security dilemmas, dangerous arms races, and rivalries even less likely."[20] This security commitment sometimes extends to the nuclear realm in which strategies to prevent nuclear proliferation involve assurances to both allies and adversaries. By providing a forward presence and preventing the need for rearmament by these former belligerents, US military power serves as a pacifying force in the region.

The second way in which major powers use assurance to influence their allies is by leveraging defense treaties and forward presence to affect the domestic politics or public opinion of the ally. US alliance strategy in the late 1940s and early 1950s reveals how a major power signed defense pacts to not only warn potential aggressors, but also to affect the internal dynamics of the target state. American policymakers worried not only about the return of militant sentiments in Germany and Japan, but also about the political systems of other states as communism became more attractive in war-depressed economies. As discussed below in the case study, in addition to a potential Soviet conventional attack, one of the gravest concerns for European statesmen in the immediate post-World War II period was the potential for communist or Soviet-sympathetic parties to win election or convince their governments to succumb to Russian demands. In East Asia, the United States employed asymmetric bilateral alliances for similar reasons. According to Victor Cha, US security guarantees to Japan, South Korea, and Taiwan were driven by the desire to constrain the aggressive, authoritarian leaders from waging wars in which the United States would become embroiled. To achieve this goal, the Eisenhower administration intentionally created economic and political dependencies to restrain its unpredictable allies from aggressive action intended to shore up their domestic legitimacy.[21] Although the United States pursed a multilateral approach in Europe and bilateral one in East Asia, the overall logic was a desire to control the behavior or domestic politics of allied states. US-led alliances are not the only ones in which this applies: as one team of scholars point out, many alliance commitments require consultations and deliberations during crises, which provides an opportunity to convince the ally to back down and preserve the peace.[22]

## The Dark Side of Assurance: "Entangling Alliances" and the Problem of Burden-Sharing

German Chancellor Otto Von Bismarck once quipped that the best alliances are those in which one state is a "rider" and one is the "horse," not one in which there are two riders vying for leadership.[23] The desire for control by major powers over smaller states through assurance is obvious, yet alliances require constraints for both parties, which results in negative consequences for the major power. George Washington and Thomas Jefferson famously cautioned against joining entangling alliances and these concerns about the negative consequences of security commitments remain today. Several potential undesirable outcomes arise from a major power's security guarantee: notably, entrapment, moral hazard, and free-riding. As mentioned above, entrapment (or "chain-ganging") occurs when one member of an alliance engages in war only because it fears the loss of an ally would leave it isolated and prone to further aggression. German and Russian leaders' fear of the military defeat of their allies—Austria-Hungary and France, respectively—in 1914 is often cited as an example of great powers being dragged into war.[24] The American fear over entangling alliances was demonstrated by US Senators in 1948, who were initially unwilling to ratify NATO's Atlantic Treaty because that would result in a loss of control over the decision to declare war.[25]

The second two dangers are captured by Barry Posen in what he labels "dangerous drivers" and "cheap-riders": US allies that take advantage of America's concern with credibility of commitments. On the one hand, weaker allies may exploit a major power's patronage as a blank check to engage in aggressive behavior, as Posen claims Israeli behavior toward its Arab neighbors indicates. On the other, allies may under-produce security for themselves since protection is guaranteed by the major power: wealthy Europe and Japan need not invest in expensive nuclear weapons or tanks if the United States is willing to provide them.[26] Again, this concern emanated among postwar American leaders: Robert Taft and former president Herbert Hoover opposed the deployment of US Army divisions to Europe because it would produce the undesirable consequence of absolving European responsibility for its own defense while burdening the United States.[27] One study partially supports this burden-sharing concern by demonstrating that US troop presence in allied and non-allied states results in a decrease in that state's defense spending; this is, however, excluding NATO members which increase their proportion of defense spending when troops are stationed within or near their borders.[28]

Despite these potential negative consequences for assurance-through alliances, most American leaders since World War II have committed to defending its European and Asian allies, determining that the benefits generally outweigh the costs. Although the fear of entrapment will always be present, Michael Beckley argues that out of all the militarized interstate disputes in which the United States participated from 1948 to 2010, he could find only five cases in which the United States was somewhat entangled. In fact, most of these conflicts were driven by other motives, served US interests, and sometimes allowed the United States to restrain the allies' behavior.[29] Moreover, as noted above, NATO allies actually increase their defense spending when the US forward-stations troops in its territory. Forward presence provides additional benefits, including operational access during crises, which is explored below.

## FORWARD PRESENCE AND OPERATIONAL ACCESS

America's security commitments and forward presence, which increased following the end of World War II, not only assuages an ally's fear of abandonment, but also provides additional operational benefits. Before the war, the United States maintained no peacetime alliances and only a limited presence abroad, with most of its bases located in US territories or dependencies such as Guam, the Philippines, Hawaii, and Puerto Rico. However, German expansion in the 1930s forced American policymakers to seek air bases in the Western Hemisphere, and by war's end, defense planners determined that the United States needed a strong network of foreign bases to protect the homeland and contain the spread of communism.[30] Although American presence in foreign territory has diminished since its height in the 1950s, the United States still stations hundreds of thousands of soldiers abroad, as well as, by one count, approximately 800 bases outside of the 50 US states in 2015.[31]

The sheer number of US troops and bases abroad may be startling, yet Robert Art argues that one of the most efficient ways of signaling assurance to allies is through the forward presence of soldiers. By placing thousands of troops in key regions, this visible form of American presence dampens conflict and removes the need for costly arms races. Yet, the forward-stationing of troops provides an additional benefit in case war becomes necessary. If shaping and coercion fail, military units with pre-positioned equipment are ready to engage in battle with allies bound by treaty to support each other in case of an attack. For instance, American bases in the Persian Gulf were available and beneficial during the invasion of Afghanistan after the 9/11 attacks. As Art notes, "Forward-based, alliance-embedded forces can react more quickly, be reinforced more effectively, and fight better than forces that have to be introduced into the region from scratch."[32] Another benefit of peacetime forward presence is the ability to place heavy military equipment in foreign land before war breaks out. The US Army maintains at least three "Prepositioned Stock" (APS) sites in Europe, which allows units to deploy their soldiers and occupy the tanks, artillery, and other fighting vehicles when they arrive in theater for training or combat.[33]

In addition to having forward-stationed troops prepared for contingencies, another benefit of assurance is the ability to gain operational access for military missions. According to US military doctrine, operational access is the ability to project military forces into a region with limited constraints.[34] This access relies on legal agreements between the United States and the host country for the permission to fly through its air space, transit over its land, or occupy bases, ports, logistics hubs within their sovereign territories, either during peacetime or contingently during a crisis. As a RAND study of US access requests from 1945 to 2014 points out, forward presence does not always result in assured access: in one salient example, despite peacetime presence, all the members of NATO—excluding Portugal—refused to allow the United States to use their air bases to resupply Israel during the Yom Kippur War in 1973. However, those states with a permanent American presence were more likely to grant greater freedom of action to US operations and twice as likely to allow US combat forces to operate from their territories.[35] The study also found that the United States is more likely to gain operational access if its operations are viewed as internationally legitimate and the target state is a mutual defense ally or "enduring partner"; that is, states with an elite consensus on the stabilizing role of US presence and those that continue to host foreign troops after an immediate threat has passed. Conversely, access is less likely when domestic opposition is high.[36] Unfavorable domestic politics sometimes thwart US efforts to gain operational access for missions, even from allies. NATO member Turkey's 1982 constitution requires that only its Grand National Assembly may permit foreign troops to be stationed in its territory, which frustrated American efforts to gain access during both Gulf Wars in 1991 and 2003.[37] These findings suggest that the United States has an interest in building enduring partners and convincing domestic populations that its presence and operations are legitimate.

## China and Russia's Efforts to Reduce US Access

Major powers, especially the United States with its expansive grand strategy and power-projection capabilities, hold a high interest in assuring peacetime and contingency access. The rise of long-range weapon technologies, such as anti-air, ant-shipping, and surface-to-surface ballistic and cruise missiles, has provided states with the ability to deny others from encroaching on their borders or sphere of influence. Understanding the US asymmetric advantage in deploying power abroad, rising powers such as China and Russia began investing in these technologies to develop what came to be known as "Anti-Access/Area-Denial" (A2/AD) strategies, which has caused US policymakers to become more concerned about the ability for the United States to gain and maintain access in contested zones.

China's growing use of A2/AD to deny or complicate America's freedom of action in East Asia and the South China Sea has received the bulk of the attention. However, Russia has also invested in these technologies and even placed some in the strategically located Kaliningrad exclave, which could deny US freedom of maneuver and ability to reinforce its forward-stationed troops even within NATO member states such as the Baltic states and Poland.[38] Russia's invasion of eastern Ukraine in 2014 heightened Western fears of its ability to impose its will through subversive tactics or neutralizing NATO's influence in the region. The case study below unpacks the initial American response to Russia's intervention, which surprisingly was dedicated more toward influencing the minds of NATO publics than to send a strong deterrent signal toward its rival.

## CASE STUDY: THE US "OPERATION DRAGOON RIDE" IN EASTERN EUROPE

As the origins of NATO reveal, American and British leaders were just as concerned about the ability for the Soviet Union to sow disunion from within the alliance (through promoting communism) than from outside (through a conventional or nuclear attack). As Sayle recounts, although the postwar Marshall Plan improved Western Europeans' standard of living, prominent British officials believed that a defense treaty was necessary to provide a "psychological boost" to the weary Europeans. The communist takeover in Prague in 1948 buttressed the fear that communism may take root in an economically-deprived Western Europe, while Norwegian officials were warning of an imminent Russian demand to negotiate a security pact favorable to Soviet expansion in the Baltic Sea. A security guarantee through a multilateral alliance—with the United States as the powerful bedrock—was viewed as the best option to prevent threats from emerging both inside and out.[39]

Despite the end of the Cold War, the United States still practices the logic of assurance daily in its forward presence and military exercises in Europe and East Asia. Below is a description of one highly visible expression of assurance after Russia invaded and annexed the Ukrainian province of Crimea. Known as "Operation Dragoon Ride," the vehicle march that travelled over thousands of miles was intended to reassure an uncertain Eastern European public and resist Russian influence through annexation or less-visible tactics to undermine their democracies. This case is exemplary because of its clear assurance logic: the vehicular road march, which was not even initially planned to take place, became a symbol of solidarity as American soldiers drove into civilian shopping areas merely to demonstrate the level of US commitment.

### The Spark: Russia Invades and Annexes Crimea

In November of 2013, the Ukrainian government under President Viktor Yanukovych announced that it would not sign an economic agreement with the European Union (EU), referencing the negative consequences for its relations with Moscow. According to *Reuters*, Yanukovych was convinced by his deputies and business executives—especially those from the Russian-speaking east of the country—that signing the EU deal would provoke Russia to cause damage to the Ukrainian economy.[40] In Russia, President Vladimir Putin claimed that the EU was "blackmailing" Ukraine into joining the agreement and instead encouraged Ukrainian leaders to develop greater economic ties with Russia, potentially by joining its customs union. The decision to turn down the deal with the EU sparked massive protests—estimated at 100,000—in the Ukrainian capital Kiev.[41] By early December, protestors had occupied the city hall located in Independence Square with thousands demanding the resignation of President Yanukovych.[42] Putin agreed to purchase $15 billion-worth of Ukrainian debt and reduce the price of gas by a third, further angering the protestors. By late January 2014, rallies swelled, police responded with violence, and protestors began storming regional government offices. Despite compromise deals signed by the Ukrainian president and opposition leaders in mid-February, the protests became overwhelming and Yanukovych fled the country on February 22 while demonstrators occupied the presidential building. Shortly thereafter, the Ukrainian parliament named an interim president and arranged an arrest warrant for Yanukovych.[43]

Despite the anti-Russian sentiment expressed through the "Maiden Revolution" in Kiev, the situation was quite different in the eastern peninsula of Crimea. Between 27 and 28 February, unmarked Russian troops began occupying the regional parliament building and local airports amid pro-Russian protestors calling for Moscow's protection against Ukraine's new leadership.[44] On March 6, 2014, the Crimean parliament voted to join the Russian Federation and set a public referendum on the issue for March 16. In the following days, additional troops continued to reinforce its positions with hundreds of vehicles transported by land and sea, disarming and occupying Ukrainian military bases on the peninsula. According to the Crimean prime minister Sergei Aksyonov, pro-Russian forces numbered roughly 11,000, controlled most of the peninsula, and blockaded any bases that had not yet surrendered.[45]

The physical occupation was buttressed by Russia's social media presence and neutralization of Ukrainian-language broadcasts in eastern Ukraine, leaving Russian-owned *RT* (formerly Russia Today) as the only television news-source available to locals.[46] Not only did these media platforms demonize the Maiden protestors and place a positive spin on Crimea's newfound "independence," *RT* reported that the March 16 referendum resulted in nearly a 97 percent vote for integration with Russia, with an 83 percent turnout.[47] Russian lawmakers largely endorsed Crimea's independence and possible reunification with Russia, as the Russian parliament's lower house welcomed a delegation from Crimea's legislative body in Moscow on March 7.[48] Despite Russia's support, the international reaction was swift: the United States sponsored a UN Security Council resolution to declare the referendum illegal, claiming that it violated both international and Ukrainian law.

Although thirteen countries were in favor of the declaration, Russia vetoed the measure and China abstained. Additionally, the US administration under President Barack Obama immediately implemented travel restrictions and other economic sanctions against Russian leaders and elites.[49] Russia officially denied that Russian troops were directly involved in Crimea or Eastern Ukraine, though witnesses and even Putin himself later admitted its military was involved.[50] Russia also used the pretext of defending Russian speakers in its intervention in the regions of South Ossetia and Abkhazia, Georgia in 2008, and later signed military agreements to align policies and exert de facto sovereignty over these regions.[51]

Although the invasion was surprising—US Secretary of State John Kerry claimed territorial conquest was a "stunning" nineteenth century tactic inappropriate for the contemporary era[52]—Crimea has long occupied an intersection of great power politics and strategy. Seeking a warm-water base for its navy and commerce, Russia seized the Crimean Peninsula from Turkey in 1783 and the port was vital for the Russian and Soviet navies throughout the nineteenth and twentieth centuries. Soviet leader Nikita Khrushchev signed the peninsula over to the Soviet Republic Ukraine in 1954, which was largely a formality throughout the Cold War. However, after the fall of the Soviet Union, Crimea was located in the now-sovereign country of Ukraine, even though 300 Russian naval vessels of the Black Sea fleet were based in the naval base at Sevastopol. In 1992, Russian nationals—who comprised 70 percent of the peninsula's population of 3 million—gathered almost 250,000 signatures to force a referendum on declaring independence from Ukraine. As one Russian living in Crimea told a reporter: "They want to introduce their language, and that is no good for us. They want us to be their colony . . . There is danger the tension here could be transformed into armed conflict."[53] The Crimean lawyer responsible for drafting the resolution argued that the referendum should go beyond independence: "For many, it's not a question of independence, but a desire to return to Russia." Russian president Boris Yeltsin even endorsed the Russian nationalist party's resolution to annul the 1954 transfer of Crimea to Ukraine.[54] The Ukrainian government vetoed the referendum in 1992 and another similar referendum in 1994.[55]

## Russian Information Operations and "Hybrid" Tactics

Crimea's complex history provided good reason for the United States to fear Russian influence in the former Soviet Union and Eastern Europe, especially for its NATO allies Estonia, Latvia, Lithuania, and Poland. As a team of scholars note: since the end of the Cold War, Russia lost most of its "strategic depth" as former Soviet Republic and Warsaw Pact states joined NATO. In response, "Russia has had to implement alternative strategies—notably, hybrid warfare and the extension of A2/AD capabilities—as part of a large manoeuvre to exercise influence in what it considers to be its backyard."[56] Russia's actions alarmed the military alliance, as Robbie Gramer describes, "And NATO, initially created to prevent such a catastrophe from ever happening, was caught off guard."[57]

What made policymakers particularly worried was how Russia was so effective in annexing a piece of sovereign territory, so quickly, and without much resistance. Part of its success is attributable to Russia's effective implementation of "information warfare" to control the narrative and defend Russian nationalism in the news and on social media, what one group of researchers regard as a "manipulative form of Russian 'soft power.'" In this sense, the limited conventional military operations—such as the physical annexation of Crimea—are merely supporting a broader political and information strategy to prevent countries within its sphere of influence from aligning with the West by sowing discord, confusion, and division in target states.[58] Although the term is often used ambiguously, other observers were claiming that Russia was engaging in a form of "hybrid" war that allowed it to achieve its goals under the threshold of open violence. Alexander Lanoszka provides one of the most sophisticated definitions of the concept, which he defines as a strategy that combines regular and irregular military means to "undermine its target's territorial integrity, subvert its internal political cohesion and disrupt its economy." For hybrid tactics to be successful, the initiator relies on military means a little as possible and instead leverages subversion, propaganda, agitation, and fomenting disorder, yet contains enough military strength to deter a forceful reaction by the target or its allies.[59]

Unfortunately for the United States and NATO, Lanoszka argues that the former Soviet Union—including the Baltics—are particularly prone to hybrid tactics. Given the ethnic heterogeneity, historical grievances, weakness of civil society, and regional complexity, these countries are ripe for successful hybrid tactics. The demographic composition of Estonia and Latvia is about a quarter Russian and contain a large Russian stateless population, providing an opportunity for Russia to foment nationalist secessionist movements and serve as the guarantor of these ethnic groups' security.[60] Russian nationalist groups in the Baltic states are active in the region; for instance, in August 2014, the Latvian Union of Russians signed a cooperative agreement with the Russian Unity political party in Crimea, intended to "strengthen the unity of the Russian world" through economic and cultural projects.[61] Other reports feared that Russia would attempt to bring separatist regions into "de facto" control through economic and political agreements, though stopping short of physical annexation.[62] As British defence secretary Michael Fallon told reporters in early 2015, he was "worried about [Putin's] pressure on the Baltics, the way he is testing NATO."[63] The alliance would need to act in order to prevent its Eastern flank from becoming attractive to Russian influence.

## The US Responds: The European Reassurance Initiative and Operation Atlantic Resolve

One of the consequences of Russia's invasion of Ukraine was how it reversed a decline of US troop presence—and attention—in Europe. Given the relative stability in Europe in the late 2000s, the Obama administration believed that American interests would be better served by focusing on East Asia to manage a rising China. To support the administration's "Pivot to Asia," the US Army inactivated two combat brigades in Europe in 2012 and 2013. The plan was to remove the permanently stationed troops from Europe, but create a set of pre-positioned equipment known as the European Activity Set to augment a battalion-sized combat task force with equipment in case of a crisis.[64] In fact, as of March 2014 the United States retained less than 70,000 troops in European NATO countries; by the time Russia invaded, there was not a single American tank in Europe. However, in the immediate weeks after Russia's invasion, the United States deployed fighter jets to assist in NATO's Baltic Air Policing mission, dispatched naval surface vessels to the Black Sea, and ordered paratroopers from the 173rd Infantry Brigade to expand land exercises in the Baltic countries and Poland.[65]

In addition to these immediate measures, American leaders began developing a strategy to assure its European allies against potential Crimea-style Russian intervention. In June 2014, President Obama scheduled a four-day visit to Europe and joined the Polish president in a news conference to "reaffirm the enduring commitment of the United States to the security of Poland"; additionally, he announced his desire to dedicate $1 billion for assurance activities through the European Reassurance Initiative (ERI).[66] American lawmakers were also supportive of this program. During the first fiscal year, Congress even funded the effort with $985 million: $60 million more than the $925 million requested by the White House. Funding would support the following goals: increase US presence in Europe, host more exercises with allies and partners, improve the stock of pre-positioned equipment, enhance forward bases, and build partner capacity.[67] The first goal—presence—would be achieved primarily through the nine-month rotational deployment of an Armored Brigade Combat Team (ABCT) under the mission of Operation Atlantic Resolve, which would supplement the airborne and Stryker brigades already stationed in Germany and Italy.[68] The initiative also increased funding for major US-led and NATO exercises, to include Swift Response, Anakonda, BALTOPS, and Trident Juncture.

In September 2014, NATO officials met in Wales to determine how the alliance should respond to and prevent future Russian aggression. The delegates developed a "Readiness Action Plan" to increase air, sea, and land presence in Eastern Europe and establish a Very High Readiness Joint Task Force (VJTF) capable of deploying on short notice.[69] These efforts were challenging given NATO's current political divides, decreased defense budgets, and war-weariness from Afghanistan. Leaders pledged to increase their defense spending at the Wales summit, yet few followed through and NATO's Rapid Reaction Force would need time to develop.[70] In the meantime, the United States would increase its presence in the Baltics and develop a creative strategy to assure its European partners.

## Operation Dragoon Ride

In March 2015, a year after Russia's invasion of Crimea, an American battalion from the 2nd Stryker Calvary Regiment concluded its three-month OAR rotation in the Baltics and Poland. During the training, military leaders at US Army Europe were assessing how best to increase assurance among its anxious European allies in addition to the military maneuvers. As the US Army Europe Commander, Lieutenant General Ben Hodges, watched the Russian military increase its training program to incorporate massive "snap exercises," he decided that the United States needed to send a message not only to Russia, but also to Eastern European publics who were growing concerned about the potential for Russia to intervene militarily or politically through subversion. After Army units are complete with the training rotation, it is common to load their vehicles onto railcars and fly the soldiers back to the home station (in this case, Vilseck, Germany). However, Lieutenant General Hodges developed a different idea: he ordered them to drive home instead, a journey of 1,100 miles across six European countries—the longest convoy in Europe since the Battle of the Bulge in 1944—which included about 500 US troops and 120 vehicles.[71] He came to the idea from a British colleague who , in a prior exercise in North Africa, chose to transport soldiers by land through France and Spain instead of by air.[72] By convincing the European public that America was committed to its security, he hoped these states would be assured and less susceptible to Russian meddling.

Lieutenant General Hodges' fear of potential Russian intervention in NATO's eastern flank is apparent in a report he drafted with two colleagues at the Center for European Analysis several years after he retired from active duty. The document describes seven scenarios in which Russia could creatively exploit shaping to close the "Suwalki Gap" that separates its ally Belarus from the Russian strategic exclave of Kaliningrad, which hosts the Russian Baltic Fleet and S-400 air defense missiles. Four of these scenarios stand out: two involve Russian attempts to gain access through a Lithuanian overland route if Kaliningrad becomes vulnerable to external attack, ethnic unrest rises, or the electric grid becomes compromised. Another includes an irredentist group in Kaliningrad asking Moscow to intervene so it can expand its borders to incorporate Russian-speaking portions of Poland and Lithuania to correct a historical injustice, a pretext which the authors argue "would be similar to the dubious territorial assertions Moscow made in advance of its illegal annexation in Crimea." An alternative situation imagines that Moscow would agitate Russian speakers in the Baltics and intervene to protect these minorities against their repressive governments, which the authors fear would fall below NATO's Article V security guarantee.[73] In each of these scenarios, Russia relies on its ability to foment ethnic discord below the threshold of open violence to achieve its goal of creating a land bridge between Belarus and the Kaliningrad oblast, which would also cut off land reinforcements from the majority of NATO countries to the Baltics.

Hodges' goal for the long vehicle movement was far more about political influence than achieving tactical military readiness. Hodges told a reporter, "The whole purpose . . . is to assure those allies that live closest to the Bear that we are here . . . You heard our president say very clearly, we will defend our allies, Lithuania, Latvia, Estonia, and Poland." By demonstrating physical presence, he argued, the locals "will be able to literally see Stryker vehicles, talk to American soldiers," moreover, he noted "I envision kids crawling over those vehicles, sort of a public awareness kind of thing as well."[74] There were, of course, tactical and training value to this demanding road march: practicing long-range maintenance and logistics is challenging and a rare opportunity for units eager to improve and test their readiness. Moreover, the unit needed get its vehicles back to Germany somehow (though railhead is the usual method). Nonetheless, the emphasis on public diplomacy was central, as journalist Robbie Gramer notes, "Although Dragoon Ride's primary audience wasn't Russia, it did exhibit that military commanders in Europe are thinking about how to incorporate public relations and communications into their planning and the value they are placing on European citizens' views of the alliance."[75] The target of the convoy was more for the hearts and minds of the European public than the calculations of Russian military planners.

## Assuring the Eastern European Public

Since the OAR maneuvers took place in the Baltic states, the convoy first stopped in major cities Estonia, Latvia, and Lithuania to interact with the cheering crowds. American soldiers were greeted emphatically during their stays in the Baltic states and Poland, especially among those with memories of the Soviet occupation after World War II. One video released by the unit

reveals a visit at a shopping area in Vilnius, Lithuania, where American soldiers were welcomed by enthusiastic locals.[76] An 81-year-old Lithuanian man
who once served in the Soviet Army came out to support the visit and told
a reporter, "American soldier is our friend." One of the American soldiers
recounts: "The older people start getting emotional. I had one lady came up
to me crying . . ..They were all really grateful."[77] When the convoy stopped
in Poland, one 69-year-old woman noted, "I am very worried and afraid
about what Russia might do next . . . It gives us all comfort to see these
American soldiers and to know they are here for us." In the northeastern city
of Bialystock, Poland, hundreds of locals brought the American soldiers cake
and vodka.[78] By assuring the public of America's support, US Army Europe
hoped that the publics would continue to support US and NATO interests
against Russia.

Yet as the convoy moved West and the threat of Russian invasion was less
intense, the public relations campaign needed to convince a more skeptical
crowd. The hard test for the journey was the Czech Republic, with its high-
level of anti-American sentiment and a president who enjoyed warm relations with Russia. A few days prior to the convoy's arrival in the country,
former communist and leftist groups staged an anti-NATO rally in the central
Wenceslas Square in Prague. One former parliamentarian told a reporter,
"We've been considering blocking the roads but eventually decided to stage
a protest in Prague outside the base where the U.S. soldiers will be staying
. . . I will come with a banner that says 'Czechs against NATO.'"[79] This anti-
American sentiment was buttressed by pro-Russian sympathies by the Czech
president, Milos Zeman. Zeman was one of the few European leaders who
committed to attend a commemoration of the Soviet victory in World War
II in Moscow; he also openly questioned the prudence of EU sanctions on
Russia.

Moscow's influence in the Czech Republic extended beyond the presidential palace and into the public, primarily through social media. Only a
month prior to the convoy, Sputnik—a Russian-sponsored news organization—announced that it would launch a news website in Czech to provide
"alternative views" to it foreign readers.[80] A week before the convoy was set
to travel into the Czech Republic, *RT* published a story revealing Czech dis-
satisfaction with the convoy by drawing attention to a Facebook page known
as "Tanks? No thanks!" that opposed the convoy as American aggression.[81]
Another website suspected of support by Russian sympathizers, *AE News,*
illustrated its coverage of the event with photographs of Hitler Youth and
claimed that the Stryker vehicles were emanating depleted Uranium around
the countryside.[82]

Yet US Army Europe waged an online presence of its own: even Lieutenant
General Hodges filmed himself riding along with the Stryker soldiers, one of

several videos the unit posted on YouTube revealing the large crowds gathering around the vehicles.[83] The support extended even to the physical space, as an enthusiastic Czech crowd greeted the Americans along the border under sleet and heavy winds. As the *Economist* notes, "The onlookers were defying more than the inclement weather. They were also repudiating Milos Zeman, the Czech president, whose public pro-Kremlin sympathies have made him a key ally in Moscow's efforts to divide European opinion over Ukraine."[84] One survey found that 82 percent of the Czechs were supportive of the convoy's travel through the country, which surprised even the pollsters.[85] In fact, one group of Harvey-Davidson riders offered to meet the American convoy at the border and escort it through the country.[86] It appeared that US Army Europe was successful in convincing public opinion that its presence was welcome and necessary.

## Assessing the Impact of Dragoon Ride

After the soldiers returned home, there was a sense that Dragoon Ride was more of a publicity stunt than a valid operation to deter Russia.[87] By rotating only small, tactical units in the four vulnerable NATO members, the ERI and OAR seemed paltry. Several RAND simulations conducted in 2014 and 2015 determined that as currently postured, Russia could invade the Baltic capitals in under 60 hours.[88] American officials seemed to agreed: In July 2016, Department of Defense civilians and military leaders testified before Congress, requesting to increase funding for the ERI and to send a clear message that the European Command's strategy was transitioning from assurance to deterrence. As the director of strategy and policy at US European Command noted in his opening statement, "To an extent, assuring our allies has a deterrent effect in and of itself. However, as we continue to see a malign influence and a Russia acting to upset international norms, we have transitioned beyond purely assurance."[89] Moreover, for the FY 2017 budget request under the National Defense Authorization Act, the name of the program was changed to the "European *Deterrence* Initiative" (EDI) and resulted in increased funding.[90] NATO also improved its deterrence posture in 2016 by deploying four 1,000-soldier multinational rotational battlegroups in each of the Baltic states and Poland, with the bulk of troops supplied by the United States, the United Kingdom, Canada, and Germany.[91]

Clearly, moderate-sized exercises and vehicle convoys through European towns do little to deter a large-scale invasion by a near peer-adversary. However, that does not appear to be Hodges' main goal for Operation Dragoon Ride. This exercise was concerned more about attacks on European minds and less about European soil; it was more about influencing perceptions rather than demonstrating military might. Russian officials seem very attuned to these need to affect perceptions, as a Russian adviser to Vladimir Putin wrote in an op-ed in 2019, "Foreign politicians talk about Russia's interference in elections and referendums around the world. In fact, the matter is even more serious: Russia interferes in your brains, we change your conscience, and there is nothing you can do about it."[92] Russia has continued to foment dissent in the Baltics and Poland and was even suspected of supporting a failed coup attempt in one of NATO's newest members, Montenegro, in 2016. Montenegro may be ripe for interference, as one poll revealed that 47 percent of the population opposed NATO accession a month before the country joined the alliance. As the authors of a report on Russian influence in the country noted, "the risk of Russian malign influence in Montenegro has not receded following their NATO membership and efforts to join the European Union. If anything, it may be intensifying."[93] The US and NATO member militaries understand the subversive success of Russia and are attempting to combat its influence over minds. For example, the Enhanced Forward Presence battlegroup in Lithuania even generated online videos of how Lithuanian teachers are educating young students about the suffering endured under Soviet occupation. As one teacher explained to the NATO interviewer:

> For Lithuania, I think one of the best things that could have happened after it got it's [sic] independence back, is for the country to join NATO and the EU. For a long time we couldn't understand that it's beneficial for us because we were just enjoying our freedom. But the events of Crimea opened our eyes for the danger [of Russian Occupation] which is still present. The presence of NATO forces and being a member of the alliance is a warranty for us that maybe we can avoid this. But with this neighbor we don't know what can happen in the future and we have to be ready for everything.[94]

Given the rise of Russia's creative shaping strategies to undermine NATO cohesion, perhaps assurance to convince allied publics of a security commitment is an appropriate response to this complex challenge.

## SUMMARY

Assurance is a major power's attempt to manage an ally's behavior by removing a source of insecurity, usually through the extension of a security commitments, forward-stationing of troops, or verbal statements of support. Major powers leverage assurance when they become concerned about an ally's aberrant behavior, which may take the form of aggression toward its neighbors, de-alignment with the major power, or falling under the influence of a rival. One of the benefits of forward presence is also the ability to gain access through airbases or logistical hubs, which become useful if shaping and deterrence fail and war becomes necessary. As the only major power with over sixty alliance commitments, the United States occupies the bulk of the literature and examples of assurance in action. Although the most prominent studies of US assurance explore the Cold War alliances in Europe and East Asia, this chapter illustrated this logic with a more recent example to reveal how major powers may use assurance in today's environment. Operation Dragoon Ride, which was a clear attempt by US Army Europe to reassure anxious European publics about Russian overt or subversive interference after its annexation of Crimea, illustrated this logic.

Although Operation Dragoon Ride appeared to assuage weary NATO members, assessing the overall effects of assurance in practice is challenging and the results are mixed at best. In one of the few comprehensive empirical studies on the effect of US forward presence on interstate conflict, a RAND study found that from 1951 to 2007, US troop presence abroad was correlated with lower likelihoods of interstate war, yet also associated with higher levels of conflict below the threshold of open violence (such as threats or demonstrations of force). Thus, on average, although American presence may deter interstate wars, it also could incentivize more threats and demonstrations than locations without forward presence. Importantly for the discussion about assurance, troops on or near allies were associated with fewer interstate disputes initiated by the ally, which provide some evidence for the hypothesis that assurance restrains reckless ally behavior.[95] Yet, others charge that assurance results in one of the negative consequences of alliance politics explored above: notably moral hazard and entrapment. As Barry Posen notes, US security guarantees and defense spending "amounts to a subsidy to other prosperous nations that could defend themselves if they spent a little more on defense."[96] This contention reveals one of several negative consequences of shaping, which are explored in the conclusion to follow.

# Chapter 8

# Conclusion: The Significance and Future of Shaping

In early 2016, during the annual gathering of the Russian Academy of Military Sciences, Russian Chief of Staff General Vitaly Gerasimov called on the military's top thinkers to develop ideas for countering Western attempts to foment political unrest close to Russia's borders. Gerasimov concluded that any strategy must incorporate an increased use of soft power instruments to neutralize the West's hybrid tactics.[1] According to Dmitry Adamsky, this belief that a "New Generation Warfare" had emerged in which countries skillfully combine the various tools of statecraft, leveraging both hard and soft power, to achieve their goals is prevalent among Russia's senior military leaders. Describing Gerasimov's influential 2013 article on the topic, Adamsky observes that the ratio of nonmilitary to military tools in this type of competition is "4 to 1, with these forms of non-military strategic competition being under the aegis of the military organization."[2] The blending of diplomatic, information, military, and economic tools, prioritizing the indirect over the openly lethal, all under the orchestrating hand of a military leader, reveals the wide range and future trajectory of military statecraft.

The purpose of this book was to explore the rise and character of military shaping, a way of military statecraft designed to construct a more favorable environment through the management of military relationships, partner characteristics, and the behavior of allies. Shaping differs from the well-known military instruments of warfighting and coercion, tools that dominate the conventional wisdom and scholarly discourse on the use of military power. To reduce strategic uncertainty, major powers apply the four logics of shaping—attraction, socialization, delegation, and assurance—that target different aspects of their environment: the first two engagement logics rely more on a major power's persuasion, legitimacy, and values, while the second pair of security cooperation logics involve efforts to improve or commit coercive power to a partner. Although the origins of shaping are located in Sun Tzu's writing and the historical practices of statemen and military officers, the concept and primacy of these logics accelerated following the end of the Cold War. Though initially articulated in US foreign policy, now all major powers employ these logics to some degree. Civilian and military leaders have found military exercises to be a useful means to shape their environments, which is why this book illustrated the four logics through major multinational exercise programs.

The conclusion presented here attempts to illuminate the broader significance of shaping, particularly for two normative aspects of the contemporary broadening of military statecraft: how shaping fits into debates regarding US grand strategy and whether a reliance on shaping is leading to a militarization of foreign policy. The final part of this conclusion discusses the future of shaping, given the apparent return of great power competition. The appendix that follows this conclusion offers a more rigorous statistical test of the overall argument that a rise in strategic uncertainty resulted in an increase in shaping by the major powers.

## SHAPING AND AMERICAN GRAND STRATEGY

Although this book revealed how all major powers have adopted military shaping to manage their environments, there is growing interest in how the United States, in particular, leverages military power to support its overall grand strategy. In recent years, the debate about US grand strategy has "experienced a renaissance," especially as the election of President Donald Trump brought into question the long-held beliefs of most American policymakers.[3] As Nina Silove explains, the term "grand strategy" is often beset by conceptual confusion as different scholars and practitioners use the phrase differently to explain US strategic plans, principles, or behavior.[4] Yet Barry Posen offers a simple, useful definition for our purposes: "a nation-state's theory about how to produce security for itself."[5] In other words, arguments about American grand strategy often revolve around which instruments of statecraft and logics are best for protecting America against threats. As one team of scholars note, much of the grand strategy debate concentrates on the role of military power, especially in terms of force structure, security commitments, military deployments, and use of force.[6] Thus, to help inform the discussion, it may be useful to imagine which grand strategy options would prioritize the shaping logics described throughout this book.

### Shaping in Deep Engagement and Restraint

The literature offers two prominent "ideal type" strategic options that US policymakers could consider: *deep engagement* and *restraint*. These strategies are differentiated by their theoretical underpinnings, as well as the degree to which they prioritize the different logics of military statecraft. In general, the former imagines a United States that is internationally active, upholds multilateral institutions, and maintains a strong presence abroad to buttress international stability. Conversely, the latter holds that America's role and presence abroad should be limited: advocates would prefer to keep troops in the homeland, "offshore," and deploy them only if a rising power threatens regional hegemony. Theoretically, deep engagement holds that one powerful hegemon would stabilize the international order by providing public goods, while restraint views a major interstate power imbalance as threatening and prone to balancing by others.[7]

A grand strategy of deep engagement would likely include high levels of all shaping logics, though delegation would be applied selectively, and socialization would depend on the degree to which democracy promotion and the protection of human rights are viewed as necessary to America's security and values. To support deep engagement, attraction would be useful to recruit new partners to participate in multilateral missions such as peacekeeping and intervention to preclude state failure. Moreover, attraction may be beneficial to manage rivals by developing balancing coalitions or attempting to reduce tensions through cooperative programs. Deep engagement relies heavily on assurance through security commitments and the forward presence of ground troops to dampen security dilemmas, increase regional stability, and provide operational access to respond to contingencies.[8] Delegation would be applied more often to support weaker states fighting terrorism or facing state collapse rather than other major powers, who would either be allies (and assured) or rivals (who would either be deterred or attracted). The level of socialization would depend on whether the strategy prizes democracy promotion and the armed defense of human rights: the "liberal internationalist" variant of deep engagement would likely place a premium on this logic, while the "realist" version would not.[9]

Conversely, a grand strategy of restraint—which includes "offshore balancing"—would likely prioritize delegation, consider attraction only if a hegemon emerges, and eschew assurance as well as socialization. As the United States finds itself the predominant power secured by two large oceans, benign neighbors, and few great power threats, advocates of this strategy hold that there is little reason to sustain a large land-based military abroad. However, if a regional hegemon does arise in one of the three most critical regions of the world—Europe, Northeast Asia, and the Persian Gulf—the United States should first attempt to pass the buck (delegate) to allies instead of providing assurances, allowing efficient regional balancing to take place. Thus, restrainers would likely limit security commitments and forward presence on foreign territory, preferring to keep ground troops offshore and ready to deploy only if the ally is unable to check the rising hegemon.[10] Restrainers would view the logic of assurance as expensive and potentially harmful by accelerating insecurity in rivals and underwriting the security of risk-acceptant allies.[11] Moreover, assurance mixed with socialization may be counterproductive as it invites local, nationalist blowback against Western military occupation.[12] As fighting terrorism abroad and engaging in humanitarian interventions are not high priorities for a policy of restraint, attraction would only be useful to secure state alliances against emerging hegemons in the three most critical regions listed above (though, after first attempting delegation). Given the absence of a forward ground troop presence, restraint would instead rely on US naval and air power to command the global commons to ensure operational access and the free flow of commerce, especially oil. Moreover, shaping exercises in general would be kept to a minimum, as restraint advocate Barry Posen explains: "In practice, many of these exercises serve purposes that are less important to Restraint Strategy than they are to present U.S. grand strategy."[13]

The current discussion about which grand strategy is best to protect America's interests mirrors one from the 1990s as the United States found itself without a peer competitor.[14] The resurgence of the grand strategic debate has led to another debate: whether grand strategy is a useful concept at all. A few scholars have questioned the value of the idea, albeit for different reasons: some argue that grand strategy may not be possible in today's nonpolar international system and divisive America politics, while others have argued that grand strategy could even be a harmful "delusion" that inflates threats and creates unnecessary insecurity.[15] Regardless of the state of theorizing on grand strategy, the advantage of thinking in terms of statecraft is the ability to observe day-to-day military practices, identify how and why major powers use various logics, and anticipate future military behavior given the structural factors laid out in this book.

## SHAPING AND THE MILITARIZATION
## OF FOREIGN POLICY

Especially since the George W. Bush administration's two armed interventions in the wake of 9/11, a growing sense has emerged that American foreign policy is becoming "militarized"—that is, when the use of force is considered as a first resort above other tools of statecraft or when foreign policy is dominated by military officers.[16] In other words, these observers fear that leaders will favor too much *warfighting* and *coercing* on the one hand, or too much *shaping* on the other. As Rachel Maddow succinctly describes the concern: "Our military and weapons prowess is a fantastic and perfectly weighted hammer, but that doesn't make every international problem a nail."[17] One indicator of this problem is the vast disparity between US departments' funding and resources. The budget of the Defense Department vastly outweighs that of the State Department: the Fiscal Year (FY) 2019 defense budget was 13 times the size of the international affairs budget (designated for the State Department, US Agency for International Development, and the international programs of other departments).[18] Former secretary of state Condoleezza Rice complained that there were more musicians in military bands than the State Departments' entire corps of US Foreign Service Officers.[19]

Moreover, after the Cold War the American military was increasingly deployed for humanitarian purposes: to provide aid in conflict regions, enforce peacekeeping agreements, restore stability after hurricanes, contain Ebola in Africa, and even encourage agricultural development in Africa and the Middle East. As Secretary of State Madelene Albright famously asked Chairman of the Joint Chiefs of Staff General Colin Powell, "What's the point of having this superb military that you're always talking about if we can't use it?"[20] Many observers view both this dependence on combat power and the growing use of soldiers to carry out nonmilitary missions as a sign that foreign policy is being militarized to a dangerous level. The major arguments are concerned about two negative consequences for US foreign policy: (1) that war is favored over other alternatives of statecraft or (2) that the US military is too frequently assigned tasks that were previously carried out by civilian departments or agencies, such as the State Department or USAID. Observers fear that relying too heavily on the military instrument will either lead to unnecessary violence and human suffering by choosing war as the primary tool, or that excessive shaping will lead to ineffective outcomes, given that soldiers are ill-equipped to carry out nonmilitary tasks.

## Two Perspectives on the Militarization of American Foreign Policy

One of the most prominent voices of the first type of militarization is Andrew Bacevich, who argued in *The New American Militarism* that the American people—not just presidents or military officers but also local politicians, journalists, religious leaders, and intellectuals—have become enamored of American military strength and its ability to achieve the ends of American foreign policy. He locates the source of this over-reliance and fascination with military power to the 1970s, when senior officers and emerging neo-conservatives sought to reinvigorate military power after the frustrations and humiliations of the Vietnam War. This militarization is manifest in immense budgets, capabilities beyond mere territorial defense, permanent troop presence abroad, but most importantly, a normalization of war through the excessive reliance on the use of force in a post-Cold War age of superior access to battlefield information, precision technology, and "low-cost" combat. Bacevich notes:

> That even apart from fighting wars and pursuing terrorists, U.S. forces are con-stantly prowling around the globe—training, exercising, planning, and postur-ing—elicits no more notice (and in some cases less) from the average American than the presence of a cop on a city street corner. Even before the Pentagon officially assigned itself the mission of "shaping" the international environment, members of the political elite, liberals and conservatives alike, had reached a common understanding that scattering U.S. troops around the globe to restrain, inspire, influence, persuade, or cajole paid dividends.[21]

Despite this passing remark about the use of the US military for nonwar purposes, he mainly criticizes the American reliance on violent force, reach-ing its apogee in the 2003 invasion of Iraq largely to secure oil for the US homeland.[22]

The second type of militarization is typified by Rosa Brooks' *How Everything Became War and the Military Became Everything*, in which a former defense official observes the growing tendency of the US government to depend on soldiers for nonmilitary tasks, such as teaching law to Afghan officials or running health clinics in Malaysia. Brooks argues that this expan-sion resulted from the current ambiguous security environment in which the traditional distinction between war and peace has been blurred. She argues: "As the lines we have drawn between 'war' and 'nonwar' grow indistinct, the role and mission of the U.S. military have grown similarly hazy. Today, as the military struggles to respond to novel threats from novel quarters, its once seemingly straightforward raison d'être—defending America from armed attack by foreign states—is no longer clear-cut."[23] Brooks importantly asks, "And what is the *military* for, in a world in which future threats are as likely to come from computer hackers, terrorists, and other nonstate actors as from armies of foreign states?"[24] Brooks notes that despite growing prosperity and life expectancy across the world, the global increase in interconnectedness, transportation, reach of technology, and climate change has produced an environment in which the next catastrophic event is unpredictable.[25] Thus, for Brooks, the assumption of nonmilitary tasks by soldiers is largely a response to this new uncertain environment.

After four decades of government service, former Secretary of Defense Robert Gates expressed grave concerns with both types of militarization. Gates observes the reduction in budgets and manpower of the traditional "non-military tools" of state power, namely the State Department and USAID. He also laments the disbandment of the US Information Agency in 1999, which served as America's primary public diplomacy arm during the Cold War. He diagnoses the problem with the outdated structure of the US national security apparatus, especially the "stultifying bureaucracy" in the State Department and over-reliance on the ineffective "whole-of-government" approach of the National Security Council. He recommends a drastic reorganization to prioritize the nonmilitary agencies, including tasking the State Department with leading nonmilitary efforts, reinvigorating development assistance, and overhauling its public relations abroad to better compete with China and Russia.[26] Secretary Gates' thoughtful condemnation of the militarization of US foreign policy is significant, yet the analysis in this book reveals how shaping has often combined and blurred the tools of statecraft, especially when the military is often viewed as the best organization to construct a more favorable environment. As the case studies and quantitative analysis in the appendix reveals, this is unfortunately the case not only for the United States, but for all major powers. If there is an ongoing militarization of foreign policy—perhaps even through more shaping and less warfighting—it appears that this phenomenon is systemic, not confined to America.

## Shaping and Bureaucratic Rivalry

Whether a militarization of foreign policy is justified by the complex international environment, or, conversely, US policymakers have prioritized military power to an unnecessary or dangerous degree, one conclusion seems clear. The recent post-Cold War broadening of military statecraft will likely cause bureaucratic conflict within the US government and will be difficult to ameliorate. As described in chapter 3, when overlap develops between the missions of two separate bureaucracies, we can expect that each will defend its turf and seek to reduce the threat of rivals. Despite sincere efforts to engender whole-of-government approaches to reduce bureaucratic friction, some conflict is inevitable. Africa Command (AFRICOM), the newest US Combatant Command and one of the most persistent executers of shaping operations, is often perceived as a significant infringement on civilian control of foreign policy by civil servants in the State Department and USAID.[27] The question of who is responsible for governance in the aftermath of war is even more salient. After the invasion of Iraq in 2003, then Major General David Petraeus' unit in Mosul was faced with a city in shambles and little civilian support. Fred Kaplan notes that despite initial concerns about the army's role in development, "there *was* no local government, so the 101st Airborne would have to create one."[28] Especially during the ongoing civil war or in the immediate aftermath of conflict, the military is often granted powers to reshape entire governments. Although some civilian leaders or diplomats may welcome the efficient organization and resources of the military, others will push back against the shaping logics of attraction, socialization, and delegation that often mimic the activities of diplomats and development specialists.

## THE FUTURE OF SHAPING

The remarkable increase in shaping exercises since the end of the Cold War should alert scholars and practitioners alike to the growing need for a more comprehensive understanding of military statecraft. The use of shaping through multinational exercises reveals how states leverage their military to manage diverse threats in a complex environment of costly war, emerging great power competition, and the persistent threat of violent non-state actors. Although shaping was a prominent activity of all major powers since the end of the Cold War, the apparent return of great power rivalry may raise the question about whether shaping will continue to be a prominent foreign policy tool. Figure 8.1 reveals that traditional exercises are making a comeback in world politics, especially as a result of NATO's exercises as part of the European Reassurance Initiative and Operation Atlantic Resolve. In 2014, the same year in which Russia invaded and annexed the Ukrainian province of Crimea, traditional exercises eclipsed shaping for two years straight for

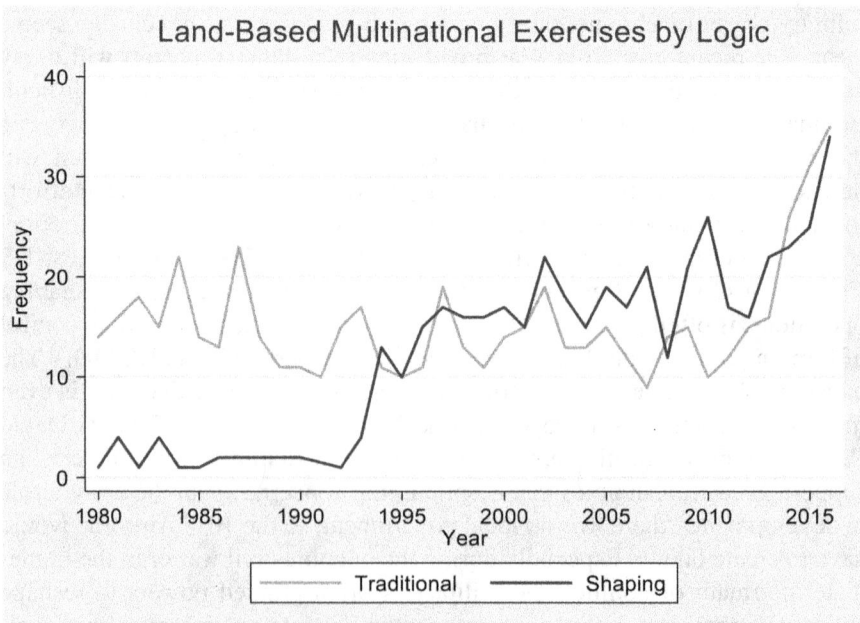

**Figure 8.1   Traditional and Shaping Exercises, 1980–2016.**

the first time since 1994. Yet what is also interesting about this graph is that *both* traditional and shaping exercises seem to be on an upward trend: that is, responses to threats known and unknown are rising.

## The Return of Traditional Exercises

In June 2016, NATO conducted its largest exercise in Eastern Europe since the Cold War. The exercise, Anakonda 2016, consisted of over 30,000 troops from 24 different countries, including non-allies such as Ukraine, Georgia, and even Kosovo. Although the US Army described the exercise as a "joint defense operation on a large scale," Russian Foreign Minister Sergei Lavrov told other reporters in response to the event, "We will invoke Russia's sovereign right to guarantee its security with measures proportionate to current risks."[29] Shortly after the exercise, NATO announced that 5,000 troops from the United States, Britain, and Germany would be stationed in Poland and the Baltics to deter possible Russian aggression. Recent Russian exercises, including the 2013 and 2017 iterations of *Zapad*, are alleged to consist of over 100,000 troops, drawing concerns about an "exercise gap" between NATO and Russia.[30] In an interview with Reuters in August 2017, a senior US exercise planner noted that by fiscal year 2020, the US military plans to conduct exercises "that involved forces from all nine U.S. combatant commands" and increase troop levels to over 40,000.[31]

The return of traditional exercises is concurrent with changes to major power military doctrine, particularly within the United States. In October 2017, the US Army released its new operations manual—*Field Manual 3-0*—to reemphasize large-scale conventional war after almost two decades of counterinsurgency and other nontraditional operations. Announcing the changes, the commander of the US Army Combined Arms Center, Lieutenant General Mike Lundy, asserted that when the previous edition of the operational doctrine was rescinded in 2011: "The world was a different place. The likelihood of large-scale ground combat against an enemy with peer capabilities seemed remote."[32] He argues that in 2017, "The strategic environment has changed significantly since then": aggressive actions by "peer adversaries" such as Russia and China have made major power war more likely and the US Army must return to a focus on massive maneuvers and higher-echelon operations.[33] However, the senior officer notes that the US Army must also maintain its ability to shape the environment while simultaneously preparing for major power war: the manual retains the "shape" and "prevent" phases before large-scale combat. General Lundy notes the vast array of enemies and scenarios the US Army must be prepared for: "Army forces do not have the luxury of focusing solely on large-scale land combat at the expense of other missions the Nation requires them to do, but at the same time, they cannot afford to be unprepared for those kinds of operations in an increasingly unstable world."[34] The Army officer's assessment highlights the need for US forces to be ready for any type of threat, state or non-state, major power or not.

## The Continued Prominence of Shaping

As detailed in chapter 2, shaping will continue to play a prominent role in major power statecraft for the foreseeable future for three reasons. First, the dominance of defensive technology, beginning first with the nuclear revolution and now buttressed by advances in missile and radar technology, will make shaping more attractive. As warfare and violent coercion have become more costly in terms of lives and treasure, major powers will look to the logics of shaping to achieve their goals below the threshold of violence: socialization to impart values and practices in partners, delegation to pass the burden of security onto others, and attraction to improve deterrence against rivals. Second, the consequences of globalization have given rise to the power of non-state actors, which are difficult to manage with warfighting or coercion. Instead, major powers will reach to the tools of shaping to build multinational peacekeeping coalitions or build capacity in weak states to contain these threats. Third, as the structure of the international system turns more multipolar, state leaders will use attraction to improve external balancing, assurance to manage allies and balance foes, and delegation to fund proxies against one another.

By illuminating the rise and future of shaping, this book hopes to serve as an impetus for scholars and a cautionary tale for practitioners. The dearth of studies on the nontraditional uses of military power provides ample space for political scientists, historians, and strategic studies scholars to discover the true extent of military shaping in world politics. In addition to exercises, major powers exploit other means of military statecraft that need to be explored: military aid, weapon sales, intelligence-sharing, and officer and student exchanges outside of the United States are only a few of the many possibilities. The important normative discussions above concerning grand strategy and the militarization of foreign policy are only brief and need to be elaborated in greater detail. For those practitioners charged with executing and managing shaping—the military officers and civilian leaders—the previous chapters should provide a better understanding of how major powers are leveraging shaping to manage various types of threats. When addressing violent non-state threats, shaping could be an option for great power cooperation: the training scenarios for India and China's "Hand-in-Hand" exercise program involved countering terrorism and improving humanitarian assistance. However, the return of great power competition will likely result in the use of shaping to undermine one another through subversion and balancing. Leaders must continue to explore and manage shaping appropriately to prevent the need for the costliest and most tragic ways of military statecraft.

# Appendix

## *Measuring Military Statecraft*

This appendix is intended to offer a more comprehensive test of the book's main argument—that an increase in strategic uncertainty incentivized major powers to increase their use of shaping exercises—as well as provide additional graphs and reference material to supplement the analysis throughout the book.[1]

### RESEARCH DESIGN: CONTENT ANALYSIS AND LARGE-N REGRESSION

In addition to the qualitative evidence provided throughout chapters 4–7, I further test my argument using textual sentiment analysis and multinomial logit models of dyads between major powers and every other state in the international system from 1980 to 2016. My outcome variable—*exercise type*, a nominal categorical variable—is the probability of conducting a certain type of exercise, which assumes one of three values: no exercise, a traditional exercise, or a shaping exercise. I derive observations from a new dataset of over 1,000 major power-led, land-based multinational military exercises from 1980 to 2016; each exercise was reported in the news or announced by a military public affairs office. I include only land-based multinational military exercises in order to separate actual exercises from workshops, seminars, or computer-simulated exercises (which are far cheaper and easier to administer). I also exclude air, air defense, and naval exercises. I exclusively test land-based exercises for two methodological reasons. First, although most states have at least a standing army, not all states have an air or naval force, which would bias the dyad observation away from these states when addressing the question of why major powers conduct exercises with non-allies.[2] Second, as opposed to training on national land, naval and air training exercises are often conducted in the global commons—against, for instance, drug traffickers or pirates—which makes it difficult to distinguish between exercises (practice) and patrols (actual operations).[3]

## Data

I borrow most observations from a dataset compiled by Vito D'Orazio,[4] but code more exercises and re-code some of his observations to reflect exercise type, training task, number of troops, organization or alliance involved, and exercise program history. Every exercise is coded by "type," which I determined by observing several indicators for each exercise: tasks that were trained, named "threat" during the exercise, number and type of troops, official and journalistic accounts, and exercise program type and history.[5] The coding criteria are available in figure A.7. The exercise types delineated in the dataset directly translate into the ways and logics of military statecraft described throughout this book. *Traditional exercises* are designed to rehearse for war or other missions, practice the coercive use of force, or signal deterrence (i.e., the logics of warfighting and coercing). *Shaping exercises* are a general category that includes *recruitment and trust-developing exercises* (logic of attraction) and *role-forming and capacity-building exercises* (logics of socialization and delegation, respectively). Importantly, the shaping logic of *assurance* is included in traditional exercises because of the observational equivalence of extended deterrence and assurance: an exercise designed to assure is also often designed to deter. By separating exercises by type (traditional vs. shaping), my study parts ways with other works that assume that all exercises serve the same purpose.[6]

I then organize these observations into about 40,000 (directed) dyad[7] years between each major power and every other state in the international system.[8] Though the concept of "major power" carries different interpretations, I include as major powers those delineated by the authors of the Correlates of War State System Membership Project: from 1945 to 2016, these countries include the United States, Great Britain, France, Germany, Russia, China, and Japan. However, I make two caveats to this list: (1) though Japan may be considered an economic major power, I exclude the country due to its constitutional inability to project military force outside of its borders;[9] (2) I include India, which, as of the most recent Correlates of War National Material Capabilities (NMC) list, had the third highest Composite of National Capabilities (CINC) behind the Unites States and China and the fourth largest military in 2012.[10] In order to be included as a partner, a state's military must comprise at least 1,000 troops, which I assume is the least amount of total national troops possible for a state to be considered a potential exercise-partner.[11]

## Variables: Explanatory, Alternatives, and Controls

Though ostensibly ambiguous, I code my primary explanatory variable—*strategic uncertainty*—using two indicators: one specifically for the United States and the other for all major powers. My first indicator—*doctrinal uncertainty*—is the perceived uncertainty expressed in US Army operational doctrine, which I determine using sentiment analysis.[12] The US Army's capstone operations manual, published about once or twice a decade, serves as the organization's formal statement of its military doctrine.[13] Each version sets out the Army's primary purpose, potential threats, and a description of how the Army plans for its forces to be employed (operating concept). Figure A.1, adapted from Jensen (2016), describes each version of the Army's

| Version of U.S. Army Operations Manual | Year of Publication | Number of Pages and Words | Major Operating Concept | Named Primary Threats | Frequency of words describing strategic uncertainty (per 10,000 words) |
|---|---|---|---|---|---|
| FM 100-5: Operations | 1976 | 69 20,971 | Active Defense | Warsaw Pact, irregular units | 0.00 |
| FM 100-5: Operations | 1982 | 51 22,606 | AirLand Battle | Warsaw Pact and Soviet-supported insurgents and terrorists | 1.91 |
| FM 100-5: Operations | 1986 | 207 94,115 | AirLand Battle | Warsaw Pact, Soviet surrogates, terrorist groups | .99 |
| FM 100-5: Operations | 1993 | 163 92,995 | Full-Dimensional Operations | Drug-trafficking, natural or man-made disasters, regional conflicts, civil wars, insurgencies, extremists | 2.12 |
| FM 3-0: Operations | 2001 | 319 125,415 | Full-Spectrum Operations (emphasizing shaping) | Potential interstate conflict, nonstate actors, regional powers, transnational groups (terrorism, illegal drug trading, illicit arms trafficking, organised crime, piracy, environmental damage). | 3.76 |
| FM 3-0: Operations | 2008 | 220 105,283 | Full-Spectrum Operations (emphasizing counterinsurgency and stability operations) | Nation-states, organizations, people, groups, coalitions, or natural phenomena able to damage or destroy life. | 6.28 |
| ADP 3-0: Unified Land Operations | 2011 | 28 7,747 | Unified Land Operations | Most likely hybrid threats (combination of regular forces, irregular forces, terrorist forces, criminal elements) | 2.69 |

Figure A.1   Textual Analysis of US Army Operations Manuals.

operations manual by year of publication, the major operating concept, the primary objective of the US Army, named threats, and the frequency of the sentiment "strategic uncertainty" described in the doctrine. The major operating concept, objectives, and threats are derived from either the preface, introduction, or chapter 1 of each manual, sections which serve as the overarching basis for the rest of the manual.

The second indicator for uncertainty—*Post-Cold War uncertainty*—measures strategic uncertainty by differentiating two time periods: the Cold War (1980–1991) and post-Cold War (1992–2016). As explained in argument section above, the threat environment changed considerably after the end of superpower rivalry and the collapse of communism. Moreover, Figure A.1 reveals the change in the US Army's perception of threats: from specifically the Soviet Union and Soviet-backed insurgents during the Cold War to ambiguous, non-state threats beginning in the early 1990s. This indicator is used to test not only United States but all major power increases in shaping operations. Below are the two hypotheses I test:

> $H_1$: An increase in doctrinal uncertainty is associated with an increase in the likelihood of conducting a shaping exercise with a partner, even when controlling for other factors (US Only).
>
> $H_2$: An increase in post-Cold War uncertainty is associated with an increase in the likelihood of conducting a shaping exercise with a partner, even when controlling for other factors (US and Non-US).

I include several covariates that represent either the alternative explanations or controls for other factors that may influence decisions to implement shaping operations. There are two main alternative explanations that challenge my account of the rise of shaping operations after the end of the Cold War. First, militaries, as self-interested organizations, may use shaping operations to procure greater organizational benefits, such as size, wealth, prestige, and autonomy. This explanation is supported by some of the most prominent works in military doctrine. From this perspective, armies favor certain doctrines in order to reduce organizational uncertainty on the battlefield and to increase the military's prestige and morale, its organizational size and wealth, and its autonomy from civilian oversight.[14] Because armies often pursue doctrines that are harmful to a state's political goals, civilian government officials are forced to intervene and change a military's doctrine to better align with the state's grand strategy.[15] Failure to intervene in unwise military doctrine can result in disintegrated foreign policy or, as was the case prior to World War I, even great power war.[16] These traditional works borrow heavily from organization theory and bureaucratic politics to explain why militaries behave in ways counter to their governments' goals.[17] Thus, major power militaries may have leveraged military exercises in the 1990s and 2000s in order to serve these parochial interests rather than achieve the ends of grand strategy established by civilian officials.

Second, major powers may have employed exercises simply as an opportunity to institutionalize cooperation among allies and prepare for multinational operations. The major increase in multinational operations in the 1990s and 2000s suggests that perhaps these exercises provided an opportunity for allies (both defense-pact and coalition) to practice interoperability in preparation for missions. Celeste Wallander, for instance, argues that exercises comprise a key element of NATO's integrated military command, which served as a specific asset that allowed the alliance to survive in the mid-1990s after the threat of the Soviet Union dissipated.[18] In this sense, major powers may use military exercises to deepen relations with allies.

The first alternative explanation—concerning organizational benefits—is indicated through two variables: *military spending*, which is the amount of money (in constant 2016 US Dollars) that the major power spent on its military for a given year, as well as *exercise size*, the average number of troop participants for all exercises in a given year.[19] States authorize military expenditures in order for militaries to fund training, purchase equipment, and provide wages for military personnel; thus, militaries may seek to increase expenditures to enjoy more resources for the organization. Moreover, we would expect militaries to prefer large-scale exercises, which would align with their "organizational essence" preference for combat and require more resources to support.[20] *Ally* represents the second alternative explanation, which indicates whether the partner was an ally: that is, a permanent, defense-pact signatory (formal alliance) that is actively protecting or deterring against adversary or mission-based ("ad hoc") coalition partner.[21] Same region, contiguity, and sovereign history serve as geographic and historical controls to determine whether major powers choose local partners or desire to institutionalize cooperation with former colonies or republics.[22] The outcome, explanatory, and control variables are described in figure A.2.

## Models

I test my argument with four multinomial logit regression models: the first two only include the United States, the third includes all non-US powers, and the fourth involves only Russia: a non-Western, non-liberal major power. Since the outcome variable is multinomial, I do not apply fixed effects, random effects, or dummy years; however, I do include lagged dependent variables and dyad-clustered, serial-correlated (robust) standard errors to account for heteroskedasticity and temporal dependence.[23] Figure A.10 provides a robustness check of the results with a different data organization and model specification: an Ordinary Least Squares (OLS) regression in which

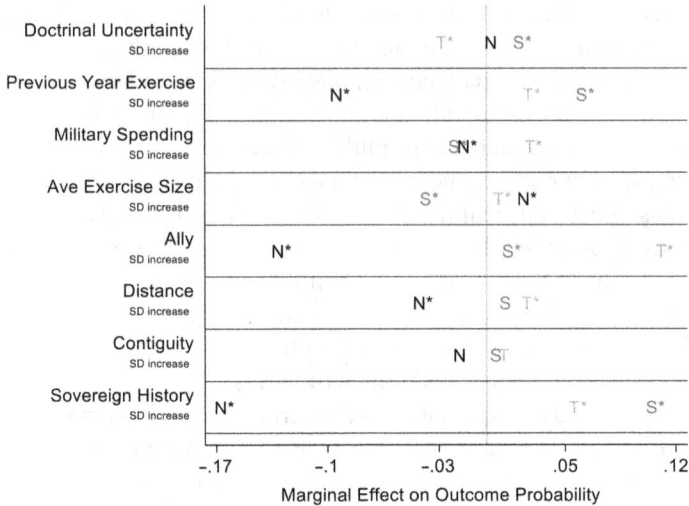

**Figure A.2    Marginal Change Plot for Model 1.**

the dependent variable is total number of shaping exercises by major power per year.[24]


# RESULTS

Tables A.1 and A.2 below show the results for the four models according to the value of the dependent variable: table A.1 for traditional exercises and table A.2 for shaping exercises (the first value—no exercise—is the base outcome and is therefore not represented). Supporting the first hypothesis, Model 1 reveals that an increase in *doctrinal uncertainty* is associated with an increase in the probability of conducting a shaping exercise. When considering the first alternative explanation, shaping is associated with a *decrease* in military spending and exercise size, which is not puzzling when considering that in comparison to traditional exercises, shaping training events are relatively small in scale and far less expensive to execute. Conversely, doctrinal uncertainty is (weakly) negatively associated with traditional exercises which makes sense considering most of these exercises are used to rehearse for missions or deter a known threat. Moreover, traditional exercises are associated with an increase in military spending and exercise size since these training events are much larger in scale and resources than shaping exercises.

Concerning the second alternative, although the probability of shaping increases slightly with an ally, traditional exercises are far more likely to be carried out between allies (since shaping is more often conducted to influence

**Table A.1   Descriptive Statistics**

| | Obs. | Mean | Std. Dev. | Min. | Max. | Description |
|---|---|---|---|---|---|---|
| **Dependent Variables** | | | | | | |
| Exercise Type | 40,708 | 0.141 | 0.476 | 0 | 2 | "0" for no exercise, "1" for traditional exercise, "2" for shaping exercise |
| **Explanatory/Control Variables** | | | | | | |
| Doctrinal Uncertainty | 6,134 | 2.565 | 1.517 | 0 | 6.28 | Frequency of the sentiment "strategic uncertainty" expressed in US Army doctrinal manuals |
| Post-Cold War Uncertainty | 40,708 | 0.727 | 0.446 | 0 | 1 | "1" if year is 1992–2016, "0" if year is 1980–1991 |
| Lag Exercise (1-Year) | 39,465 | 0.139 | 0.474 | 0 | 2 | "0" if no previous exercise, "1" if previous year traditional exercise, "2" if previous year shaping exercise |
| Military Spending | 40,708 | 11.08 | 1.094 | 8.638 | 13.552 | Logarithm of total military expenditures for each year |
| Average Exercise Size | 40,708 | 9.548 | 0.95 | 7.894 | 11.328 | Logarithm of the average of exercise size (by number of troops) for each year |
| Ally | 40,708 | 0.135 | 0.342 | 0 | 1 | "1" if ally, "0" if not |
| Geographic Distance | 40,708 | 8.171 | .753 | 5.094 | 9.392 | Logarithm of distance (in miles) between partners' state capitals |
| Contiguity | 40,708 | 0.039 | 0.194 | 0 | 1 | "1" if partners share territorial border, "0" if not |
| Sovereign History | 40,708 | 0.091 | 0.288 | 0 | 1 | "1" if partners share colonial/sovereign history, "0" if not |

non-allies). Thus, as expected, allies rehearse for multinational operations and practice deterrence, while major powers largely reserve shaping for non-allies to change the character of or relationship between militaries. Models 2, 3, and 4 display the results for the second hypothesis in which *Post-Cold War uncertainty* is the indicator for uncertainty (Model 2 for the United States;

**Table A.2  Results for H$_1$ and H$_2$ (Outcome: Traditional Exercises)**

| Dependent Variable: Exercise Type | Model 1 Doctrinal Uncertainty (US) | Model 2 Post-Cold War Uncertainty (US) | Model 3 Post-Cold War Uncertainty (All Non-US) | Model 4 Post-Cold War Uncertainty (Russia) |
|---|---|---|---|---|
| **Outcome: Traditional Exercise** | | | | |
| Doctrinal Uncertainty | −0.253*** | | | |
| | (0.05) | | | |
| Post-Cold War Uncertainty | | 0.293 | 0.315* | −0.752 |
| | | (0.20) | (0.13) | (1.36) |
| Lag Exercise (1-Year) | 0.953*** | 0.887*** | 1.024*** | 1.609*** |
| | (0.11) | (0.13) | (0.07) | (0.33) |
| Military Spending (Log) | 1.980*** | 1.187** | 0.676*** | 1.060** |
| | (0.46) | (0.38) | (0.10) | (0.39) |
| Average Exercise Size (Log) | 0.02 | 0.323*** | 0.442*** | 0.199 |
| | (0.06) | (0.07) | (0.04) | (0.23) |
| Ally | 3.268*** | 3.305*** | 3.144*** | 3.434** |
| | (0.45) | (0.45) | (0.29) | (1.09) |
| Geographic Distance | 0.885** | 0.806** | −0.719*** | −1.634* |
| | (0.30) | (0.31) | (0.15) | (0.74) |
| Contiguity | 1.733 | 1.638 | −0.666* | −3.126* |
| | (1.13) | (1.06) | (0.26) | (1.47) |
| Sovereign History | 15.102*** | 14.824*** | 0.939** | 1.712 |
| | (1.02) | (1.02) | (0.35) | (1.58) |
| N | 5,953 | 5,953 | 33,512 | 5,784 |
| BIC | 6,014 | 5,846 | 13,116 | 1,348 |

Standard errors in parentheses are clustered by dyad. *$p < 0.05$; **$p < 0.01$; ***$p < 0.001$

Model 3 for non-US major powers; Model 4 for Russia).[25] The results are similar to Model 1 with the exception that there is a slight positive correlation between military spending and the probability of holding a shaping exercise for non-US major powers. Last year's exercise (the lagged dependent variable) is also significant, given the habitual nature of exercise programs, which are often conducted on a regular annual or biannual basis.

Since the dependent variable is a nominal categorical variable, the coefficients for the results only indicate the direction and statistical significance

**Table A.3   Results for H₁ and H₂ (Outcome: Shaping Exercises)**

| Dependent Variable: Exercise Type | Model 1 Doctrinal Uncertainty (US) | Model 2 Post-Cold War Uncertainty (US) | Model 3 Post-Cold War Uncertainty (All Non-US) | Model 4 Post-Cold War Uncertainty (Russia) |
|---|---|---|---|---|
| **Outcome: Shaping Exercise** | | | | |
| Doctrinal Uncertainty | 0.111*** | | | |
| | (0.03) | | | |
| Post-Cold War Uncertainty | | 3.329*** | 3.718*** | 4.095*** |
| | | (0.54) | (0.50) | (1.16) |
| Lag Exercise (1-Year) | 1.095*** | 0.970*** | 1.200*** | 1.629*** |
| | (0.10) | (0.10) | (0.07) | (0.25) |
| Military Spending (Log) | −0.611 | −0.151 | 0.561*** | 0.690** |
| | (0.35) | (0.27) | (0.10) | (0.23) |
| Average Exercise Size (Log) | −0.475*** | −0.161*** | −0.171*** | −0.518*** |
| | (0.06) | (0.05) | (0.03) | (0.06) |
| Ally | 1.287*** | 1.453*** | 1.123*** | 0.801** |
| | (0.15) | (0.15) | (0.12) | (0.30) |
| Geographic Distance | 0.457** | 0.370* | −0.575*** | −0.336 |
| | (0.15) | (0.16) | (0.07) | (0.26) |
| Contiguity | 0.988 | 0.923 | −0.159 | −0.887 |
| | (0.94) | (0.90) | (0.26) | (0.92) |
| Sovereign History | 15.507*** | 15.592*** | 0.763*** | 2.111** |
| | (1.01) | (1.02) | (0.16) | (0.66) |
| N | 5,953 | 5,953 | 33,512 | 5,784 |
| BIC | 6,014 | 5,846 | 13,116 | 1,348 |

Standard errors in parentheses are clustered by dyad. *$p < 0.05$; **$p < 0.01$; ***$p < 0.001$

for the relationship between the variables. Therefore, figures A.2 through A.5 display the marginal effects of each of the explanatory variables and covariates on the values of the dependent variable.[26] The plots depict the estimated impact of a one standard deviation increase in an explanatory variable on the outcome variable. "S" refers to the impact of the variable on shaping exercises, "T" refers to traditional exercises, and "N" refers to no exercise. Figure A.2 displays the marginal effect of the two explanatory variables and

**Table A.4 Results for OLS Robustness Check (Dependent Variable: Total Number of Shaping Exercises)**

| Dependent Variable: Number of Shaping Exercises | Model 1 Doctrinal Uncertainty (US) | Model 2 Doctrinal Uncertainty (US w/Lag) | Model 3 Post-Cold War Uncertainty (US) | Model 4 Post-Cold War Uncertainty (US w/Lag) | Model 5 Post-Cold War Uncertainty (All Non-US) | Model 6 Post-Cold War Uncertainty (All Non-US w/Lag) | Model7 Post-Cold War Uncertainty (Russia) | Model 8 Post-Cold War Uncertainty (Russia w/Lag) |
|---|---|---|---|---|---|---|---|---|
| Doctrinal Uncertainty | 1.582* | 0.872 | | | | | | |
| | (0.71) | (0.54) | | | | | | |
| Post-Cold War Uncertainty | | | 6.777*** | 5.503** | 1.936* | 0.627* | 9.823*** | 5.417* |
| | | | (1.54) | (1.78) | (0.66) | (0.21) | (2.37) | (2.47) |
| Lag Number of Shaping Exercises (1 Year) | | 0.442** | | 0.201 | | 0.734*** | | 0.498** |
| | | (0.15) | | (0.19) | | (0.07) | | (0.18) |
| Military Spending (Log) | −7.881 | −5.224 | −1.858 | −1.825 | 0.444 | 0.244* | 3.603** | 2.225* |
| | (4.62) | (3.41) | (2.28) | (2.46) | (0.18) | (0.07) | (1.22) | (0.97) |
| Average Exercise Size (Log) | −1.951 | −1.101 | −1.412 | −1.11 | −0.432* | −0.157* | −0.686 | −0.497 |
| | (1.00) | (0.74) | (0.96) | (0.81) | (0.13) | (0.06) | (0.56) | (0.44) |
| Total Number of Traditional Exercises | 0.296*** | 0.182 | 0.158* | 0.133 | 0.05 | −0.036 | −0.192 | −0.21 |
| | (0.07) | (0.1) | (0.07) | (0.08) | (0.10) | (0.05) | (0.17) | (0.30) |
| $R^2$ | 0.591 | 0.674 | 0.752 | 0.757 | 0.29 | 0.588 | 0.606 | 0.68 |
| N | 37 | 36 | 37 | 36 | 212 | 206 | 37 | 36 |
| BIC | 208 | 197 | 189 | 187 | 899 | 764 | 176 | 168 |

Standard errors in parentheses are clustered by dyad. *$p < 0.05$; **$p < 0.01$; ***$p < 0.001$

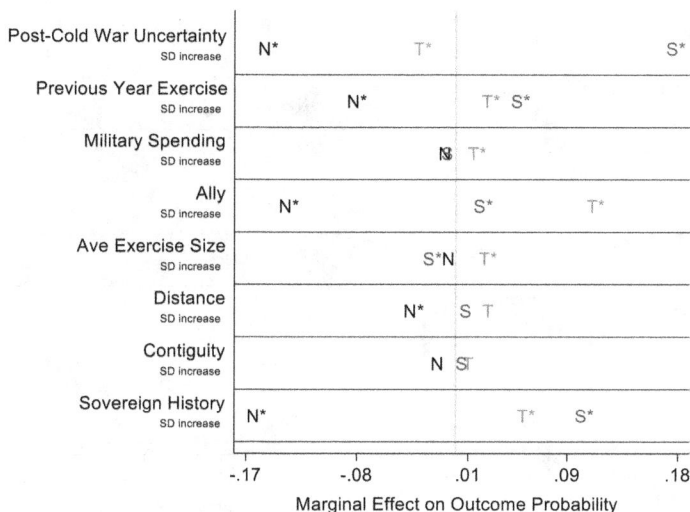

**Figure A.3    Marginal Change Plot for Model 2.**

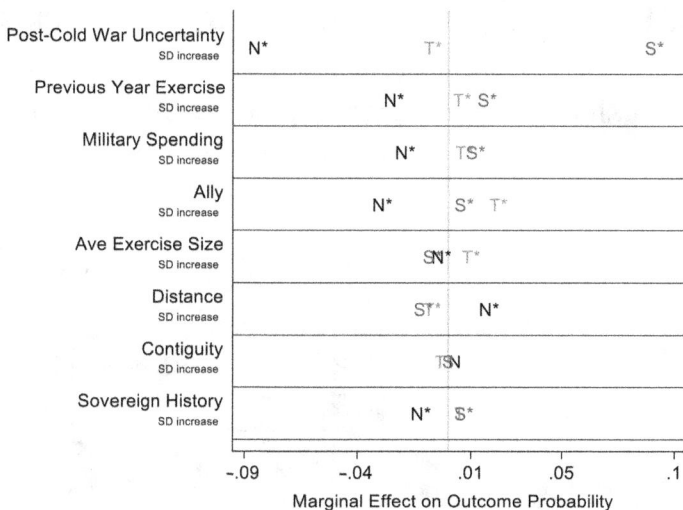

**Figure A.4    Marginal Change Plot for Model 3.**

the alternatives on the nominal outcomes for Model 1: a standard deviation increase in doctrinal uncertainty is associated with a stronger influence on shaping than military spending or being an ally, though a previous year's exercise is also a strong predictor. Figures A.4 and A.5 are especially instructive: non-US powers, including Russia, were affected by strategic uncertainty, even controlling for other explanations.

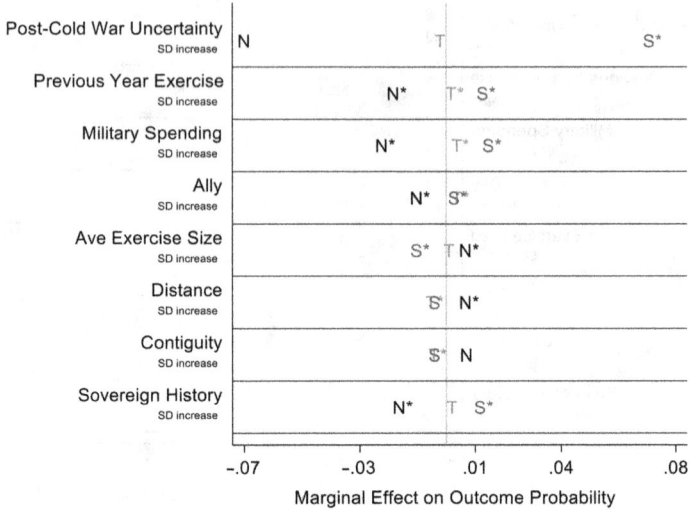

Figure A.5    Marginal Change Plot for Model 4.

# ADDITIONAL FIGURES AND REFERENCE MATERIAL

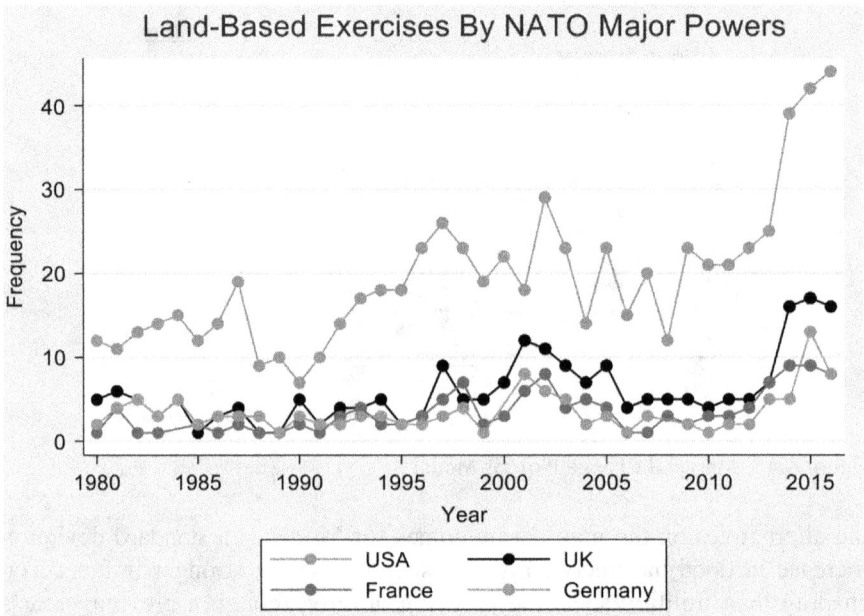

Figure A.6    Multinational Exercises by Major Power, 1980–2016 (NATO Powers).

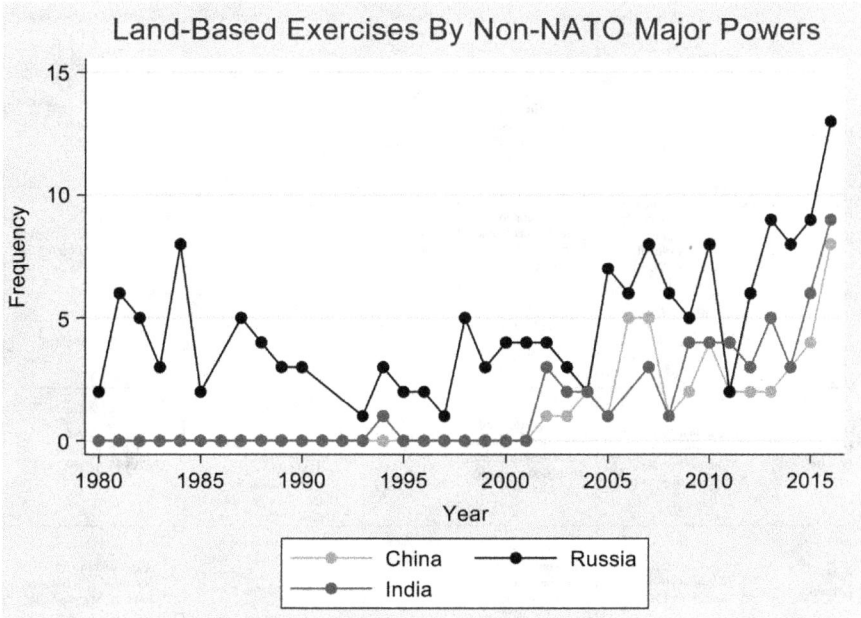

Figure A.7 **Multinational Exercises by Major Power, 1980–2016 (Non-NATO Powers).**

| | Training Tasks Exercised | Number of Troops | Named Exercise Threat | Official Statements and News Coverage | Exercise Program and History |
|---|---|---|---|---|---|
| **Deterrence** | Conventional-Maneuver Only | Significant for deterrence (usually more than 5,000 troops) | External to Partners | " Defend our interests" " Deterrence" " Reassure Allies" | e.g. " NATO REFORGER" |
| **Rehearsal** | Conventional-Maneuver, Counterinsurgency-Counterterrorism, Peacekeeping-Stability, Humanitarian-Disaster Relief | Approximately the number that would be used during deployment | External to Partners | " Interoperability" " Preparation for deployment" " Test Ability to Work Together" | Usually no exercise program; used as preparation for deployment or potential mission |
| **Trust-Developing** | Counterinsurgency-Counterterrorism, Peacekeeping, Humanitarian-Disaster Relief | Small, largely symbolic (100-500 troops) | External or Internal to Partners | " Building Trust" " History of Hostility" | e.g. " Hand-in-Hand" |
| **Capacity-Building** | Conventional-Maneuver, Counterinsurgency-Counterterrorism | Major power sends small units or limited number of trainers compared to partner military | Internal to Partners or Regional Peacekeeping | " Building Partner Capacity" " Strengthen Ability to Defend Itself" " Upgrading fighting capabilities" " Bolster Foreign Troops" " Special Forces Trainers" | e.g. " Flintlock, RECAMP" , " BMATT" |
| **Role-Forming** | Counterinsurgency-Counterterror, Peacekeeping-Stability | Major power sends small units or limited number of trainers compared to partner military | Internal to Partners | Similar to capacity-building, but partner militaries are more advanced and major power influence more subtle. " Familiarize with new weaponry" | e.g. " Interaction" , " Frontier" , " Balance Piston" , " Steppe Eagle" |
| **Recruitment** | Conventional-Maneuver, Counterinsurgency-Counterterrorism, Peacekeeping-Stability, Humanitarian-Disaster Relief | Small, largely symbolic (100-500 troops) | External to Partners | " Gathering Support" " Build Relationship" " Friendship" " Improve military cooperation" | e.g. " Partnership for Peace" , " INDRA" , " Yudh Abhyas" |

**Figure A.8   Coding Criteria for Multinational Exercise Type.**

| War/Coalition Name | Chad Intervention | Chad Intervention | Gulf War | Somalia Intervention (Op. Restore Hope) | Haiti Intervention (Op. Uphold Democracy) | Bosnia Intervention IFOR | Bosnia Intervention SFOR |
|---|---|---|---|---|---|---|---|
| Date Start | 1982 | 1986 | 11/1/1990 | 12/3/1992 | 7/xx/1994 | 12/xx/1995 | 12/xx/1996 |
| Date End | | 1987 | 2/1/1991 | 5/xx/1993 | 3/31/1995 | 12/xx/1996 | 12/xx/2005 |
| Organization | | | | UNITAF | UN | NATO | NATO |
| Type of Operation | Conventional, Peacekeeping | Conventional, Peacekeeping | Conventional | Humanitarian-Disaster Relief | Conventional, Peacekeeping | Peacekeeping | Peacekeeping |
| Source | Finnemore, 132 | Wolford, 50; Nolushingu, 12 | Finnemore, 138 | "Somalia-UNOSOM I." | Finnemore, 138; Kreps, 78-79 | Yost, 195-196 | Yost, 195-196 |
| Major Powers | France | France | USA, UK, France, Germany | USA, UK, France, Germany | USA | USA, UK, France, Germany | USA, UK, France, Germany |
| Non-Allied Coalition Partner 1 | Zaire (DRC) | Chad | Saudi Arabia | Australia | Belize | Albania | Albania |
| Partner 2 | Chad | | Egypt | Botswana | Jamaica | Austria | Austria |
| Partner 3 | | | Syria | Egypt | Barbados | Bulgaria | Bulgaria |
| Partner 4 | | | Morocco | India | Antigua and Barbuda | Czech Republic | Czech Republic (member MAR 1999) |
| Partner 5 | | | Kuwait | Kuwait | Guyana | Egypt | Egypt (left 1998) |
| Partner 6 | | | Oman | Morocco | Trinidad and Tobago | Estonia | Estonia |
| Partner 7 | | | Pakistan | New Zealand | Bahamas | Finland | Finland |
| Partner 8 | | | UAE | Nigeria | Argentina | Hungary | Hungary (member MAR 1999) |
| Partner 9 | | | Qatar | Pakistan | | Jordan | Iceland |
| Partner 10 | | | Bangladesh | Saudi Arabia | | Latvia | Jordan (left 1998) |
| Partner 11 | | | Niger | Sweden | | Lithuania | Latvia |
| Partner 12 | | | Sweden | Tunisia | | Malaysia | Lithuania |
| Partner 13 | | | Argentina | UAE | | Morocco | Malaysia (left 1998) |
| Partner 14 | | | Senegal | Zimbabwe | | Poland | Morocco |
| Partner 15 | | | Bahrain | | | Romania | Poland (member MAR 1999) |
| Partner 16 | | | Czechoslovakia | | | Russia | Romania |
| Partner 17 | | | | | | Sweden | Russia |
| Partner 18 | | | | | | Ukraine | Slovenia |
| Partner 19 | | | | | | | Sweden |
| Partner 20 | | | | | | | Ukraine |
| Partner 21 | | | | | | | |
| Partner 22 | | | | | | | |
| Partner 23 | | | | | | | |
| Partner 24 | | | | | | | |
| Partner 25 | | | | | | | |
| Partner 26 | | | | | | | |
| Partner 27 | | | | | | | |
| Partner 28 | | | | | | | |
| Partner 29 | | | | | | | |
| Partner 30 | | | | | | | |

Figure A.9   Major Power-Led Coalitions (Part 1).

| War/Coalition Name | Kosovo Intervention KFOR | NATO Peacekeeping Macedonia | | NATO ISAF/OEF/Res. Support. | Multi-National Force- Iraq 2003 | Anti-ISIS (Op. Inherent Resolve) |
|---|---|---|---|---|---|---|
| Date Start | xx/xx/1999 | 8/xx/2001 | | 10/xx/2001 | 3/xx/2003 | 8/8/2014 |
| Date End | - | 3/xx/2003 | | - | 12/31/2011 | - |
| Organization | NATO | NATO | | NATO | | |
| Type of Operation | Peacekeeping | Peacekeeping | | Conventional, COIN | Conventional, COIN | Conventional, COIN |
| Source | Bescht, 95. NATO Online- "KFOR Troop Contributions" | NATO Online- "Operations and Missions: Past and Present." | | NATO Online- "ISAF Troop Contributing Nations." | Carney- *Allied Participation in Operation Iraqi Freedom* | McGinnis- "Coalition Contributions to Countering the Islamic State." |
| Major Powers | USA, UK, France, Germany | USA, UK, France, Germany | | USA, UK, France, Germany | USA, UK | USA, UK, France, Germany |
| Non-Allied Coalition Partner 1 | Albania (after 2000) | Macedonia | | Armenia | Albania (APR 2003-DEC 2008) | Australia |
| Partner 2 | Armenia (after 2000) | | | Australia | Armenia (JAN 2005-OCT 2008) | Finland |
| Partner 3 | Austria | | | Austria | Australia (2003, JUN 2005-JUL 2009) | New Zealand |
| Partner 4 | Azerbaijan (left in 2008) | | | Azerbaijan | Azerbaijan (MAY 2003 - DEC 2008) | Jordan (Training Grounds) |
| Partner 5 | Bulgaria (member MAR 2004) | | | Bosnia | Bosnia (JUN 2005 - NOV 2008) | Qatar (Training Grounds) |
| Partner 6 | Croatia (after 2000) (member 2009) | | | Finland | Bulgaria (AUG 2003 - DEC 2005, MAR 2006 - DEC 2008) | Saudi Arabia (Training Grounds) |
| Partner 7 | Estonia (member MAR 2004) | | | Georgia | Czech Republic | Sweden |
| Partner 8 | Finland | | | Ireland | Denmark | UAE |
| Partner 9 | Georgia (left in 2008) | | | Jordan | Dominican Republic (APR 2003 - MAY 2004) | |

Figure A.10    Major Power-Led Coalitions (Part 2).

# Notes

## CHAPTER 1

1. "Vostok 2018: Russia Lets the War Games With China Begin," *Deustche Welle Online,* September 10, 2018, https://www.dw.com/en/vostok-2018-russia -lets-the-war-games-with-china-begin/a-45435748; Danila Galperovich, "Analysts: Russia's Vostok '18 Troop Numbers, 'China Alliance' Claims Questionable," *Voice of America*, September 11, 2018, https://www.voanews.com/europe/ana-lysts-russias-vostok-18-troop-numbers-china-alliance-claims-questionable. Kevin Klose, "Brezhnev, in a Signal to Chinese, Watches Maneuvers Near Border," *The Washington Post*, April 6,1978, Nexis Uni. China similarly carried out exercises to deter a potential Soviet invasion; for instance, see "China Simulates Atomic Blast in War Games Aimed at Soviet," *The New York Times,* July 14, 1982, Nexis Uni.

2. David A. Baldwin, *Economic Statecraft* (Princeton: Princeton University Press, 1985), 8–9, 18–24.

3. For instance, see Robert M. Gates, "The Overmilitarization of American Foreign Policy," *Foreign Affairs* 99, no. 4 (July–August 2020): 121–32.

4. H. Richard Yarger, "Toward a Theory of Strategy: Art Lykke and the U.S. Army War College Strategy Model," in *US Army War College Guide to National Security Issues Vol. I: Theory of War and Strategy,* ed. J. Boone Bartholomees, Jr. (Carlisle: US Army War College Press, 2012), 45.

5. Lisa Ferdinando, "Annual 'Cobra Gold' Exercise Commences in Thailand," *US Department of Defense News,* February 14, 2017, accessed January 8, 2018, https://www.defense.gov/News/Article/Article/1083001/annual-cobra-gold-exercise -commences-in-thailand/.

6. Matthew Southerland, "The Chinese Military's Role in Overseas Humanitarian Assistance and Disaster Relief: Contributions and Concerns," *US-China Economic and Security Review Commission,* July 11, 2019, https://www.uscc.gov/sites/ default/files/Research/USCC%20Staff%20Report_The%20Chinese%20Military%E2

%80%99s%20Role%20in%20Overseas%20Humanitarian%20Assistance%20and %20Disaster%20Relief_7.11.19.pdf, 6–7.

7. Max Bearak, "In Strategic Djibouti, a Microcosm of China's Growing Foothold in Africa," *The Washington Post,* December 30, 2019, https://www.washingtonpost.com/world/africa/in-strategic-djibouti-a-microcosm-of-chinas-growing -foothold-in-africa/2019/12/29/a6e664ea-beab-11e9-a8b0-7ed8a0d5dc5d_story .html.

8. "Russia Finalizes Plans to Set Up Naval Base in Somaliland," *Defence Monitor Worldwide,* February 1, 2020, Nexi Uni; Eric Schmitt and Thomas Gibbons-Neff, "Russia Exerts Growing Influence in Africa, Worrying Many in the West," *The New York Times,* January 28, 2020, https://www.nytimes.com/2020/01/28/world/ africa/russia-africa-troops.html.

9. William Clinton, *A National Security Strategy of Engagement and Enlargement* (Washington, DC: The White House, 1995); for grand strategies that apply the term engagement, see Stephen G. Brooks and William C. Wohlforth, *America Abroad: The United States' Global Role in the 21st Century* (Oxford: Oxford University Press, 2016) and Robert J. Art, "Geopolitics Updated: The Strategy of Selective Engagement," *International Security* 23, no. 3 (Winter 1998–1999): 79–113.

10. United Kingdom Ministry of Defence, *Strategic Defence Review: Presented to Parliament by the Secretary of State for Defence by Command of her Majesty,* July 1998, http://webarchive.nationalarchives.gov.uk/20121018172816/http://www.mod.uk /NR/rdonlyres/65F3D7AC-4340-4119-93A2-20825848E50E/0/sdr1998_complete.pdf, 19; UK Ministry of Defence, *UK Defence Doctrine,* Joint Doctrine Publication 0-01, Fifth Edition, November 2014, 59–60; Andrew Cottey and Anthony Forster, *Reshaping Defence Diplomacy: New Roles for Military Cooperation and Assistance*, Adelphi Papers 44, no. 365 (May 1, 2004); See Juan Emilio Cheyre, "Defence Diplomacy," in *The Oxford Handbook of Modern Diplomacy*, eds. Andrew F. Cooper, Jorge Heine, and Ramesh Thakur (Oxford: Oxford University Press, 2013).

11. Kenneth Allen, Phillip C. Saunders, and John Chen, *Chinese Military Diplomacy, 2003-2016: Trends and Implications* (Washington, DC: National Defense University Press, 2017), 8–11.

12. Ministry of Defence, Government of India, *Annual Report 2018-2019,* 197–204.

13. A 2008 manual on shaping cautions, "Commanders and their staffs have to operate in a world of ambiguity and complex relationships with a wide range of partners and where progress toward goals is very difficult to measure." *Military Contribution to Cooperative Security (CS) Joint Operating Concept*, version 1.0 (Washington, DC: Joint Chiefs of Staff, 2008), 8n11. On the difficulty in assessing deterrence effectiveness, due largely to selection bias, see James D. Fearon, "Selection Effects and Deterrence," *International Interactions* 28, no. 5 (2002): 5–29.

14. Ben Werner, "China's Past Participation in RIMPAC Didn't Yield Intended Benefits of Easing Tensions," *USNI News,* May 24, 2018, https://news.usni.org/2018 /05/24/33834.

15. Robert Jervis, *System Effects: Complexity in Political and Social Life* (Princeton: Princeton University Press, 1997), 61–69. See also Chalmers Johnson,

"American Militarism and Blowback: The Costs of Letting the Pentagon Dominate Foreign Policy," *New Political Science* 24, no. 1 (2002): 21–38.

16. *Military Contribution to Cooperative Security (CS) Joint Operating Concept*, iii.

17. Derek Grossman, "General Robert Brown on the U.S. Army's Role in Asia," *The RAND Blog*, October 25, 2017, accessed January 19, 2018, https://www.rand.org /blog/2017/10/general-robert-brown-on-the-us-armys-role-in-asia.html.

18. *The US Army Operating Concept- Win in a Complex World*, TRADOC Pamphlet 525-3-1 (Washington DC: Government Printing Office, 7 October 2014), iii, https://usacac.army.mil/publication/us-army-operating-concept.

19. Jim Garamone, "Dunford Details Implications of Today's Threats on Tomorrow's Strategy," US Department of Defense News, August 23, 2016, accessed August 26, 2017, https://www.defense.gov/News/Article/Article/923685/dunford -details-implications-of-todays-threats-on-tomorrows-strategy/.

20. Tim Blanning, *Frederick the Great: King of Prussia* (New York: Random House, 2016), 287; Jeremy Black, *Western Warfare: 1775-1882* (New York: Routledge, 2014), 26.

21. The data for these graphs are explained in detail in the Appendix. In general, exercises primarily intended to rehearse for missions or signal deterrence are coded as "traditional exercises," while training events that follow the shaping logics noted above are coded as "shaping exercises." Notably, because of the observational equivalence of "deterrence" and "assurance" exercises (given the overlap between assurance and extended deterrence), the latter are coded as "traditional" exercises. See also Kyle J. Wolfley, "Military Statecraft and the Use of Multinational Exercises in World Politics," *Foreign Policy Analysis* 17, no. 2 (2021): oraa022, https://doi. org/10.1093/fpa/oraa022.

22. By *allies* I refer to permanent, defense-pact signatories (formal alliances) as well as mission-based, "ad hoc" coalition partners, while *non-allies* fall into one of the following categories: (1) partners that are not treaty allies or ad hoc coalition partners; or (2) defense-pact signatories that do not actually operate together in missions or actively deter an adversary. For defense-pact signatories, I use "Type I" formal defense pacts according to the Correlates of War typology; see Douglas M. Gibler, *International Military Alliances, 1648–2008*, Volume 2 (Washington, DC: CQ Press, 2009). Ground-based multilateral coalitions that I apply in my dataset from 1980-2016 is listed in the Appendix. I include in this group Russia and the CSTO, since the CSTO represents more of a security organization intended to regulate member behavior and respond to non-state threats, there have been no CSTO deployments since the organization's inception, and the Central Asian states are of little use for deterrence against NATO. See Gregory Gleason and Marat E. Shaihutdinov, "Collective Security and Non-State Actors in Eurasia," *International Studies Perspectives* 6 (2005): 274–84.

23. Other notable studies include Carol Atkinson, *Military Soft Power: Public Diplomacy through Military Educational Exchange* (Lanham: Rowman & Littlefield, 2014); Derek S. Reveron, *Exporting Security: International Engagement, Security Cooperation, and the Changing Face of the US Military* (Washington, DC:

Georgetown University Press, 2016); Alexandra I. Gheciu, *NATO in the "New Europe": The Politics of International Socialization After the Cold War* (Stanford: Stanford University Press, 2005).

24. The major works on military doctrine include: Barry R. Posen, *The Sources of Military Doctrine: France, Britain, and Germany Between the World Wars* (Ithaca: Cornell University Press, 1984); Jack Snyder, *The Ideology of the Offensive: Military Decision Making and the Disasters of 1914* (Ithaca: Cornell University Press, 1984); Stephen Peter Rosen, *Winning the Next War: Innovation and the Modern Military* (Ithaca: Cornell University Press, 1991); *Elizabeth Kier, Imagining War: French and British Military Doctrine Between the Wars* (Princeton: Princeton University Press, 1997); Stephen Biddle, *Military Power: Explaining Victory and Defeat in Modern Battle* (Princeton: Princeton University Press, 2004); Benjamin M. Jensen, *Forging the Sword: Doctrinal Change in the US Army* (Stanford, CA: Stanford University Press, 2016).

25. See Norrin M. Ripsman and T.V. Paul, *Globalization and the National Security State* (Oxford: Oxford University Press, 2010); Patrick Porter, *The Global Village Myth* (Washington, DC: Georgetown University Press, 2015).

26. I use the term "illustrative case study" in the manner described by Jack Levy, which is a type of plausibility probe of whether a theory or hypothesis is generally supported by the evidence in a relevant case. My cases could also be considered exploratory or "hypothesis generating" since they illustrate the four logics that are consequently tested more rigorously in the statistical models in the appendix. Jack Levy, "Case Studies: Types, Designs, and Logics of Inference," *Conflict Management and Peace Science* 25 (2008): 1–18.

# CHAPTER 2

1.  Paul Gordon Lauren, Gordon A. Craig, and Alexander L. George, *Force and Statecraft: Diplomatic Challenges of our Time* (Oxford: Oxford University Press, 2014), 5.

2.  David Baldwin uses the terms propaganda, diplomacy, economics, and military, which builds on Harold Laswell's classic framework closest to the DIME construct today (albeit exchanging "military" with "force"). See Harold Laswell: *Politics: Who Gets What, When, and How* (New York: Meridian Books, 1958), 204–5; see also David A. Baldwin, *Economic Statecraft* (Princeton: Princeton University Press, 1985), 13.

3.  Interview with Colin Powell by Walter Isaacson, "General Colin Powell on the American Diplomatic Toolbox," The Aspen Institute and Khan Academy, https://www.khanacademy.org/partner-content/arts-humanities-partners/aspeninstitute/american-diplomatic-toolbox/gen-colin-powell/v/isaacson-with-powell.

4.  H. Richard Yarger, "Toward a Theory of Strategy: Art Lykke and the U.S. Army War College Strategy Model," in *US Army War College Guide to National Security Issues Vol. I: Theory of War and Strategy,* ed. J. Boone Bartholomees, Jr. (Carlisle: US Army War College Press, 2012), 45.

5.  J. Boone Bartholomees, Jr., "A Survey of the Theory of Strategy," in *US Army War College Guide to National Security Issues Vol. I: Theory of War and*

*Strategy,* ed. J. Boone Bartholomees, Jr. (Carlisle: US Army War College Press, 2012), 14–15. See also Yarger, "Toward a Theory of Strategy," 49.

6. I use the term "mechanism" loosely to describe, in general, the attempt to "cause" something to happen or attempt to explain causation from an observation using the tools of political science. For a description of the ambiguity and many specific definitions of this term, see John Gerring, "Causal Mechanisms, Yes But . . ." *Comparative Politics Studies* 43, no. 11 (2010): 1499–526.

7. Lawrence Freedman, *Strategy: A History* (Oxford: Oxford University Press, 2013), xii.

8. Baldwin, *Economic Statecraft*, 13–14. In a separate work, Baldwin highlights the preoccupation with "military force" in the majority of IR scholarship on power, most of which assumes military statecraft is used as the threat or use of force. David A. Baldwin, *Power and International Relations: A Conceptual Approach* (Princeton: Princeton University Press, 2016), 109–11, 178–88.

9. Robert A. Dahl, "The Concept of Power," *Behavioral Science* 2, no. 3 (1957): 202–3.

10. David A. Baldwin, *Power and International Relations* (Princeton: Princeton University Press, 2016), 50.

11. The costs and benefits of both approaches are nicely described by Michael Beckley, "The Power of Nations: Measuring What Matters," *International Security* 43, no. 2 (Fall 2018): 11–14.

12. J. David Singer, Stuart Bremer, and John Stuckey, "Capability Distribution, Uncertainty, and Major Power War, 1820-1965," in Bruce Russett (ed) Peace, War, and Numbers (Beverly Hills: Sage, 1972), 19–48. The current dataset can be accessed at https://correlatesofwar.org/data-sets/national-material-capabilities.

13. Michael Beckley, "The Power of Nations: Measuring What Matters," *International Security* 43, no. 2 (Fall 2018): 7–44.

14. Joseph S. Nye Jr., *Soft Power: The Means to Success in World Politics* (New York: Public Affairs, 2004), 5–15.

15. Joseph S. Nye Jr., *The Future of Power* (New York: Public Affairs, 2011), 25–49.

16. Edward Hallett Carr, *The Twenty Years' Crisis: 1919-1938,* 2nd Edition (London: The MacMillan Press, 1981), 132–38.

17. Hans J. Morgenthau, *Politics Among Nations: The Struggle for Power and Peace,* 5th Edition (Knopf: New York, 1973), 112–49.

18. Arnold Wolfers, "Power and Influence: The Means of Foreign Policy," in *Collaboration and Discord: Essays on International Politics* (Baltimore: Johns Hopkins Press, 1962), 103–5.

19. Joseph S. Nye Jr. *Soft Power: The Means to Success in World Politics* (New York: Public Affairs, 2004), 33–72.

20. Carol Atkinson, "Does Soft Power Matter? A Comparative Analysis of Student Exchange Programs 1980-2006," *Foreign Policy Analysis* 6, no. 1 (2010): 1–22.

21. Jonathan McClory, *The Soft Power 30: A Global Ranking of Soft Power (2019)*, Portland and the University of California Center on Public Diplomacy, https://softpower30.com/find-out-more/.

22. See David W. Kearn, "The Hard Truths about Soft Power," *Journal of Political Power* 4, no. 1 (2011): 70–71.

23. Kenneth N. Waltz, *Theory of International Politics* (Reading, MA: Addison-Wesley Publishing Company, 1979), 113–14.

24. John J. Mearsheimer, *The Tragedy of Great Power Competition* (New York: W.W. Norton, 2014), 55–67.

25. Mearsheimer, *Tragedy of Great Power Competition*, 83–87.

26. The literature on offense-defense theory is vast, but two works stand out: Charles L. Glaser and Chaim Kaufmann, "What is the Offense-Defense Balance and Can We Measure It?" *International Security* 22, no. 4 (Spring 1998): 44–82; Steven Van Evera, *Causes of War: Power and the Roots of Conflict* (Ithaca: Cornell University Press, 2001).

27. See, for instance, John J. Mearsheimer, Barry R. Posen, Eliot A. Cohen, Steven J. Zologa, Malcom Chalmers, and Lutz Unterseher, "Correspondence: Reassessing Net Assessment and the Tank Gap Data Flap," *International Security* 13, no. 4 (Spring 1989): 128–79.

28. Stephen D. Biddle, *Military Power: Explaining Victory and Defeat in Modern Battle* (Princeton: Princeton University Press, 2004).

29. These other factors are nicely described in Michael J. Meese, Suzanne C. Nielsen, and Rachel M. Sondheimer eds., *American National Security,* 7th Edition (Baltimore: Johns Hopkins Press, 2018), 323–24.

30. Robert J. Art, "To What Ends Military Power?" *International Security* 4, no. 4 (Spring 1980): 3–35.

31. Robert Jervis, *The Meaning of the Nuclear Revolution: Statecraft and the Prospect of Armageddon* (Ithaca: Cornell University Press, 1989); Richard K. Betts, "Nuclear Peace and Conventional War," *Journal of Strategic Studies* 11, no. 1 (1988): 79–95.

32. Barry R. Posen, "Command of the Commons: The Military Foundation of U.S. Hegemony," *International Security* 29, no. 1 (Summer 2003): 5–46.

33. Robert J. Art, "American Foreign Policy and the Fungibility of Force," *Security Studies* 5, no 4 (Summer 1996): 7–42.

34. Atkinson, *Military Soft Power,* 3.

35. The first inclusion of shaping as a military "way" was in the 1997 US National Military Strategy, along with two other ways: responding to the full spectrum of crises and preparing now for an uncertain future. *National Military Strategy* (Washington, DC: Government Printing Office, 1997). For a more detailed description of the emergence of shaping in military strategy, see chapter 3.

36. Robert Pape makes the following distinction between compellence and warfighting, but admits the overlap: "Although coercers and warfighters may seek identical goals . . . how they attain them is quite different. Brute force first routs opposing forces on the battlefield and then imposes political demands on a defenseless victim. . . .. By contrast coercion seeks to change the behavior of states that still retain the capacity for organized military resistance." Robert A. Pape, *Bombing to Win: Air Power and Coercion in War* (Ithaca: Cornell University Press, 1996), 13. Though deterrence and shaping share the goal of conflict prevention, the former's reliance

on threats and hard power parts ways with most logics of shaping, except assurance, which is described in the next section.

37. Robert Art provides an alternative categorization of the uses of military power: defense, deterrence, compellence, and swaggering. "Physical" defense and some forms of "physical" compellence are essentially warfighting, while "peaceful" defense, deterrence, and peaceful compellence are consistent with coercing. Although this framework is somewhat useful for understanding the more traditional tools of warfighting and coercion, this framework has little to say about shaping. "Swaggering" seems to come close through its description as the "peaceful use of force and is expressed usually in one of two ways: displaying one's military strength at military exercises and national demonstrations and buying or build the era's most prestigious weapons" (10). However, swaggering appears to rely on the threat or use of force (traditional power), but more so to achieve nonmaterial goals such as prestige and respect instead of mere power and security. Even the author admits that swaggering is "the most difficult to be precise about" and "elusive to describe" (11). Art, "To What Ends Military Power?"

38. Carl von Clausewitz, *On War,* ed. Michael Howard and Peter Paret (Princeton, NJ: Princeton University Press, 1976), 75.

39. Clausewitz, *On War,* 75.

40. Clausewitz, *On War,* 607.

41. See, for instance, John J. Mearsheimer, *Conventional Deterrence* (Ithaca, NY: Cornell University Press, 1984), 28–30. Clausewitz also hinted at this distinction in an incomplete plan for revision: Carl von Clausewitz, *On War*, "Two Notes by the Author on His Plans for Revising *On War*," (1827), 69.

42. *Doctrine for the Armed Forces of the United States,* Joint Publication 1, Change 1 (Washington, DC: Department of Defense, 12 July 2017), x, I-4 through I-5.

43. Robert Art's use of the term "defense" somewhat confusingly includes both attacks into enemy territory as well as protection of one's own; he notes that states could attack in a first strike *preemptively* or *preventatively* as a form of "defense." See Art, "To What Ends Military Power?" 4–8, 11–13.

44. Richard K. Betts, *Military Readiness* (Washington, DC: Brookings Institution Press, 1995).

45. *Doctrine for the Armed Forces of the United States*, I–6.

46. For the former, see Martin Van Creveld, *The Transformation of War* (New York: The Free Press, 1991), 18–25; for the latter, see Jason Lyall and Isaiah Wilson III, "Rage Against the Machines: Explaining Outcomes in Counterinsurgency Wars," *International Organization* 63, no. 1 (Winter 2009): 70.

47. *Counterinsurgency,* US Army Field Manual 3-24 (Washington, DC: Headquarters, Department of the Army, December 2006), 5-1 through 5-6.

48. Although war and diplomacy are not opposites (even Clausewitz argued that diplomacy should continue during war to ensure the violence is not divorced from politics), the literature on diplomacy implies that interstate dialogue is primarily intended to prevent war or negotiate its settlement on favorable terms. As one of the few American foreign service officers to reach the rank of Career Ambassador, William Burns argues, "Short of war, diplomacy is the main instrument we employ

to manage foreign relations, reduce external risks, and exploit opportunities to advance our security and prosperity." William Burns, *The Back Channel: A Memoir of American Diplomacy and the Case for Its Renewal* (New York: Random House, 2019), 9–10. Some of the most prominent works in diplomacy seem to agree that one of diplomacy's main goals is the prevention of war. See Adam Watson, *Diplomacy: The Dialogue Between States* (New York: Routledge, 1982), 9, as well as Hans Morgenthau, *Politics Among Nations*, 519–21.

49. James D. Fearon, "Rationalist Explanations for War," *International Organization* 49, no. 3 (1995): 379–83.

50. Robert J. Art and Kelly M. Greenhill, "Coercion: An Analytical Overview," in *Coercion: The Power to Hurt in International Politics* (Oxford: Oxford University Press, 2018), 4–5.

51. Thomas Schelling, *Arms and Influence* (New Haven: Yale University Press, 1966), 2–6, 69–78.

52. Glenn H. Snyder, *Deterrence and Defense: Toward a Theory of National Security* (Princeton: Princeton University Press, 1961), 14–16. Snyder attributes this distinction to Robert E. Osgood, "A Theory of Deterrence," unpublished manuscript, 1960.

53. Patrick M. Morgan, *Deterrence: A Conceptual Analysis* (Beverly Hills: Sage Publications, 1983), chapters 1 and 3.

54. Daryl Press argues that past actions have little influence on assessments of credibility, while Weisiger and Yahri-Milo argue the opposite. Daryl G. Press, "The Credibility of Power: Assessing Threats During the 'Appeasement' Crises of the 1930s," *International Security* 29, no. 3 (2004/2005): 136–69; Alex Weisiger and Keren Yahri-Milo, "Revisiting Reputation: How Past Actions Matter in International Politics," *International Organization* 69, no. 2 (2015): 473–95.

55. James D. Fearon, "Domestic Political Audiences and the Escalation of International Disputes," *The American Political Science Review* 88/3 (September 1994), 579–80.

56. Robert A. Pape, *Bombing to Win: Airpower and Coercion in War* (Ithaca, NY: Cornell University Press, 1996), 12–19.

57. Robert J. Art and Kelly M. Greenhill, "Coercion: An Analytical Overview," in *Coercion: The Power to Hurt in International Politics* (Oxford: Oxford University Press, 2018), 14.

58. Andrew H. Kydd and Barbara F. Walter, "The Strategies of Terrorism" *International Security* 31, no. 1 (2006): 49–80.

59. Andrea Ruggeri, Han Dorussen, and Theodora-Ismene Giezelis, "Winning the Peace Locally: UN Peacekeeping and Local Conflict," *International Organization* 71 (Winter 2017): 163–85.

60. Quoted in Michael J. Meese, Suzanne C. Nielsen, and Rachel M. Sondheimer, *American National Security* (Baltimore, MD: Johns Hopkins University Press, 2018), 401.

61. Alexander L. George, "Coercive Diplomacy: Definition and Characteristics," in *The Limits of Coercive Diplomacy*, eds. Alexander L. George and William E. Simons (Boulder: Westview Press, 1994), 10.

62. Author's emphasis. Henry A. Kissinger, *Diplomacy* (New York: Simon and Schuster, 1994), 17.

63. Joseph S. Nye Jr., "Public Diplomacy and Soft Power," *The Annals of the American Academy of Social Science* 616 (March 2008), 95.

64. *Joint Operations*, Joint Publication 3-0 (Washington, DC: Government Printing Office, 2017), VI-1.

65. Derek S. Reveron, "Shaping the Security Environment," in *Shaping the Security Environment*, ed. Derek S. Reveron (Newport: Naval War College Press, 2007), 2–3.

66. *Military Contribution to Cooperative Security (CS) Joint Operating Concept*, version 1.0 (Washington, DC: Joint Chiefs of Staff, 2008), 3.

67. Edmunds, Timothy Anthony Forster, and Andrew Cottey, "Armed Forces and Society: A Framework for Analysis," in *Soldiers and Societies in Postcommunist Europe*, eds. Timothy Edmunds, Anthony Forster, and Andrew Cottey (Basingstoke, United Kingdom: Palgrave MacMillan, 2003), 8–15.

68. See *JP 3-0*, VI-3. Derek Reveron, however, argues that these terms often merely reflect the current US administration's preference of language to describe shaping activities. He notes how the George W. Bush administration attempted to limit Clinton-era engagement activities that were not tied to specific security objectives, thus using the term "security cooperation" instead of "engagement." Reveron, *Exporting Security*, 49–50.

69. Evan Resnick, "Defining Engagement," *Journal of International Affairs* 54, no. 2 (Spring 2001): 559–61. Several authors have described and advocated for US grand strategic options that use the term engagement, notably "selective engagement" and "deep engagement"; these grand strategies would place a high emphasis on both forms of shaping. The conclusion of this book better explains the intersection between grand strategy and the ways of military statecraft, for not only the United States but also other major powers.

70. Nye, *The Future of Power*, 47–48, 99–109.

71. Janice Gross Stein, "Reassurance in International Conflict Management," *Political Science Quarterly* 106, no. 3 (Spring 1991): 431–51.

72. My use of socialization mirrors that of Alexandra Gheciu, who builds on other constructivists in IR. See Alexandra Gheciu, *NATO in the 'New Europe': The Politics of International Socialization after the Cold War* (Stanford: Stanford University Press, 2006), 10–14. Regarding how communities instill practices, see Emmanuel Adler, "The Spread of Security Communities: Communities of Practice, Self-Restraint, and NATO's Post-Cold War Transformation," *European Journal of International Relations* 14, no. 2 (2008): 195–230; and Vincent Pouliot, "The Logic of Practicality: A Theory of Practice of Security Communities," *International Organization* 62, no. 2 (Spring 2008): 257–88.

73. Derek Reveron, *Exporting Security*, 27.

74. Mearsheimer, *Tragedy*, 157–62.

75. Roseanne W. McManus and Mark David Nieman, "Identifying the Level of Major Power Support Signaled for Protégés: A Latent Measure Approach," *Journal of Peace Research* 56, no. 3 (2019): 365–66.

76.   See Robert Jervis, "Cooperation Under the Security Dilemma," *World Politics* 30, no. 2 (January 1978): 167–70.

77.   Robert J. Art, "Geopolitics Updated: The Strategy of Selective Engagement," *International Security* 23, no. 3 (Winter 1998–1999): 82.

78.   Kenneth Waltz, *Theory of International Politics* (Reading: Addison-Wesley, 1979), 67–71. See also Jonathan Kirshner, "Globalization, American Power, and International Security," *Political Science Quarterly* 123, no. 3 (Fall 2008): 365.

79.   Frank Knight, *Risk, Uncertainty, and Profit* (Ithaca: Cornell University Press, 1921), 19–20, 259–60; For an extended discussion on uncertainty, see Kyle J. Wolfley, "Military Statecraft and the Use of Multinational Exercises in World Politics," *Foreign Policy Analysis,* forthcoming.

80.   Morgenthau, *Politics Among Nations,* 205.

81.   Waltz, *Theory of International Politics,* 176–83. See also Robert Jervis, *System Effects: Complexity in Political and Social Life* (Princeton: Princeton University Press, 1997), 110–22.

82.   Jervis, *System Effects,* 111.

83.   Thomas Christensen and Jack Snyder, "Chain Gangs and Passed Bucks: Predicting Alliance Patterns in Multipolarity," *International Organization* 44, no. 2 (Spring 1990): 137–68.

84.   Stephen G. Brooks and William C. Wohlforth, *World Out of Balance: International Relations and the Challenge of American Primacy* (Princeton: Princeton University Press, 2008).

85.   Kenneth N. Waltz, "The Emerging Structure of International Politics," *International Security* 18, no. 2 (Fall 1993): 44–79.

86.   Nuno Monteiro, "Unrest Assured: Why Unipolarity is not Peaceful," *International Security* 36, no. 3 (Winter 2011/2012): 9–40.

87.   Jonathan Kirshner, "Globalization and National Security," in *Globalization and National Security* (New York: Routledge, 2006), 1.

88.   Kenneth N. Waltz, "Globalization and Governance," *Politics Science and Politics* 32, no. 4 (Dec. 1999), 693–94.

89.   Stephen G. Brooks, *Producing Security: Multinational Corporations, Globalization, and the Changing Calculus of Conquest* (Princeton: Princeton University Press, 2005).

90.   David Held and Anthony McGrew, David Goldblatt and Jonathan Perraton, *Global Transformations: Politics, Economic and Culture* (Stanford, CA: Stanford University Press, 1999), 341–46, 421–24.

91.   Geoffrey L. Herrera, "New Media for a New World? Information Technology and Threats to National Security," in *Globalization and National Security,* ed. Jonathan Kirshner (New York: Routledge, 2006), 88–98.

92.   Martin Rudner, "'Electronic Jihad': The Internet as Al Qaeda's Catalyst for Global Terror," *Studies in Conflict and Terrorism* 40, no. 1 (2017): 10–23.

93.   Held et al., *Global Transformations,* 314, 424–26.

94.   Karl P. Mueller, "The Paradox of Liberal Hegemony: Globalization and U.S. National Security," in *Globalization and National Security,* ed. Jonathan Kirshner (New York: Routledge, 2006), 143–69.

95. Audrey Kurth Cronin, "Behind the Curve: Globalization and International Terrorism," *International Security* 27, no. 3 (Winter 2002/2003): 30–58.

96. Andrew E. Kramer, "C.I.A. Helped Thwart Terrorist Attack in Russia, Kremlin Says," *The New York Times,* December 17, 2017, https://www.nytimes.com /2017/12/17/world/europe/putin-trump-cia-terrorism.html.

97. Philip P. Pan, "Russia Braces for Terrorism's Return as 3 Die in Subway Bombings," *Washington Post Foreign Service,* March 30, 2010, http://www.wash-ingtonpost.com/wp-dyn/content/article/2010/03/29/AR2010032900007_pf.html.

98. Adam Taylor, "The Recent History of Terrorist Attacks in Russia," *The Washington Post,* April 3, 2017, https://www.washingtonpost.com/news/worldviews /wp/2017/04/03/the-recent-history-of-terrorist-attacks-in-russia/.

99. Megha Rajagopalan, "China Security Chief Blames Uighur Islamists for Tiananmen Attack," *Reuters*, November 1, 2013, https://www.reuters.com/article/us -china-tiananmen/china-security-chief-blames-uighur-islamists-for-tiananmen-attack -idUSBRE9A003L20131101.

100. Rina Chandran, "Mumbai's Taj Hotel Reopens Sunday After 2008 Attacks," *Reuters,* October 15, 2010, https://www.reuters.com/article/uk-india-taj-idUSLNE 69E04I20101015.

101. Neta C. Crawford, "United States Budgetary Costs and Obligations of Post-9/11 Wars through FY2020: $6.4 Trillion," *Brown University Cost of War Project,* November 13, 2019, https://watson.brown.edu/costsofwar/files/cow/imce/papers /2019/US%20Budgetary%20Costs%20of%20Wars%20November%202019.pdf.

102. Neta C. Crawford and Catherine Lutz, "Human Cost of Post-9/11 Wars," *Brown University Cost of War Project,* November 13, 2019, https://watson.brown .edu/costsofwar/files/cow/imce/papers/2019/Direct%20War%20Deaths%20COW %20Estimate%20November%2013%202019%20FINAL.pdf.

103. Robert Jervis, *The Meaning of the Nuclear Revolution: Statecraft and the Prospect of Armageddon* (Ithaca: Cornell University Press, 1989), 23–38; Steven Van Evera, *Causes of War: Power and the Roots of Conflict* (Ithaca: Cornell University Press, 1999), 240–54.

104. Michael Beckley, "The Emerging Military Balance in East Asia: How China's Neighbors Can Check Chinese Naval Expansion," *International Security* 42, no. 2 (Fall 2017): 77–119. Stephen Biddle and Ivan Oelrich, "Future Warfare in the Western Pacific: Chinese Antiaccess/Area Denial, U.S. AirSea Battle, and Command of the Commons in East Asia," *International Security* 41, no. 1 (Summer 2016): 19–22, 47.

105. Alexander Lanoszka, "Russian Hybrid Warfare and Extended Deterrence in Eastern Europe," *International Affairs* 92, no. 1 (2016): 177–81.

# CHAPTER 3

1. "Perkins: Army Must Win in a Complex and unpredictable World," *Association of the United States Army,* May 29, 2015, https://www.ausa.org/articles/ perkins-army-must-win-complex-and-unpredictable-world.

2.   *The U.S. Army Operating Concept- Win in a Complex World*, TRADOC Pamphlet 525-3-1, 7 October, https://usacac.army.mil/publication/us-army-operating -concept, i.

3.   Victor H. Mair, "Introduction," in *The Art of War: Sun Zi's Military Methods*, trans. Victor H. Mair (New York: Columbia University Press, 2007), 1, 9–23.

4.   Sun Zi, *The Art of War: Sun Zi's Military Methods*, trans. Victor H. Mair (New York: Columbia University Press, 2007), 86.

5.   Sun Zi, *The Art of War*, 76, 80–83.

6.   Sun Zi, *The Art of War*, 85.

7.   David Lai, *Learning from the Stones: A Go Approach to Mastering China's Strategic Concept, Shi* (Carlisle: Army War College, Strategic Studies Institute, 2004), 3–4.

8.   Mair, "Introduction" and "Key Terms," in *The Art of War: Sun Zi's Military Methods*, xlv, 11, 78.

9.   Arthur Waldron, "Foreword," in *The Art of War: Sun Zi's Military Methods*, xxiv–xxv.

10.   Lai, *Learning from the Stones: A Go Approach to Mastering China's Strategic Concept, Shi*, quote on 28.

11.   The US military's use of "coercive" shaping (described later in this chapter) is also identified by Sun Tzu; that is, by placing your army in an advantageous posi- tion right before attacking, using spies to collect information on the enemy's plans and disposition, apply deception to confuse the enemy, and using incendiary fire to weaken the opponent during an assault. See, respectively, Sun Zi, *The Art of War: Sun Zi's Military Methods*, 78, 88–90, 128–131, 124, 125–27.

12.   Lawrence Freedman, *Strategy: A History* (Oxford: Oxford University Press, 2013), 44.

13.   B.H. Liddell Hart, "Foreword," in *Sun Tzu: The Art of War*, trans. Samuel B. Griffith (Oxford: Oxford University Press, 1963), v–vii.

14.   Most notably, see John J. Mearsheimer, *Liddell Hart and the Weight of History* (Ithaca: Cornell University Press, 1988).

15.   Freedman, *Strategy,* 134–39.

16.   B.H. Liddell Hart, *Strategy,* 2nd Revised Edition (New York: Frederick A. Praeger, 1967), 15–18, 338–39, 368–69.

17.   Quoted in Timothy Andrew Sayle, *Enduring Alliance: A History of NATO and the Postwar Global Order* (Ithaca: Cornell University Press, 2019), 1.

18.   B.H. Liddell Hart, *Strategy,* 333.

19.   Ibid., 334–35.

20.   Brian Bond and Martin Alexander, "Liddell Hart and De Gaulle: The Doctrines of Limited Liability and Mobile Defense," in *Makers of Modern Strategy,* ed. Peter Paret (Princeton, NJ: Princeton University Press, 1986), 612–13.

21.   Lawrence Freedman, "Alliance and the British Way in Warfare," *Review of International Studies* 21, no. 2 (1995): 145–46; Brian Holden Reid, "The British Way in Warfare: Liddell Hart's Idea and Its Legacy," *RUSI Journal* 156, no. 6 (2011): 70–76.

22.   Alfred Vagts, *The Military Attaché* (Princeton: Princeton University Press, 1967), 3–14.

23.   Juan Emilio Cheyre, "Defence Diplomacy," in *The Oxford Handbook of Modern Diplomacy* eds. Andrew F. Cooper, Jorge Heine, and Ramesh Thakur (Oxford: Oxford University Press, 2013), 369–71.

24.   Jonathan R. Dull, *The French Navy and American Independence: A Study of Arms and Diplomacy, 1774-1787* (Princeton: Princeton University Press, 1975), 33–49; Hajo Holborn, "The Prusso-German School: Moltke and the Rise of the General Staff," in *Makers of Modern Strategy,* ed. Peter Paret (Princeton, NJ: Princeton University Press, 1986), 284–85.

25.   Andrew Cottey and Anthony Forster, *Reshaping Defence Diplomacy: New Roles for Military Cooperation and Assistance*, Adelphi Papers 44, no. 365 (May 1, 2004), 6.

26.   Jesse Dillon Savage and Jonathan D. Caverley, "When Human Capital Threatens the Capitol: Foreign Aid in the Form of Military Training and Coups," *Journal of Peace Research* 54, no. 4 (2017): 542–57.

27.   Peter Paret, "Napoleon and the Revolution in War," in *Makers of Modern Strategy: From Machiavelli to the Nuclear Age*, ed. Peter Paret (Princeton, NJ: Princeton University Press, 1986), 129–30.

28.   George Kennan, *The Fateful Alliance: France, Russia, and the Coming of the First World War* (New York: Pantheon Books, 1984), 35, 42–44.

29.   William L. Langer, "The Franco-Russian Alliance (1890-1894)," *The Slavonic Review* 3, no. 9 (March 1925): 554–55.

30.   Gerhard Ritter, *The Schlieffen Plan* (London, 1958), 18; quoted in Gunther E. Rothenberg, "Moltke, Schlieffen, and the Doctrine of Strategic Envelopment," in *Makers of Modern Strategy,* ed. Peter Paret (Princeton, NJ: Princeton University Press, 1986), 306.

31.   Kennan, *The Fateful Alliance,* 45–51.

32.   Kennan, *The Fateful Alliance,* 50.

33.   Kennan, *The Fateful Alliance,* 16.

34.   For several analyses of balances of forces during the Cold War, see John J. Mearsheimer, Barry R. Posen, Eliot A. Cohen, Steven J. Zaloga, Malcom Chalmers, and Lutz Unterseher, "Correspondence: Reassessing Net Assessment and the Tank Gap Data Flap," 128–79.

35.   Lawrence Freedman, *Strategy: A History,* 198–201.

36.   Michael E. Latham, "The Cold War in the Third World, 1963-1975," in *The Cambridge History of the Cold War,* Vol. 2, eds. Melvyn P. Leffler and Odd Arne Westad (Cambridge, UK: Cambridge University Press, 2010), 258–280.

37.   William Rosenau, *US Internal Security Assistance to South Vietnam: Insurgency, Subversion, and Public Order* (New York: Routledge, 2005), 11.

38.   Ibid., 28–33, 77–84.

39.   Michael E. Latham, "The Cold War in the Third World, 1963-1975," 274.

40.   John M. Caravelli, "Soviet and Joint Warsaw Pact Exercises: Functions and Utility," *Armed Forces and Society* 9, no. 3 (Spring 1983): 399, 407–12.

41.   James H. Baker, Testimony Before the Senate Finance Subcommittee on International Trade, February 19, 1987, pg. 14. See also Hal Brands, *Making the*

*Unipolar Moment: US Foreign Policy and the Rise of the Post-Cold War Order* (Ithaca, NY: Cornell University Press, 2016), 222–23.

42.   Lloyd M. Bensten, Statement Before the Senate Finance Subcommittee on International Trade, February 19, 1987, pgs. 1–2.

43.   Bob Dole, Statement Before the Senate Finance Subcommittee on International Trade, February 19, 1987, pg. 2.

44.   Bensten, Statement Before the Senate Finance Subcommittee on International Trade, February 19, 1987, pgs. 1–2.

45.   James H. Baker, Testimony Before the Senate Finance Subcommittee on International Trade, February 19, 1987, pg. 14, 19–33.

46.   George H.W. Bush and Brent Scowcroft, *A World Transformed* (New York: Alfred Knopf, 1999), 208.

47.   Hal Brands, *Making the Unipolar* Moment, 274–335.

48.   My emphasis. George Bush and Brent Scowcroft, *A World Transformed,* 564.

49.   James H. Baker, Remarks to Chicago Council on Foreign Relations, April 2, 1992, Box 169, Baker Papers. See also Brands, *Making the Unipolar Moment,* 327.

50.   *The National Military Strategy of the United States of America* (Washington, DC: Government Printing Office, 1992), 17.

51.   Patrick E. Tyler, "U.S. Strategy Plan Calls for Insuring No Rivals Develop," *The New York Times,* March 8, 1992, https://www.nytimes.com/1992/03/08/world/us -strategy-plan-calls-for-insuring-no-rivals-develop.html.

52.   Brands, *Making the Unipolar Moment,* 326–32.

53.   Quoted in Douglas Brinkley, "Democratic Enlargement: The Clinton Doctrine," *Foreign Policy* no. 106 (Spring 1997), 113.

54.   Brinkley, "Democratic Enlargement: The Clinton Doctrine," 113.

55.   Ibid., 115.

56.   William Clinton, *A National Security Strategy of Engagement and Enlargement* (Washington, DC: The White House, 1995), 8–17.

57.   Clinton, *A National Security Strategy of Engagement and Enlargement,* 2–7.

58.   Eric V. Larson, David T. Orletsky, and Kristin Leuschner, *Defense Planning in a Decade of Change: Lessons from the Base Force, Bottom-Up Review, and Quadrennial Defense Review* (Santa Monica, CA: Project Air Force RAND, 2001), 73.

59.   *The National Military Strategy of the of the United States of America* (Washington, DC: Government Printing Office, 1995), 8–9.

60.   "1997 National Military Strategy Released," *Department of Defense New Release,* FDCH Federal Department and Agency Documents, September 27, 1997.

61.   *The National Military Strategy of the United States of America* (Washington, DC: Government Printing Office, 1997), preface.

62.   *National Military Strategy, 1997,* Chapter 1.

63.   *National Military Strategy, 1997,* Chapter 2.

64.   *National Military Strategy, 1997,* Chapter 2.

65.   Author's emphasis. William S. Cohen, *Report of the Quadrennial Defense Review* (Washington, DC: Government Printing Office, 1997), 7–8.

66. Cohen, *Report of the Quadrennial Defense Review*, 9. See also Derek S. Reveron, "Shaping the Security Environment," in *Shaping the Security Environment*, ed. Derek S. Reveron, (Newport: Naval War College Press, 2007), 4–5.

67. *National Military Strategy, 1997*, preface.

68. *National Military Strategy, 1992*, 2.

69. For an overview of the phasing construct, see Paul Scharre, "American Strategy and the Six Phases of Grief," *War on the Rocks,* October 6, 2016, https://warontherocks.com/2016/10/american-strategy-and-the-six-phases-of-grief/.

70. Lauren Fish, "Painting by Numbers: A History of the U.S. Military's Phasing Construct," *War on the Rocks,* November 1, 2016, https://warontherocks.com/2016/11/painting-by-numbers-a-history-of-the-u-s-militarys-phasing-construct/.

71. Dmitry Adamsky, "The Revolution in Military Affairs," in *Net Assessment and Military Strategy: Retrospective and Prospective Essays,* ed. Thomas G. Mahnken (Amherst, NY: Cambria Press, 2020), 153–60.

72. Adamsky, "The Revolution in Military Affairs," 160–63. See also Freedman, *Strategy: A History,* 214–20.

73. John M. Shalikashvili, "Joint Vision 2010: America's Military—Preparing for Tomorrow," *Joint Forces Quarterly* 12 (Summer 1996): 34.

74. *Joint Vision 2010* (Washington, DC: The Joint Chiefs of Staff, 1996), 21.

75. *The National Military Strategy of the United States*, preface, 3–4.

76. Rick Rowlett, "Joint Publication 3-0, Joint Operations," *Joint Forces Quarterly 86,* no. 3 (2017): 122–23.

77. *Operations,* US Army Field Manual 100-5 (Washington, DC: Government Printing Office, 1986).

78. *Joint Operations*, Joint Publication 3-0 (Washington, DC: Government Printing Office, 1993), I-3 through I-5. Brands, *Making the Unipolar Moment,* 274–75.

79. *Joint Operations* (1993), V-1, V-5.

80. *Joint Operations* (1993), Chapter V. The first joint doctrinal manual specifically dedicated to MOOTW- *Joint Publication 3-07*—was published in June 1995.

81. *Military Operations Other Than War,* Joint Publication 3-07 (Washington, DC: Government Printing Office, June 1995).

82. *Military Operations Other Than War,* Joint Publication 3-07, I-2, III-3, IV-4.

83. *Joint Operations*, Joint Publication 3-0 (Washington, DC: Government Printing Office, 1995), Chapter V; *Joint Operations*, Joint Publication 3-0 (Washington, DC: Government Printing Office, 2001), V-6.

84. *Army Vision 2010* (Washington, DC: The Joint Chiefs of Staff, 1996), 3.

85. *Army Vision 2010,* 13, 18.

86. *Concept for Future Joint Operations: Expanding Joint Vision 2010* (Washington, DC: Government Printing Office, May 1997), forward.

87. *Concept for Future Joint Operations: Expanding Joint Vision 2010*, 11.

88. *JP 3-0 (2001),* Figure III-4.

89. Charles F. Wald, "The Phase Zero Campaign," *Joint Forces Quarterly* 43, no. 4 (2006): 72–73.

90.   Wald, "The Phase Zero Campaign," 73–75.

91.   Quoted in Derek S. Reveron, "Shaping the Security Environment," in *Shaping the Security Environment*, ed. Derek S. Reveron (Newport: Naval War College Press, 2007), 6.

92.   *Capstone Concept for Joint Operations*, version 2.0 (Washington, DC: Joint Chiefs of Staff, 2005), 2.

93.   *Capstone Concept for Joint Operations*, version 2.0 (Washington, D.C.: Joint Chiefs of Staff, 2005), 9.

94.   *Capstone Concept for Joint Operations*, version 2.0 (Washington, D.C.: Joint Chiefs of Staff, 2005), 9, D-1 through D-3.

95.   *Joint Operations,* US Joint Publication 3-0 (Washington, DC: Government Printing Office, 2006), IV-27.

96.   This manual also consolidated the former manual dedicated solely to MOOTW (JP 3-07) into JP 3-0. *Joint Operations*, Joint Publication 3-0 (Washington, DC: Government Printing Office, 2006), iii.

97.   *Joint Operations*, 2006, I-13.

98.   Douglas J. Feith, "Transformation and Security Cooperation," National Press Club, Washington, DC, September 8, 2004, http://www.dougfeith.com/docs/2004_09_08_National_Press_Club_Transformation.pdf.

99.   Reveron, *Exporting Security*, 49–50.

100. *Military Contribution to Cooperative Security (CS) Joint Operating Concept*, version 1.0 (Washington, DC: Joint Chiefs of Staff, 2008), iii; *Joint Operations*, Joint Publication 3-0 (Washington, DC: Government Printing Office, 2011), V-8.

101. For an overview of the phasing construct, see Paul Scharre, "American Strategy and the Six Phases of Grief," *War on the Rocks,* October 6, 2016, https://warontherocks.com/2016/10/american-strategy-and-the-six-phases-of-grief/.

102. *Joint Planning,* Joint Publication 5-0 (Washington, DC: Government Printing Office, 16 June 2017), iii.

103. David G. Perkins, "Multi-Domain Battle: The Advent of Twenty-First Century War," *Military Review* (November-December 2017): 9–10.

104. *Joint Operations*, Joint Publication 3-0 (Washington, DC: Government Printing Office, 2018), V-5.

105. See *Security Cooperation,* Joint Publication 3-20 (Washington, DC: Government Printing Office, 2017), I-1 through I-4.

106. "Building Partner Capacity: Inventory of Department of Defense Security Cooperation and Department of State Security Assistance Efforts," *Government Accountability Office,* GAO-17-255R, March 24, 2017, https://www.gao.gov/assets/690/683682.pdf, 1–6, 11–13. See also Taylor P. White, "Security Cooperation: How it All Fits," *Joint Forces Quarterly* 71, no. 1 (2014): 106–8.

107. A recent Army doctrinal manual defines a shaping operation as essentially support to the main effort in combat: "an operation that establishes conditions for the decisive operation through effects on the enemy, other actors, and the terrain." See Army Doctrine Publication 3-0, *Operations,* 2017, pgs. 13–14.

108. See, for instance, Army Field Manual 100-5: Operations (1993), 6–6.

109. Terrence J. O'Shaughnessy, Matthew D. Strohmeyer, and Christopher D. Forrest, "Strategic Shaping: Expanding the Competitive Space," *Joint Forces Quarterly* 90, no. 3 (2018): 10–15.

110. *Military Deception,* Joint Publication 3-13.4 (Washington, DC: Government Printing Office, 2012).

111. *Joint Operations*, Joint Publication 3-0, Change 1 (Washington, DC: Government Printing Office, 2018), V-9.

112. James Q. Wilson, *Bureaucracy: What Government Agencies Do and Why They Do It* (New York: Basic Books, 1989), 23–27, 179–95.

113. Although Posen offers a "balance-of-power" perspective that anticipates some different outcomes than this "organization theory" perspective, his case studies reiterate that militaries prefer offensive operations and doctrines only become defensive after civilian intervention. Even in the case of the French defensive "Maginot Line," the French army only assented to the defense because of the French legislature's reduction of the length of conscription in 1928, preventing enough trained troops for effective offensive campaigns. Posen, *The Sources of Military Doctrine,* 41–54, 74–78, 116–21, 173, 222–24; Posen, "Foreword: Military Doctrine and the Management of Uncertainty" 159–73.

114. Jack Snyder, "Civil-Military Relations and the Cult of the Offensive, 1914 and 1984," *International Security*, Vol. 9, no. 1 (Summer 1984): 108–46.

115. Allan Mallison, *Too Important for the Generals: How Britain Nearly Lost the First World War* (London: Bantam Press, 2017), preface.

116. Reveron, *Exporting Security*, 77–89.

117. Morton H. Halperin, Priscilla A. Clapp, and Arnold Kantor, *Bureaucratic Politics and Foreign Policy* (Washington, DC: Brookings Institution Press, 2006) and Krasner, *Defending the National Interest,* 33.

118. James J.F. Forest and Rebecca Crispin, "AFRICOM: Troubled Infancy, Promising Future," *Contemporary Security Policy* 30, no. 1 (2009): 5, 7–10.

119. United States Government Accountability Office, "Defense Management: Actions Needed to Address Stakeholder Concerns, Improve Interagency Collaboration, and Determine Full Costs Associated with the U.S. Africa Command," GAO 09-181, February 2009, pg. 3, https://www.gao.gov/new.items/d09181.pdf.

120. Quoted in Forest and Crispin, "AFRICOM: Troubled Infancy, Promising Future," 12–13. See also Mark Malan, "AFRICOM: A Wolf in Sheep's Clothing?" Testimony Before the Subcommittee on African Affairs, Committee on Foreign Relations, US Senate, August 1, 2007, https://www.foreign.senate.gov/imo/media/doc/MalanTestimony070801.pdf.

121. Quoted in Derek S. Reveron, *Exporting Security: International Engagement, Security Cooperation, and the Changing Face of the US Military* (Washington, DC: Georgetown University Press, 2016), 73.

122. Reveron, *Exporting Security,* 75.

123. David G. Perkins, "Win in a Complex World—But How?" *Army AL&T Magazine,* January-March 2015, https://usacac.army.mil/sites/default/files/documents/cact/GEN%20PERKINS%20HOW%20TO%20WIN%20IN%20COMPLEX%20WORLD.pdf, 106.

## CHAPTER 4

1. Gary Fields, "East, West Practice Partnership for Peace," *USA Today*, August 25, 1995, LexisNexis Academic.

2. John Valceanu, "Centrazbat '98'," *Soldiers,* 52.2, February 1999, LexisNexis Academic.

3. Stephen M. Walt, *The Origins of Alliances* (Ithaca: Cornell University Press, 1987).

4. Brett Ashley Leeds, "Do Alliances Deter? The Influence of Military Alliances on the Initiation of Militarized Interstate Disputes," *American Journal of Political Science* 47, no. 3 (Jul 2003): 427–39; Paul Huth, "Extended Deterrence and the Outbreak of War," *American Political Science Review* 82, no. 2 (Jun 1988): 423–43.

5. For competing explanations, see Thomas Christensen and Jack Snyder, "Chain Gangs and Passed Bucks: Predicting Alliance Patterns in Multipolarity," *International Organization* 44, no. 2 (Spring 1990): 137–68; and Randall Schweller, *Unanswered Threats: Political Constraints on the Balance of Power* (Princeton: Princeton University Press, 2006).

6. Kenneth Waltz, *Theory of International Politics* (Reading: Addison-Wesley, 1979), 176–83. See also Robert Jervis, *System Effects: Complexity in Political and Social Life* (Princeton: Princeton University Press, 1997), 110–22.

7. Martha Finnemore, *The Purpose of Intervention: Changing Beliefs of Intervention* (Ithaca: Cornell University Press, 2003); Sarah E. Kreps, *Coalitions of Convenience: United States Military Interventions After the Cold War* (Oxford, UK: Oxford University Press, 2011).

8. George Kennan, *The Fateful Alliance: France, Russia, and the Coming of the First World War* (New York: Pantheon Books, 1984), 97–99.

9. Joseph S. Nye Jr., "Public Diplomacy and Soft Power." *The ANNALS of the American Academy of Political and Social Science* 616, no. 1 (March 2008): 94–109.

10. Carol Atkinson, *Military Soft Power: Public Diplomacy through Military Educational Exchange* (Lanham: Rowman & Littlefield, 2014), 4.

11. *Military Contribution to Cooperative Security (CS) Joint Operating Concept*, version 1.0 (Washington, DC: Joint Chiefs of Staff, 2008), 24–25.

12. *Military Contribution to Cooperative Security (CS) Joint Operating Concept*, 11.

13. *Military Contribution to Cooperative Security (CS) Joint Operating Concept*, 11–16, quotes on 11–12.

14. Sun Tzu, *The Art of War,* trans. Samuel B. Griffith (Oxford: Oxford University Press, 1963), 69.

15. Timothy Crawford, "Preventing Enemy Coalitions: How Wedge Strategies Shape Power Politics," *International Security* 35, no. 4 (Spring 2011): 155–89.

16. Janice Gross Stein, "Reassurance in International Conflict Management," *Political Science Quarterly* 106, no. 3 (Spring 1991): 431–32.

17. For the former, see Andrew Kydd, "Trust, Reassurance, and Cooperation," *International Organization* 54, 2 (Spring 2000): 325–57; for the latter, see Volker

Rittberger, Manfred Efinger, and Martin Mendler, "Toward an East-West Security Regime: The Case of Confidence- and Security-Building Measures," *Journal of Peace Research* 27, no. 1 (Feb, 1990): 55–74.

18.   Stacie Goddard, *When Right Makes Might: Rising Powers and World Order* (Ithaca, NY: Cornell University Press, 2018).

19.   See, for instance, phases 3 and 4 of Kupchan's pathways to durable peace between rivals. Charles Kupchan, *How Enemies Become Friends: The Sources of Stable Peace* (Princeton, NJ: Princeton University Press, 2010),

20.   Michael J. Mazarr, Arthur Chan, Alyssa Demus, Bryan Frederick, Alireza Nader, Stephanie Pezard, Julia A. Thompson, and Elina Treyger, *What Deters and Why: Exploring Requirements for Effective Deterrence of Interstate Aggression* (Santa Monica, CA: RAND Corporation, 2018), 2–5. The authors also note that dissuasion is similar to Huth's "firm but flexible" deterrence strategy. See Paul Huth, "Deterrence and International Conflict: Empirical Findings and Theoretical Debates," *Annual Review of Political Science* 2 (1999): 29, 38.

21.   Jeffrey W. Knopf, "Varieties of Assurance," *Journal of Strategic Studies* 35, no. 3 (2012): 379–80.

22.   Lisa Ferdinando, "Annual 'Cobra Gold' Exercise Commences in Thailand," *U.S. Department of Defense News,* February 14, 2017, accessed January 8, 2018, https://www.defense.gov/News/Article/Article/1083001/annual-cobra-gold-exercise -commences-in-thailand/.

23.   "Chinese Official Hails 'Pioneering Significance' of Joint Thai Drill," *BBC Monitoring Asia Pacific*, July 30, 2007. LexisNexis Academic.

24.   "Thai Special Forces Join Training in China to Boost Cooperation, Regional Peace," *BBC Monitoring Asia Pacific,* July 18, 2007; "Chinese Official Hails 'Pioneering Significance' of Joint Thai Drill," *BBC Monitoring Asia Pacific*, July 30, 2007. LexisNexis Academic.

25.   "Thai, Chinese Military to Conduct Joint Military Exercise, USA to Observe," *BBC Monitoring Asia Pacific*, December 3, 2009. LexisNexis Academic.

26.   "Thai, Chinese Military to Conduct Joint Military Exercise, USA to Observe," *BBC Monitoring Asia Pacific*, December 3, 2009. LexisNexis Academic.

27.   Ibid.

28.   *Multinational Operations,* US Joint Publication 3-16 (Washington, DC: Government Printing Office, July 16, 2013), I-9.

29.   Brigadier General (Danish Army, retired) Michael Clemmesen, former Defence Attaché to the Baltics and Commandant of the Baltic Defence College, Skype interview by author, June 12, 2017.

30.   Colonel (US Air Force, retired) Sam Gardiner, former NATO staff officer and Chairman of the Department of Joint and Combined Operations at the National War College, phone interview by author, June 9, 2017.

31.   Joseph S. Nye Jr., "Public Diplomacy and Soft Power," *The Annals of the American Academy of Social Science* 616 (March 2008): 99.

32.   Joseph Albright, "Joint U.S.-Russian Maneuvers May Be Moved to State of Georgia Nunn Seeks to Rescue Exercises after Attack by Ultranationalists," *The Atlanta Journal and Constitution,* June 1, 1994, LexisNexis Academic.

33.    James Brooke, "Russians Have Landed in Kansas! But They've Come to Make Peace," *The New York Times*, October 27, 1995, LexisNexis Academic.

34.    "Russians Invade Kansas Soldiers Involved in Joint Exercise," *The Denver Post,* October 27, 1995, LexisNexis Academic.

35.    "Military Exercise Back for U.S., Russians," *Omaha World Herald*, October 10, 1995, LexisNexis Academic.

36.    Richard Halloran, "U.S. Rapid Deployment Operation in Egypt Shows Readiness Problem," *The New York Times*, November 21, 1980, LexisNexis Academic.

37.    "Soviet Union, Syria to Hold First Joint Military Exercises," *Xinhua General News Service,* July 3, 1981, LexisNexis Academic.

38.    "Bangladesh, India to begin joint military training 4 Nov," *BBC Monitoring South Asia – Political*, November 4, 2010, LexisNexis Academic.

39.    Ben Blanchard, "Freedom of Navigation Patrols in South China Sea May End in Disaster, Chinese Admiral Warns," *Reuters*, July 18, 2017, accessed January 13, 2018, https://www.reuters.com/article/us-southchinasea-ruling/freedom-of-navigation-patrols-may-end-in-disaster-chinese-admiral-idUSKCN0ZY0FJ.

40.    Ronald D. Asmus, *Opening NATO's Door: How the Alliance Remade Itself for a New Era* (New York, NY: Columbia University Press, 2002), 18–19.

41.    William Clinton, "Remarks to the 48th Session of the United Nations General Assembly in New York City," *The American Presidency Project,* September 27, 1993, http://www.presidency.ucsb.edu/ws/index.php?pid=47119.

42.    "State of the Union; Excerpts from President Clinton's Message on the State of the Union," *The New York Times,* January 26, 1994, http://www.nytimes.com /1994/01/26/us/state-union-excerpts-president-clinton-s-message-state-union.html ?pagewanted=all.

43.    James Goldgeier, *Not Whether But When: The U.S. Decision to Enlarge NATO* (Washington, DC: Brookings Institution Press, 1999), 20.

44.    Ibid., 2.

45.    Thomas Risse-Kappen, "Collective Identity in a Democratic Community: The Case of NATO," in *The Culture of National Security: Norms and Identity in World Politics*, ed. Peter J. Katzenstein (New York: Columbia University Press, 1996), 357–99. Also see Rebecca Moore, *NATO's New Mission: Projecting Stability in a Post-Cold War World* (Connecticut: Praeger, 2007), 9–25.

46.    "The Alliance's New Strategic Concept," North Atlantic Treaty Organization, original publication November 1991, last modified August 26, 2010, accessed January 11, 2017, http://www.nato.int/cps/en/natolive/official_texts_23847.htm.

47.    Goldgeier, 56.

48.    Richard C. Holbrooke, "America, A European Power," *Foreign Affairs* 74, no. 2 (March/April 1995): 40. See also Asmus, 21.

49.    Press briefing by Anthony Lake and General Wesley Clark, The White House, Office of the Press Secretary, May 5, 1994.

50.    Asmus, 22.

51.    *NATO Handbook,* North Atlantic Treaty Organization (Brussels: NATO Office of Information and Press, 1995): 237.

52. Goldgeier, 19–24.

53. Ibid., 4.

54. Ibid., 36.

55. Anonymous former US official at NATO familiar with PfP, phone interview by author, July 26, 2017.

56. Goldgeier, 26–29.

57. Ibid.

58. In Asmus, 52.

59. "Aspin's News Conference of October 20, 1993," United States Information Agency Wireless File, October 22, 1993.

60. The CSCE is the Conference on Security and Cooperation in Europe. Warren Christopher, US Department of State Dispatch, 4.9, U.S. Government Printing Office, (March 1, 1993): 119.

61. William Clinton, "The President's News Conference in Brussels," January 11, 1994, *Public Papers*, Book I, (1994), 29.

62. "Partnership for Peace: Framework Document," North Atlantic Treaty Organization, original publication January 11, 1994, modified October 31, 2000, accessed January 7, 2017, https://www.nato.int/docu/comm/49-95/c940110b.htm.

63. The title of the "Conference on Security and Cooperation in Europe" (CSCE) was changed to the "Organization for Security and Co-Operation in Europe" (OSCE) in 1994. See "History," *The Organization for Security and Cooperation in Europe,* accessed January 20, 2017, http://www.osce.org/history.

64. "Signatures of Partnership for Peace Framework Document," North Atlantic Treaty Organization, modified January 10, 2012, accessed January 7, 2017, http://www.nato.int/cps/en/natolive/topics_82584.htm.

65. "Partnership for Peace Framework Document."

66. To a lesser extent, multinational exercises helped encourage democratic civilian control of the military and transparency through exercise planning. For instance, when asked about how the US is encouraging civilian control, the NATO Atlantic Commander, General John Sheehan replied: "The other way has to do with the legal status of the forces that are participating in PFP exercises. For example, if a nation is providing forces for a PFP exercise, oftentimes the decision to send those forces has to be passed by the parliament. The parliament also has to vote on the status of forces agreement for those particular nations." "Partnership for Peace: An Interview with General John J. Sheehan," *Issues of Democracy, USIA Electronic Journal* 2, no. 3 (July 1997): 23.

67. Moore, *NATO's New Mission,* 18.

68. Michael Ruhle and Nicholas Williams, "Partnership for Peace: A Personal View from NATO," *Parameters* 24, no. 4 (1994): 69.

69. Government Accountability Office, "NATO: U.S. Assistance to the Partnership for Peace," GAO-01-734, July 2001, pg. 4.

70. Hugh De Santis, "Romancing NATO: Partnership for Peace and East European Stability," *The Journal of Strategic Studies* 17, no. 4 (1994): 65–68.

71. Jane Perlez, "The Cold War Armies Meet, Just to Link Arms," *New York Times*, September 15, 1994, accessed January 8, 2017, http://www.nytimes.com/1994/09/15/world/biedrusko-journal-the-cold-war-armies-meet-just-to-link-arms.html.

72. Ibid.

73. Rick Atkinson, "Former Foes Find Common Cause, Different Styles in NATO Games," *The Washington Post*, September 18, 1994, LexisNexis Academic.

74. My emphasis. Anonymous former US official at NATO familiar with PfP, phone interview by author, July 26, 2017.

75. Brigadier General (Danish Army, retired) Michael Clemmesen, former Defence Attaché to the Baltics and Commandant of the Baltic Defence College, Skype interview by author, June 12, 2017.

76. Jim Garamone, "Fort Polk hosts Cooperative Nugget," *Army Communicator* 21, no. 1 (Winter 1996): 39–40.

77. "Questions & Answers about Exercise Cooperative Nugget," Interview with Brigadier General Michael Sherfield, Defense no. 6 (1995): 28–31.

78. Jim Garamone, "Fort Polk hosts Cooperative Nugget," *Army Communicator* 21, no. 1 (Winter 1996): 39–40.

79. Garamone, "Fort Polk hosts Cooperative Nugget."

80. Gheciu, *NATO in the 'New Europe,'* 123.

81. Thomas S. Szayna and Ronald D. Asmus, *German and Polish Views of the Partnership for Peace* (Santa Monica: RAND Arroyo Center, 1995), 15, 22, 38–39.

82. Government Accountability Office, "NATO: U.S. Assistance to the Partnership for Peace," GAO-01-734, July 2001, 12–14.

83. Ibid, 14.

84. Charles Skinner, former Deputy Political Advisor to US Mission to NATO, phone interview by author, June 27, 2017.

85. Yaroslav Razumov, "The Genuine Significance of the Centrasbat 2000 Exercises Is Yet to Be Discussed," in Panorama, 5. Quoted in Lyle Goldstein, "Beyond the Steppe: Projecting Power into the New Central Asia," *The Journal of Slavic Military Studies* 17, no. 2 (2004): 194. See also Michael McCarthy, *The Limits of Friendship: US Security Cooperation in Central Asia* (Maxwell Air Force Base, Alabama: Air University Press, 2007), 68–69.

86. "Why Border Stand-Offs Between India and China are Increasing," *BBC News*, September 26, 2014, accessed January 13, 2018, www.bbc.com/news/world-asia-india-29373304.

87. Jonathan Holslag, "The Persistent Military Security Dilemma Between China and India," *The Journal of Strategic Studies* 32, no. 6 (December 2009): 811–40.

88. Bérénice Guyot-Réchard, *Shadow States: India, China and the Himalayas, 1910-1962* (Cambridge: Cambridge University Press, 2017), 1–28. Though many sources claim that China invaded into Indian territory to begin the 1962 Sino-Indian War, Chinese Premier Zhou Enlai claimed China's actions were in self-defense in response to Indian incursions. See B.R. Depak, *India & China, 1904-2004: A Century of Peace and Conflict* (New Delhi: Manak Publications, 2005): 255–59.

89. B.R. Depak, *India & China, 1904-2004: A Century of Peace and Conflict,* 259–64.

90. "Agreement Between the Government of the Republic of India and the Government of the People's Republic of China on Confidence Building Measures in the Military Field Along the Line of Actual Control," *United Nations Peacemaker*

*Online,* September 7, 1993, http://peacemaker.un.org/sites/peacemaker.un.org/files /CN%20IN_930907_Agreement%20on%20India-China%20Border%20Areas.pdf. See also Rup Narayan Das, *India-China Relations: A New Paradigm,* the Institute for Defence Studies and Analysis Monograph Series, no. 19 (May 2013): 43–44.

91. "Agreement Between the Government of the Republic of India and the Government of the People's Republic of China on Confidence Building Measures in the Military Field Along the Line of Actual Control in the India-China Border Areas," First Published May 1, 1997, *China Report* 33, no. 2 (1997): 241–47.

92. "Global Outrage as India Says: We Can Build a Bomb; Desert Test Sparks Fears of Asian Arms Race," *Daily Mail,* May 12, 1998, LexisNexis Academic. See also Rollie Lal, *Understanding India and China: Security Implications for the United States and the World* (Westport: Praeger Security International, 2006), 135–36.

93. "Declaration on Principles for Relations and Comprehensive Cooperation Between the Republic of India and the People's Republic of China," Ministry of External Affairs, Government of India, June 23, 2003, accessed April 21, 2017, http://www.mea.gov.in/in-focus-article.htm?7679/Declaration+on+Principles+for +Relations+and+Comprehensive+Cooperation+Between+the+Republic+of+India +and+the+Peoples+Republic+of+China.

94. "India, China Make 2006 'Friendship Year'," *BBC Monitoring South Asia,* January 24, 2006, LexisNexis Academic.

95. "China, India to Hold Annual Defence Dialogue," BBC Monitoring Asia Pacific, May 29, 2006, LexisNexis Academic.

96. "Memorandum of Understanding between the Ministry of Defence of the Republic of India and the Ministry of National Defence of the People's Republic of China for Exchanges and Cooperation in the Field of Defence, 29 May 2006," *China Report* 42, no. 4 (November 2006): 419–21.

97. Major General (Indian Army, retired) Dipankar Banerjee, former infantry Division Commander in Jammu and Kashmir, phone interview by author, June 19, 2017.

98. Lieutenant General (Indian Army, retired) J.S. Bajwa, former director general of the Infantry, phone interview by author, June 21, 2017.

99. Ibid.

100. Ibid.

101. Major General (Indian Army, retired) Dipankar Banerjee, former infantry Division Commander in Jammu and Kashmir, phone interview by author, June 19, 2017.

102. Lieutenant General (Indian Army, retired) J.S. Bajwa, former director general of the Infantry, phone interview by author, June 21, 2017.

103. "India, China to Hold First-Ever Army Exercises in December," *BBC Monitoring Asia Pacific,* November 21, 2007, LexisNexis Academic.

104. Mark Sappenfield and Anuj Chopra, "Sino-Indian Army Exercises Bring Two Asian Powers Closer," *Christian Science Monitor,* December 26, 2007, LexisNexis Academic.

105. Li Jianmin, "Bonhomie Marks India-China Joint Exercises," *The Hindu,* December 27, 2007, accessed April 22, 2017, http://www.thehindu.com/todays-paper /Bonhomie-marks-India-China-joint-exercises/article14902587.ece.

106. "China-India Joint Anti-Terror Training Begins," *BBC Monitoring Asia Pacific,* December 6, 2008, LexisNexis Academic.

107. Major General (Indian Army, retired) Dipankar Banerjee, former infantry Division Commander in Jammu and Kashmir, phone interview by author, June 19, 2017.

108. "Chinese Army Arrives in India for Joint Exercises," *BBC Monitoring South Asia*, December 5, 2007, LexisNexis Academic.

109. "India Keen on Joint Exercise with China- Air Force Chief," *BBC Monitoring South Asia,* November 10, 2009, LexisNexis Academic. See also "India Says No Army Exercise with China Scheduled This Year," *BBC Monitoring South Asia,* September 24, 2009, LexisNexis Academic.

110. "India Cancels China Defence Exchanges After Visa Row," *Right Vision News,* August 28, 2010, LexisNexis Academic.

111. "Easing India-China Tensions," *The New York Times,* November 1, 2013, LexisNexis Academic.

112. "600 Border Violations by China Along Line of Actual Control since 2010," April 24, 2013, LexisNexis Academic.

113. "Students Hold Protest Against Chinese Incursion," *The Northlines*, April 21, 2013, LexisNexis Academic.

114. "Face-off in Ladakh Area Ends; India, China Withdraw Soldiers," *New India Express*, May 6, 2013, LexisNexis Academic.

115. "Militaries of India, China to Boost Ties," *Times of India,* July 7, 2013, LexisNexis Academic.

116. Press Information Bureau, Government of India, Prime Minister's Office, "Border Defense Cooperation Agreement between India and China," October 23, 2013, accessed March 25, 2017, http://pib.nic.in/newsite/PrintRelease.aspx?relid=100178.

117. "Managing the Border," *Indian Express,* October 24, 2013.

118. "Settling Border Disputes with China to Take Time," *Assam Tribune,* September 21, 2014, LexisNexis Academic.

119. "India, China to Resume Military Drills After 5 Yrs," *Free Press Journal,* August 13, 2013, LexisNexis Academic.

120. Rajat Pandit, "India, China to Hold Military Exercises from November 4 After Five Years," *The Times of India,* August 24, 2013, LexisNexis Academic.

121. "China, India End Anti-Terror Joint Training," *China Daily European Edition,* November 13, 2013, LexisNexis Academic.

122. "Indian, Chinese Armies Wrap Up Joint Military Drill," *One News Page,* November 14, 2013, accessed April 22, 2017. News Report Video from Asian News International recovered at http://www.onenewspage.com/video/20131114/1495792/Indian-Chinese-armies-wrap-up-joint-military-drill.htm.

123. "China, India Agree Joint Military Training," *China Daily,* February 27, 2014, LexisNexis Academic.

124. "Joint India China Exercise Hand in Hand 2014 Culminates," *The Times of India,* November 29, 2014, LexisNexis Academic.

125. "China, India Are Two Bodies with One Spirit," *The Times of India*, November 18, 2014, LexisNexis Academic.

126. "Jawans Prevent PLA from Building Road in Arunachal," The *Times of India,* October 28, 2014, LexisNexis Academic.

127. "India, China Join Hands Again," *Mirror Publications,* November 18, 2014, LexisNexis Academic.

128. "Indian Army, PLA Personnel Meet; Agree to Maintain Peace," *Free Press Journal,* September 16, 2015, LexisNexis Academic.

129. "India-China Armies to Hold Joint Drill," *BBC Monitoring South Asia,* September 27, 2015, LexisNexis Academic.

130. "Indian, Chinese Troops Participate in Joint Exercise in Yunnan," *Times of India,* October 2015, Video accessed April 22, 2017, http://timesofindia.indiatimes .com/videos/news/Indian-Chinese-troops-participate-in-joint-exercise-in-Yunnan/ videoshow/49430390.cms.

131. "Joint Military Exercise 'Hand-in-Hand'- 2015 Commences, *IPR,* October 12, 2015, LexisNexis Academic.

132. "India-China Joint Military Exercise," *Ministry of Defence, Government of India,* October 13, 2015, accessed April 22, 2017, Video at https://www.youtube.com /watch?v=sQkkyOi3QQs.

133. "India, China to Hold Joint Military Exercises," *BBC Monitoring South Asia,* October 14, 2016, LexisNexis Academic.

134. An NCO is a Non-Commissioned (or enlisted) Officer. "A Closer Look at India-China Army Exercise," *India Today Television,* December 3, 2016, http:// indiatoday.intoday.in/video/a-closer-look-at-india-china-army-exercise/1/825969 .html.

135. Brigadier (ret.) Arun Sahgal, "Sino-Indian Military CBMs—Reducing Tensions, Building Confidence," in *Military Confidence-Building and India-China Relations: Fighting Distrust,* eds. Dipankar Banerjee and Jabin T. Jacob (New Delhi: Pentagon Press, 2013), 48.

136. Senior Colonel Wang Guifang, "Viewpoints on Enhancing Military CBMs Along the China-India Border," in *Military Confidence-Building and India-China Relations: Fighting Distrust,* eds. Dipankar Banerjee and Jabin T. Jacob (New Delhi: Pentagon Press, 2013), 59.

137. "India Army Officer Says No Compromise Was Made to End Border 'Standoff' with China," *BBC Monitoring South Asia,* June 17, 2013, LexisNexis Academic.

138. Ibid.

139. Jagannath P. Panda, "China-India Joint Military Drill: Time for a Review," *Institute for Defence Studies and Analyses Comment,* September 2, 2013, accessed April 23, 2017, http://www.idsa.in/idsacomments/ChinaIndiaJointMilitaryDrill_ jppanda_020913.

140. "Global Attitudes and Trends, Chapter 4: How Asians View Each Other," *Pew Research Center,* July 14, 2014, accessed April 22, 2017, http://www.pewglobal .org/2014/07/14/chapter-4-how-asians-view-each-other/.

141. Sanjeev Miglani, "India, China Set for More Talks to De-Escalate Himalayan Standoff," *Reuters,* July 24, 2020, https://www.reuters.com/article/us-india-china -idUSKCN24P0LY.

## CHAPTER 5

1. Pavel Felgenhauer, "Russia Begins Tsentr 2011 Military Exercises," *The Jamestown Foundation Eurasian Daily Monitor,* September 15, 2011, accessed January 11, 2017, accessible at https://jamestown.org/program/russia-begins-tsentr -2011-military-exercises/.

2. Eva Bellin, "Reconsidering the Robustness of Authoritarianism in the Middle East: Lessons from the Arab Spring," *Comparative Politics* 44, no. 2 (January 2012): 127.

3. "CSTO Wants to Monitor the Internet to Prevent a Repeat of Arab Revolutions," *The Moscow News,* September 13, 2011, LexisNexis Academic.

4. "Russia: Military Security Achievable Only Through Coalition Force Contingents," *BBC Monitoring Former Soviet Union,* September 27, 2011, LexisNexis Academic.

5. Lucan Way, "Weakness of Autocracy Promotion," *Journal of Democracy* 27, no. 1 (2016): 64–75.

6. Alexander Cooley, "Countering Democratic Norms," *Journal of Democracy* 26, no. 3 (2015): 50–53. See also Thomas Ambrosio, "Catching the 'Shanghai Spirit': How the Shanghai Cooperation Organization Promotes Authoritarian Norms in Central Asia," *Europe-Asia Studies* 60, no. 8 (2008): 1321–44; and Roy Allison, "Virtual Regionalism, Regional Structures, and Regime Security in Central Asia," *Central Asian Survey* 27, no. 2 (2008): 185–202.

7. My use of socialization mirrors that of Alexandra Gheciu, who builds on other constructivists in IR. See Alexandra Gheciu, *NATO in the 'New Europe': The Politics of International Socialization after the Cold War* (Stanford: Stanford University Press, 2006), 10–14.

8. Emanuel Adler and Vincent Pouliot, "International Practices," *International Theory* 3, no. 1(2001): 4–8. Regarding how communities instill practices, see Emmanuel Adler, "The Spread of Security Communities: Communities of Practice, Self-Restraint, and NATO's Post-Cold War Transformation," *European Journal of International Relations* 14, no. 2 (2008): 195–230; and Vincent Pouliot, "The Logic of Practicality: A Theory of Practice of Security Communities," *International Organization* 62, no. 2 (Spring 2008): 257–88.

9. Carol Atkinson, "Constructivist Implications of Material Power: Military Engagement and the Socialization of States," *International Studies Quarterly* 50 (2006): 509–37; Carol Atkinson, "Does Soft Power Matter? A Comparative Analysis of Student Exchange Programs," *Foreign Policy Analysis* 6, no. 1 (2010): 1–22.

10. Sun Tzu, *The Art of War,* ed. Dallas Galvin and translated by Lionel Giles (New York: Barnes & Noble Books, 2003), 141, 179.

11. Anthony King, "On Combat Effectiveness in the Infantry Platoon: Beyond the Primary Group Thesis," *Security Studies* 25, no. 4 (2016): 709–14.

12. Edmunds, Timothy Anthony Forster, and Andrew Cottey, "Armed Forces and Society: A Framework for Analysis," in *Soldiers and Societies in Postcommunist Europe*, eds. Timothy Edmunds, Anthony Forster, and Andrew Cottey (Basingstoke, United Kingdom: Palgrave MacMillan, 2003), 8–15.

13. See Lesley Gill, *The School of the Americas: Military Training and Political Violence in the Americas* (Durham: Duke University Press, 2004); John H. Coatsworth, "The Cold War in Central America, 1975-1991," in *The Cambridge History of the Cold War,* Vol. 3, eds. Melvyn P. Leffler and Odd Arne Westad (Cambridge: Cambridge University Press, 2010), 216–18.

14. For NATO PfP socialization at the ministerial level, see Gheciu, "Security Institutions as Agents of Socialization? NATO and the 'New Europe.'" See chapter 4 case study for the practice of democratic peacekeeping tactics during training.

15. For normative and structural causes of the democratic peace, see Zeev Maoz and Bruce Russett, "Normative and Structural Causes of Democratic Peace, 1946-1986," *American Political Science Review* 87, no. 3 (September 1993): 624–38; for the impact of democratic audience costs, see James Fearon, "Domestic Political Audiences and the Escalation of International Disputes," *American Political Science Review* 88, no. 3 (1994): 577–92; for an institutional-performance explanation, see Bruce Bueno de Mesquita, James Morrow, Randolph Siverson, and Alaister Smith, "An Institutional Explanation of the Democratic Peace," *American Political Science Review* 93, no. 4 (1999): 791–807; for a critique, see Sebastian Rosato, "The Flawed Logic of Democratic Peace Theory," *American Political Science Review* 97, no. 4 (2003): 585–602.

16. John M. Owen, "How Liberalism Produces the Democratic Peace," *International Security* 19, no. 2 (Autumn 1994): 87–125.

17. Jon C. Pevehouse, "Democracy from the Outside-in? International Organizations and Democratization," *International Organization* 56, no. 3 (2002): 515–19, 527–29. See also Geoffrey Pridham, "The Politics of the European Community, Transnational Networks and Democratic Transition in Southern Europe," in *Encouraging Democracy: The International Context of Regime Transition in Southern Europe*, ed. Geoffrey Pridham (New York: St. Martins Press, 1991), 228.

18. Pevehouse, 528–29.

19. "State of the Union; Excerpts from President Clinton's Message on the State of the Union," *The New York Times,* January 26, 1994, http://www.nytimes.com /1994/01/26/us/state-union-excerpts-president-clinton-s-message-state-union.html ?pagewanted=all.

20. Thomas Ambrosio, "Beyond the Transition Paradigm: A Research Agenda for Authoritarian Consolidation," *Demokratizatsiya* 22, no. 3 (Summer 2014): 471–94.

21. Nicole Jackson, "The Role of External Factors in Advancing Non-Liberal Democratic Forms of Political Rule: A Case Study of Russia's Influence on Central Asian Regimes," *Contemporary Politics* 16, no. 1 (March 2010): 101–2.

22. "The North Atlantic Treaty," North Atlantic Treaty Organization, original publication April 4, 1949, last modified March 21, 2016, accessed January 11, 2017, http://www.nato.int/cps/en/natolive/official_texts_17120.htm.

23. Moore, *NATO's New Mission*, 26–27.

24. Marcel de Haas, "War Games of the Shanghai Cooperation Organization and the Collective Security Treaty Organization: Drills on the Move!" *The Journal of Slavic Military Studies* 29, no. 3 (July 2016): 378–406.

25.   Gregory Gleason and Marat E. Shaihutdinov, "Collective Security and Non-State Actors in Eurasia," *International Studies Perspectives* 6 (2005): 274–84.

26.   David Kerr and Laura C. Swinton, "China, Xinjiang, and the Transnational Security of Central Asia," *Critical Asian Studies* 40, no. 1 (2008): 126–30.

27.   Roy Allison, *Russia, the West, and Military Intervention* (Oxford: Oxford University Press, 2013), 138–47.

28.   Richard Weitz, "Eurasian Security Institutions: the CSTO and SCO," *World Politics Review,* June 29, 2010, accessed January 3, 2018, accessible at https:// www.worldpoliticsreview.com/articles/5916/eurasian-security-institutions-the-csto -and-sco.

29.   Gregory Gleason and Marat E. Shaihutdinov, "Collective Security and Non-State Actors in Eurasia," 278–80.

30.   Shanghai Cooperation Organization, "Declaration on The Establishment of The Shanghai Cooperation Organization," June 15, 2001, http://eng.sectsco.org/ documents/.

31.   Shanghai Cooperation Organization. "The Shanghai Convention on Combating Terrorism, Separatism and Extremism," June 15, 2001, http://eng.sectsco .org/documents/.

32.   Shanghai Cooperation Organization. "Statement by the Heads of Government of the Member States of the Shanghai Cooperation Organization," September 14, 2001, http://eng.sectsco.org/documents/.

33.   Dennis J. Blasko, "People's Liberation Army and People's Armed Police Ground Exercises with Foreign Forces, 2002-2009," in *The PLA at Home and Abroad: Assessing the Operational Capabilities of China's Military*, eds. Roy Kamphausen, David Lai, and Andrew Scobell (US Army War College: Strategic Studies Institute, 2010), 381–82.

34.   "CIS Force Chief: Russian Exercises in Tajikistan Not Linked to Iraq Situation," *ITAR-ITASS*, April 3, 2003, World News Connection; "Experts Praise CIS Anti-Terror Drills in Kyrgyzstan," *ITAR-ITASS*, September 27, 2003, World News Connection.

35.   Lieutenant Colonel (Royal Netherlands Army, retired) Marcel De Haas, former professor at Nazarbayev University, Kazakhstan and current Senior Researcher at the Russian Studies Center, University of Groningen, Skype interview by author, June 29, 2017.

36.   De Haas, 401–2.

37.   Not without opportunity: Kyrgyzstan even requested assistance during the Tulip Revolution in 2005 and an uprising in 2010, yet was denied both times by CSTO leadership. Allison, *Russia, the West, and Military Intervention,* 143–45.

38.   Ted Hopf, "Identity, Legitimacy, and the Use of Military Force: Russia's Great Power Identities and Military Intervention in Abkhazia," *Review of International Studies* 31 (December 2005): 226.

39.   Latvia, Lithuania, and Estonia refused to participate, while Ukraine and Turkmenistan became associate member states.

40.   The Collective Security Treaty was signed in 1992 by Armenia, Kazakhstan, Kyrgyzstan, Russia, Tajikistan, and Uzbekistan. Azerbaijan, Georgia, and Belarus

joined in 1993. "Collective Security Treaty Organization," Ministry of Foreign Affairs of the Republic of Belarus, accessed January 9, 2017, http://mfa.gov.by/en/organizations/membership/list/cddd96a3f70190b1.html.

41.  Collective Security Treaty Organization, "Tashkent Treaty," original publication 1992, accessed January 8, 2017, http://odkb-csto.org/documents/detail.php?ELEMENT_ID=1897.

42.  Speech to the Federation Council, *Rossiyskaya gazeta,* January 12, 1994; cited in Elizabeth Teague, 'Yeltsin: Russia "First Among Equals" in Commonwealth', RFE/RL Daily Report, January 20, 1994. See also Allison, *Russia, the West, and Military Intervention*, 120–23.

43.  Ian Brzezinski, former US deputy assistant secretary of defense for Europe and NATO policy and Advisor to the Ukrainian National Security Council and Foreign Ministry, phone interview by author, September 19, 2017.

44.  Ted Hopf argues that before or during May 1992, incursions into Moldova and Abkhazia were the result of locally stationed (and stranded) Russian military officers who intervened without direction from Moscow, which lacked a "unitary actor" until May 1992. Regardless, the fact that Soviet officers, and the Russian state after May 1992, intervened highlights the Russian view that it is responsible for stability in the former Soviet region. See Hopf, "Identity, Legitimacy, and the Use of Military Force."

45.  Russia TV, 28 February 1993, in *BBC Summary of World Broadcasts.* See also Allison, *Russia, the West, and Military Intervention,* 123.

46.  Allison, *Russia, the West, and Military Intervention*, 124.

47.  Allison, *Russia, the West, and Military Intervention,* 130.

48.  Deborah Larson and Alexei Shevchenko argue that during the 1990s and early 2000s, Russia attempted to join the "Western Club" to be accepted as a great power and point to Russia's desire to join NATO in 1992 as well as other international organizations. Only after the United States refused to recognize their great power status, as well as encourage the color revolutions, did Russia turn to other creative strategies to reassert its status. Though I agree that Russia was interested in joining these organizations in the 1990s, I argue that Russia still sought primacy in the former Soviet Union without Western interference. See Deborah Welch Larson and Alexei Shevchenko, "Status Seekers: Chinese and Russian Responses to U.S. Primacy," *International Security* 34, no. 4 (Spring 2010): 63–95.

49.  Russian Ministry of Foreign Affairs, "National Security Concept of the Russian Federation," January 10, 2000, accessed January 9, 2017, http://www.mid.ru/en/foreign_policy/official_documents/-/asset_publisher/CptICkB6BZ29/content/id/589768.

50.  McCarthy, *The Limits of Friendship,* 85.

51.  Lieutenant Colonel (Royal Netherlands Army, retired) Marcel De Haas, former professor at Nazarbayev University, Kazakhstan, and current Senior Researcher at the Russian Studies Center, University of Groningen, Skype interview by author, June 29, 2017.

52.  Richard Giragosian, "The US Military Engagement in Central Asia and the Southern Caucasus: An Overview," *Journal of Slavic Military Studies* 17, no. 1 (2004): 51–52.

53. The original name for the organization was the Collective Security Organization but was changed to Collective Security Treaty Organization in 2003. Uzbekistan did not become a member of the CSTO until 2006, but again withdrew in 2012.

54. Collective Security Treaty Organization, "Charter of the Collective Security Treaty Organization," original publication 2002, accessed January 8, 2017, http://www.odkb-csto.org/documents/detail.php?ELEMENT_ID=1896.

55. Allison, *Russia, the West, and Military Intervention,* 139–40.

56. Brigadier General (Danish Army, retired) Michael Clemmesen, former Defence Attaché to the Baltics and Commandant of the Baltic Defence College, Skype interview by author, June 12, 2017.

57. Boris Yamshanov, "We Defend the Border in a Neighborly Way," Defense and Security (Russia), November 16, 2012, accessed January 12, 2017, LexisNexis Academic.

58. "Collective Rapid Deployment Forces" are also known as "Collective Prompt Reaction Forces in some translations." See Yulia Nikitina, "The Collective Security Treaty Organization Through the Looking Glass," *Problems of Post-Communism* 59, no. 3 (2012): 43. See also Marcel de Haas, "War Games of the Shanghai Cooperation Organization and the Collective Security Treaty Organization: Drills on the Move!" *The Journal of Slavic Military Studies* 29, no. 3 (July 2016): 390–91.

59. Ian Brzezinski, former US deputy assistant secretary of defense for Europe and NATO policy and Advisor to the Ukrainian National Security Council and Foreign Ministry, phone interview by author, September 19, 2017.

60. Yuri Sharkov, "'Color Revolutions': Uniformity in Diversity," *International Affairs (Moscow)* 54, no. 4 (2008): 25–31.

61. "Council on Foreign Relations Inaugural Annual Lecture on Russia and Russian-American Relations, *Federal News Service,* 13 January 2005. See also Thomas Ambrosio, "Insulating Russia from a Colour Revolution: How the Kremlin Resists Regional Democratic Trends," *Democratization* 14, no. 2 (April 2007): 232–52.

62. "Russia Condemns US Decisions to 'Sanction' Belarus over Referendum', *Agence France Presse,* 21 October 2004. See Ambrosio, "Insulating Russia from a Colour Revolution: How the Kremlin Resists Regional Democratic Trends," 242. See also Allison, 137.

63. Lucan Way, "The Real Causes of the Color Revolutions," *Journal of Democracy* 19, no. 3 (July 2008): 63.

64. Steven Levitsky and Lucan Way, *Competitive Authoritarianism: Hybrid Regimes after the Cold War,* (Cambridge: Cambridge University Press, 2010), 211–12.

65. Human Rights Watch, "Bullets Were Falling Like Rain: The Andijan Massacre, May, 13, 2005," accessed January 16, 2017, https://www.hrw.org/report/2005/06/06/bullets-were-falling-rain/andijan-massacre-may-13-2005.

66. Vitali Silitski, "Preempting Democracy: The Case of Belarus," *Journal of Democracy* 16, no. 4 (2005): 94.

67. "Kyrgyz Defence Chief on Military Reform, Cooperation with Russia, USA," *BBC Monitoring Central Asia Unit,* February 24, 2011, LexisNexis Academic.

68. Ibid.

69. "Surkov: In His Own Words" *The Wall Street Journal,* December 18, 2006, accessed January 12, 2017, http://www.wsj.com/articles/SB116646992809753610.

70. Roy Allison, "Virtual Regionalism, Regional Structures, and Regime Security in Central Asia," *Central Asian Survey* 27, no. 2 (June 2008): 186–95.

71. "A Tulip Revolution," *The Economist,* March 24, 2005, accessed January 11, 2017, http://www.economist.com/node/3785139. See also Paul Baev, *Russian Energy Policy and Military Power: Putin's Quest for Greatness* (London: Routledge, 2008), 71.

72. De Haas, "War Games of the Shanghai Cooperation Organization and the Collective Security Treaty Organization: Drills on the Move!", 393.

73. Vitali Silitski, "'Survival of the Fittest:' Domestic and International Dimensions of the Authoritarian Reaction in the Former Soviet Union Following the Colored Revolutions," *Communist and Post-Communist Studies* 43, no. 4 (December 2010): 348.

74. Erica Marat, *The Military and the State in Central Asia: From Red Army to Independence* (New York: Routledge, 2010), 94.

75. The Collective Rapid Deployment Forces would conduct their first anti-terror multinational exercise in October 2009, called "Collaboration" or "Interaction" '09. The exercise consisted of a computer-based staff rehearsal followed by large tactical operations conducted by the rapid forces, consisting of Russian paratroopers, Russian OMON (special purpose police), Kazakh paratroopers, SWAT teams, Kazakhstani Ministry of Internal Affairs, an Armenia motorized company, and Kyrgyz "Scorpion" special forces. "Maneuvers 1,500 by 300 Clicks Wide," *Defense and Security (Moscow),* September 2, 2009, LexisNexis Academic. "Russian Capital Hosts Regional Security Organization's Command-Staff Drill," *BBC Monitoring Former Soviet Union,* September 2, 2009, LexisNexis Academic.

76. Alexander Pinchuk, "To the New 'Rubezh'," *Defense and Security,* July 31, 2006, LexisNexis Academic.

77. "Kyrgyz Servicemen to Participate in Regional Military Training," *BBC Monitoring Central Asia Unit,* August 12, 2006, LexisNexis Academic. See also Kathleen Collins, "Kyrgyzstan's Latest Revolution," *Journal of Democracy* 22, no. 3 (July 2011): 156; and Michael Steen, "Kyrgyzstani Protestors Kill Police; At Least Four Officers Beaten to Death After Demonstrators Seize Control of Town," *The Globe and Mail,* March 21, 2005, LexisNexis Academic.

78. Ibid.

79. "Uzbekistan Sends Observers to CIS Security Bloc's Drill in Kazakhstan," *BBC Monitoring Central Asia Unit,* August 23, 2006, LexisNexis Academic.

80. Vasily Kashin and Alexei Nikolsky, "The 'Red' Will Suppress the Mutiny of the 'Blue'; Russia and its Allies Learn to Defend Central Asian Regimes," *Defense and Security,* August 28, 2006, LexisNexis Academic.

81. "Russian TV Shows Major Joint Antiterrorist Drill in Kazakstan," *BBC Monitoring Former Soviet Union,* October 22, 2016, LexisNexis Academic.

82. Richard Weitz, "The CSTO Deepens Military Ties," *The Central Asia-Caucasus Analyst,* October 18, 2006, accessed January 13, 2017, https://www.cacianalyst.org/publications/analytical-articles/item/11149-analytical-articles-caci-analyst -2006-10-18-art-11149.html?tmpl=component&print=1.

83. Anna Neistat, "The Andijan Massacre Remembered," *Amnesty International,* July 2, 2015, accessed January 12, 2017, https://www.amnesty.org/en/latest/news /2015/07/the-andijan-massacre-remembered/.

84. Marat, *The Military and the State in Central Asia: From Red Army to Independence,* 94.

85. Vasily Kashin and Alexei Nikolsky, "The 'Red' Will Suppress the Mutiny of the 'Blue'; Russia and its Allies Learn to Defend Central Asian Regimes," *Defense and Security,* August 28, 2006, LexisNexis Academic.

86. Nargis Hamroboyeva, "Tajik Military Officers Participate in CSTO Drill in Kazakhstan," *Asia-Plus,* October 17, 2012, accessed January 11, 2017, http://news .tj/en/news/tajikistan/security/20121017/tajik-military-officers-participate-csto-drill -kazakhstan-0.

87. Ibid.

88. Joshua Kucera, "CSTO Holds First-Ever Peacekeeping Exercises," *Eurasia Net,* October 8, 2012, accessed January 12, 2017, http://www.eurasianet.org/node /66023.

89. For a sampling, see Valerie J. Bunce and Sharon L. Wolchik, "Defeating Dictators: Electoral Change and Stability in Competitive Authoritarian Regimes," *World Politics* 62, no. 1 (January 2010): 43–86; Steven Levitsky and Lucan Way, *Competitive Authoritarianism: Hybrid Regimes after the Cold War* (New York: Cambridge University Press, 2010), 3–21; Eva Bellin, "Reconsidering the Robustness of Authoritarianism in the Middle East: Lessons from the Arab Spring," *Comparative Politics* 44, no. 2 (January 2012): 128–29.

90. For an argument about the important of a loyal and effective coercive capacity in authoritarian stability, see Eva Bellin, "Reconsidering the Robustness of Authoritarianism in the Middle East: Lessons from the Arab Spring," *Comparative Politics* 44, no. 2 (January 2012): 127–49.

91. "Freedom in the World: Democracy in Retreat," *Freedom House,* 2019, https://freedomhouse.org/sites/default/files/Feb2019_FH_FITW_2019_Report_ ForWeb-compressed.pdf.

92. Way, "The Real Causes of the Color Revolutions," 69.

## CHAPTER 6

1. As SFABs are only comprised of leaders, the units are approximately 10 percent of a typical combat brigade's end strength. Matthew Cox, "Army Stands Up 6 Brigades to Advise Foreign Militaries," *Military.com,* February 16, 2017, accessed May 18, 2017, http://www.military.com/daily-news/2017/02/16/army-stands-up-6 -brigades-advise-foreign-militaries.html.

2.   Michelle Tan, "Interview: US Army Chief of Staff Gen. Mark Milley," *Defense News,* October 14, 2015, accessed May 18, 2017, http://www.defensenews.com/story/defense/policy-budget/leaders/interviews/2015/10/14/interview-army-chief-of-staff-gen-mark-milley/73614752/.

3.   Derek Reveron, "Security Cooperation: A Key Pillar of Defense Policy," *Foreign Policy Research Institute E-Notes,* November 23, 2015, https://www.fpri.org/article/2015/11/security-cooperation-a-key-pillar-of-defense-policy/; see also Derek Reveron, *Exporting Security,* 126–30.

4.   Sun Zi, *The Art of War: Sun Zi's Military Methods*, trans. Victor H. Mair (New York: Columbia University Press, 2007), 80–82.

5.   Christopher Gelpi, Peter D. Feaver, and Jason Reifler, *Paying the Human Costs of War: American Public Opinion and Casualties in Military Conflict* (Princeton, NJ: Princeton University Press, 2009).

6.   Jason Lyall and Isaiah Wilson III, "Rage Against the Machines: Explaining Outcomes in Counterinsurgency Wars," *International Organization* 63, no. 1 (Winter 2009): 67–106.

7.   Paul K. MacDonald, "Retribution Must Succeed Rebellion": The Colonial Origins of Counterinsurgency Failure," *International Organization* 67, no. 2 (Spring 2013): 253–86.

8.   John J. Mearsheimer, *The Tragedy of Great Power Politics* (New York: W.W. Norton, 2014), 139.

9.   Mearsheimer, *Tragedy,* 157–62.

10.   Basil Liddell Hart, *The British Way in Warfare* (New York: Macmillan, 1933); Brian Holden Reid, "The British Way in Warfare: Liddell Hart's Idea and Its Legacy," *RUSI Journal* 156, no. 6 (2011): 71.

11.   Thomas J. Christensen and Jack Snyder, "Chain Gangs and Passed Bucks: Predicting Alliance Patterns in Multipolarity," *International Organization* 44, no. 2 (Spring 1990): 140–41, 159–65.

12.   Martin S. Alexander and William J. Philpott, "The Entente Cordiale and the Next War: Anglo-French Views on Future Military Cooperation, 1928-1939," *Intelligence and National Security* 13, no. 1 (1998): 62–65.

13.   Warren F. Kimball, *The Most Unsordid Act: Lend-Lease, 1939-1941* (Baltimore: Johns Hopkins Press, 1969), 6–11.

14.   Stathis Kalyvas and Laia Balcells, "International System and Technologies of Rebellion," *The American Political Science Review* 104, no. 3 (2010): 421–23.

15.   Martha Finnemore, *The Purpose of Intervention: Changing Beliefs of Intervention* (Ithaca: Cornell University Press, 2003), 138–39.

16.   Heidi M. Peters and Sofia Plagakis, "Department of Defense Contractor and Troop Levels in Afghanistan and Iraq: 2007-2018," Congressional Research Service, May 10, 2019, https://crsreports.congress.gov/product/pdf/R/R44116/12, 6, 12.

17.   Robert Gates, *Duty: Memoirs of a Secretary at War* (New York, NY: Alfred A. Knopf, 2014), 372.

18.   Gates, *Duty,* 364–67.

19.   The authors use the economic concept of a principal-agent problem to illustrate the political problems associated with security force assistance strategies.

Stephen Biddle, Julia Macdonald, and Ryan Baker, "Small Footprint, Small Payoff: The Military Effectiveness of Security Force Assistance," *Journal of Strategic Studies* 41, nos. 1–2 (2018): 96.

20.   Robert M. Gates, "Helping Others Defend Themselves: The Future of U.S. Security Assistance," 3.

21.   Ibid., 2.

22.   Ibid., 2–4.

23.   Kathleen J. McInnis and Nathan J. Lucas, "What Is 'Building Partner Capacity?' Issues for Congress," *Congressional Research Service*, December 18, 2015, pg. 5, https://fas.org/sgp/crs/natsec/R44313.pdf. Other authors use the term "Security Force Assistance" to describe these activities. See Stephen Biddle, Julia Macdonald, and Ryan Baker, "Small Footprint, Small Payoff: The Military Effectiveness of Security Force Assistance," *Journal of Strategic Studies* 41, nos. 1–2 (2018): 90.

24.   Robert M. Gates, "Helping Others Defend Themselves: The Future of U.S. Security Assistance," *Foreign Affairs* 89, no. 3 (May/June 2010): 2.

25.   McInnis and Lucas, 6–7.

26.   Peter Dombrowski and Simon Reich, "The Strategy of Sponsorship," *Survival* 57, no. 5 (September 3, 2015): 123.

27.   Ibid., 122–23.

28.   The US military sometimes makes a distinction between "capability" and "capacity" along these lines: "Capability refers to the [Partner Nations]'s ability to *execute a given task* while capacity refers to the PN's ability to *self-sustain* and *self-replicate* a given capability." See *Security Cooperation,* Joint Publication 3-20 (Washington, D.C.: Government Printing Office, 2017), I-2. On democratic military professionalism—that is, protection both by and from the military—see Feaver, *Armed Servants: Agency, Oversight, and Civil-Military Relations*, 1–15.

29.   "Building Partner Capacity: Inventory of Department of Defense Security Cooperation and Department of State Security Assistance Efforts," *Government Accountability Office,* GAO-17-255R, March 24, 2017, https://www.gao.gov/assets /690/683682.pdf, 2.

30.   Government Accountability Office, "Regionally Aligned Forces: DOD Could Enhance Army Brigades' Efforts in Africa by Improving Activity Coordination and Mission-Specific Preparation," August 2015, pg. 55, https://www.gao.gov/products/ GAO-15-568.

31.   Kalyvas and Balcells, "International System and Technologies of Rebellion," 415.

32.   Robert Rotberg, "Failed States in a World of Terror," *Foreign Affairs* 81, no. 4 (2002): 127–40.

33.   Eric G. Berman, "The Provision of Lethal Military Equipment: French, UK, and US Peacekeeping Policies Toward Africa," *Security Dialogue* 34, no. 2 (2003): 206.

34.   Nathaniel K. Powell, "Battling Instability? The Recurring Logic of French Military Interventions in Africa," *African Security* 10, no. 1 (2017): 47–50.

35.   Jackson, "British-African Defence and Security Connections," 362–65.

36. Lieutenant Colonel (British Royal Marines) Reggie Turner, who served as a liaison officer to the UN for the Royal Marine's 42 Commando unit during Operation Palliser, Skype interview by author, June 29, 2017.

37. General Sir Peter Wall (British Army), Chief of the General Staff, "Transcript: Defence Engagement: The British Army's Role in Building Security and Stability Overseas," Lecture at Chatham House, March 12, 2014, https://www .chathamhouse.org/sites/files/chathamhouse/home/chatham/public_html/sites/default /files/20140312Defence%20Engagement.pdf.

38. Andrew Stewart, "An Enduring Commitment: The British Military's Role in Sierra Leone," *Defence Studies* 8, no. 3 (September 2008): 352.

39. Crawford Young, *The African Colonial State in Comparative Perspective* (Yale: Yale University Press, 1994), 81. See also Stewart, 352.

40. "Hopeless Africa," *The Economist,* May 11, 2000, accessed May 12, 2017, http://www.economist.com/node/333429. See also Stewart, 351.

41. Stewart, 363.

42. Mohamed Massaquoi, "National Army Set for Somalia Mission," *Concord Times,* March 20, 2012, LexisNexis Academic.

43. "Sierra Leone Jungle Training Underlines Britain's Role in Africa," *Gov.UK,* January 7, 2017, accessed March 12, 2017, https://www.gov.uk/government/news/ sierra-leone-jungle-training-underlines-britians-role-in-africa. See also Joe Clapson, "Sierra Leonean Army Comes of Age Under British Direction," *UK Ministry of Defence* website, April 6, 2011, accessed May 22, 2017, https://www.gov.uk/govern-ment/news/sierra-leonean-army-comes-of-age-under-british-direction.

44. Albrecht and Jackson estimate that between 2005 and 2008, the cost of British military assistance and training through IMATT to the RSLAF was approxi-mately £10 million per year. Conversely, in the fiscal year 2006-2007, the British military budgeted roughly £2.4 billion on equipment procurement and £534 mil-lion on science, innovation, and technology. See Peter Albrecht and Paul Jackson, *Securing Sierra Leone, 1997-2013: Defence, Diplomacy, and Development in Action,* footnote 2, pgs. 1–2; UK Ministry of Defence, "The Government's Expenditure Plans, 2006-07 to 2007-08," July 2006, pg. 14, http://webarchive.nationalarchives .gov.uk/20070305140626/http://www.mod.uk/NR/rdonlyres/A556F11A-E9A4-4330 -A96A-898A0B760808/0/MODExpenditurePlan200607to200708.pdf.

45. David H. Ucko, "Can Limited Intervention Work? Lessons from Britain's Success Story in Sierra Leone," *Journal of Strategic Studies* 39, nos. 5–6 (2016): 848–49.

46. Email correspondence with Colonel (British Army, retired) Mike Dent, Military Advisor of the Ministry of Defence Advisory Team (MODAT) and Deputy Commander of IMATT, August 20, 2017.

47. Peter Albrecht and Paul Jackson, *Securing Sierra Leone, 1997-2013: Defence, Diplomacy, and Development in Action,* Royal United Services Institute for Defence and Security Studies (Abingdon, Oxford: Routledge Journals, 2014), vi–vii, 20.

48. Ibid.

49. Email correspondence with Colonel (British Army, retired) Mike Dent, Military Advisor of the MODAT and Deputy Commander of IMATT, August 20, 2017.

50.   Ibid.

51.   Albrecht and Jackson, *Securing Sierra Leone, 1997-2013: Defence, Diplomacy, and Development in Action,* 20–22.

52.   Email correspondence with Colonel (British Army, retired) Mike Dent, Military Advisor of the MODAT and Deputy Commander of IMATT, August 20, 2017.

53.   Ucko, 853. See also Andrew M. Dorman, *Blair's Successful War: British Military Intervention in Sierra Leone* (Farnham: Ashgate 2009), 79.

54.   Lieutenant Colonel (British Royal Marines) Andrew Muddiman, who served as an intelligence officer for Royal Marine's 42 Commando unit during Operation Palliser, Skype interview by author, July 19, 2017.

55.   "Leading Article: Our Military Needs a Mandate," *The Independent,* May 14, 2000, LexisNexis Academic.

56.   Kim Sengupta and Alex Duvall Smith, "Army Say 'We Must Take the Battle to Rebels'; Minister Accused of Misleading House; Rebels 'Will Skin UN Alive'; Peace-keepers Build Up Forces," *The Independent,* May 13, 2000, LexisNexis Academic.

57.   House of Commons, Debate, 23 May 2000, Vol. 350 cc864, https://publications.parliament.uk/pa/cm199900/cmhansrd/vo000523/debtext/00523-06.htm. See also Ucko, 855.

58.   House of Commons, Debate, 23 May 2000, Vol. 350 cc869, https://publications.parliament.uk/pa/cm199900/cmhansrd/vo000523/debtext/00523-08.htm.

59.   "Army's Freetown Retraining Role May Last Three Years," *Birmingham Post,* June 1, 2000, LexisNexis Academic.

60.   Ucko, 850–55.

61.   Alex Renton, "Making the Alco-Pop Rabble Kings of the Jungle; British Peacekeeping Troops Are Currently in the Jungle Teaching Sierra Leone's Army the Art of Warfare to Enable Them to Restore Order in Their Battered Country," *The Evening Standard,* July 21, 2000, LexisNexis Academic.

62.   Ibid.

63.   Lieutenant Colonel (British Royal Marines) Reggie Turner, who served as a liaison officer to the UN for the Royal Marine's 42 Commando unit during Operation Palliser, Skype interview by author, June 29, 2017.

64.   Richard Norton-Taylor and Ewen MacAskill, "Britain Builds Up Sierra Leone Force," *The Guardian,* October 10, 2000, accessed May 21, 2017, https://www.theguardian.com/world/2000/oct/11/sierraleone.

65.   Peter Albrecht and Paul Jackson, *Securing Sierra Leone, 1997-2013: Defence, Diplomacy, and Development in Action,* 28–29.

66.   Peter Albrecht interview with Richard Woodward, UK, August 2013, in Peter Albrecht and Paul Jackson, *Securing Sierra Leone, 1997-2013: Defence, Diplomacy, and Development in Action,* 30.

67.   Peter Albrecht interview with Richard Woodward in Peter Albrecht and Paul Jackson, *Securing Sierra Leone, 1997-2013: Defence, Diplomacy, and Development in Action,* 126.

68.   Barry J. Le Grys, "British Military Involvement in Sierra Leone, 2001-2006," in *Security Sector Reform in Sierra Leone 1997-2007: Views from the Front Line,* eds. Peter Albrecht and Paul Jackson (Berlin: Lit Verlag, 2010), 56.

69.   Peter Albrecht interview with Emmanuel Corker, June 2012, in Peter Albrecht and Paul Jackson, *Securing Sierra Leone, 1997-2013: Defence, Diplomacy, and Development in Action,* 57.

70.   Peter Albrecht interview with Richard Woodward, UK, August 2013, in Peter Albrecht and Paul Jackson, *Securing Sierra Leone, 1997-2013: Defence, Diplomacy, and Development in Action,* 30.

71.   Email correspondence with British Army Colonel (retired) Mike Dent, Military Advisor of the MODAT, and Deputy Commander of IMATT, August 20, 2017.

72.   "British Help Rebuild Sierra Leone's Army," *The Globe and Mail,* March 27, 2002, LexisNexis Academic.

73.   Ibid.

74.   Colonel (retired) Mike Dent, "Sierra Leone Background Brief, 2002" July 24, 2002.

75.   Peter Albrecht and Paul Jackson, *Securing Sierra Leone, 1997-2013: Defence, Diplomacy, and Development in Action,* 32.

76.   Peter Albrecht and Paul Jackson, *Reconstructing Security After Conflict: Security Sector Reform in Sierra Leone* (Houndmills, Basingstoke, Hampshire: Palgrave MacMillan, 2011), 74–75.

77.   Al-Hassan Kharamoh Kondeh, "Formulating Sierra Leone's Defence White Paper," in *Security Sector Reform in Sierra Leone 1997-2007: Views from the Front Line,* eds. Peter Albrecht and Paul Jackson (Berlin: Lit Verlag, 2010), 157–58.

78.   IMATT, "Plan 2010," July 17, 2004, unpublished, in Peter Albrecht and Paul Jackson, *Securing Sierra Leone, 1997-2013: Defence, Diplomacy, and Development in Action,* 32–33.

79.   Joe Clapson, "Sierra Leonean Army Comes of Age Under British Direction," *UK Ministry of Defence* website, April 6, 2011, accessed May 22, 2017, https://www .gov.uk/government/news/sierra-leonean-army-comes-of-age-under-british-direction.

80.   Peter Albrecht and Paul Jackson, *Securing Sierra Leone, 1997-2013: Defence, Diplomacy, and Development in Action,* 76.

81.   Ibid., 34–35.

82.   Barry Le Grys, 51.

83.   IMATT, "Future Delivery of RSLAF Transformation by IMATT," in Peter Albrecht and Paul Jackson, *Securing Sierra Leone, 1997-2013: Defence, Diplomacy, and Development in Action,* 36.

84.   Peter Albrecht and Paul Jackson, *Securing Sierra Leone, 1997-2013: Defence, Diplomacy, and Development in Action,* 78.

85.   Peter Albrecht email exchange with Hugh Blackman in Peter Albrecht and Paul Jackson, *Securing Sierra Leone, 1997-2013: Defence, Diplomacy, and Development in Action,* 116–17.

86.   Le Grys, 56.

87. Peter Albrecht interview with Jonathan Powe in Peter Albrecht and Paul Jackson, *Securing Sierra Leone, 1997-2013: Defence, Diplomacy, and Development in Action,* 82–83.

88. Peter Albrecht interview with Jonathan Powe in Peter Albrecht and Paul Jackson, *Securing Sierra Leone, 1997-2013: Defence, Diplomacy, and Development in Action,* 84–85.

89. Joe Clapson, "Sierra Leonean Army Comes of Age Under British Direction," *UK Ministry of Defence* website, April 6, 2011, accessed May 22, 2017, https://www.gov.uk/government/news/sierra-leonean-army-comes-of-age-under-british-direction.

90. Ibid.

91. "UK Armed Forces, RSLAF Joint Military Exercise Set to Begin in Sierra Leone," *Concord Times,* November 7, 2016, LexisNexis Academic.

92. "Jungle Training with Sierra Leone Troops," *UK Army* website, January 9, 2017, accessed May 22, 2017, http://army.mod.uk/news/28900.aspx.

93. Peter Albrecht and Paul Jackson, *Securing Sierra Leone, 1997-2013: Defence, Diplomacy, and Development in Action,* 125.

94. Mimmi Söderberg Kovacs, "Bringing the Good, the Bad, and the Ugly into the Peace Fold: the Republic of Sierra Leone's Armed Forces After the Lomé Peace Agreement," in *New Armies from Old: Merging Competing Military Forces After Civil Wars,* ed. Roy Licklider (Washington, DC: Georgetown University Press, 2014), 209.

95. Stephen Biddle, Julia Macdonald, and Ryan Baker, "Small Footprint, Small Payoff: The Military Effectiveness of Security Force Assistance," *Journal of Strategic Studies* 41, nos. 1–2 (2018): 132.

# CHAPTER 7

1. Timothy Andrew Sayle, *Enduring Alliance: A History of NATO and the Postwar Global Order* (Cornell, NY: Cornell University Press, 2019), 2.

2. Brian Blankenship, "Promises under Pressure: Statements of Reassurance in U.S. Alliances," *International Studies Quarterly,* forthcoming.

3. Michael Beckley, "The Myth of Entangling Alliances: Reassessing the Security Risks of U.S. Defense Pacts," *International Security* 39, no. 4 (Spring 2015): 21–23.

4. Jeffrey W. Knopf, "Varieties of Assurance," *Journal of Strategic Studies* 35, no. 3 (2012): 375–99.

5. The second logic of "reassurance" is more similar to the mechanism of "attraction" under Shaping I.

6. This would be considered "Assurance II- Alliance Commitment," according to Knopf. See Jeffrey W. Knopf, "Varieties of Assurance," *Journal of Strategic Studies* 35, no. 3 (2012): 375–99.

7. Paul K. Huth, "Extended Deterrence and the Outbreak of War," *American Political Science Review* 82, no. 2 (1988): 423–24.

8. Roseanne W. McManus and Mark David Nieman, "Identifying the Level of Major Power Support Signaled for Protégés: A Latent Measure Approach," *Journal of Peace Research* 56, no. 3 (2019): 365–66.

9. Glenn H. Snyder, "The Security Dilemma in Alliance Politics," *World Politics* 36, no. 4 (1984): 466–67.

10. Francis J. Gavin, "Strategies of Inhibition: U.S. Grand Strategy, the Nuclear Revolution, and Nonproliferation" *International Security* 40, no. 1 (2015): 16, 29–31.

11. Brian Blankenship, "Promises under Pressure: Statements of Reassurance in U.S. Alliances."

12. Yasuhiro Izumikawa, "Binding Strategies in Alliance Politics: The Soviet-Japanese-US Diplomatic Tug of War in the Mid-1950s," *International Studies Quarterly* 62 (2018): 108.

13. Timothy Crawford, *Pivotal Deterrence: Third-Party Statecraft and the Pursuit of Peace* (Ithaca, NY: Cornell University Press, 2003), 3.

14. Paul Schroeder, "Alliances, 1815-1945: Weapons of Power and Tools of Management," in *Historical Dimensions of National Security Problems*, ed. Klaus Knorr (Lawrence: University Press of Kansas, 1976), 230.

15. Paul Schroeder, "Alliances, 1815-1945: Weapons of Power and Tools of Management," 231.

16. James D. Morrow, "Alliances and Asymmetry: An Alternative to the Capabilitiy Aggreggation Model of Alliances," *American Journal of Political Science* 35, no. 4 (November 1991): 911–13.

17. "China Says Opposes [*sic*] U.S. THAAD defence system in South Korea," *Reuters*, May 20, 2020, https://www.reuters.com/article/us-china-south-korea-usa-thaad/china-says-opposes-u-s-thaad-defence-system-in-south-korea-idUSKBN2350XA.

18. Robert Jervis, "Cooperation Under the Security Dilemma," 186-190. See also Stephen Van Evera, "Offense, Defense, and the Causes of War," *International Security* 22, no. 4 (Spring 1998): 7–16.

19. Robert Art, *A Grand Strategy for America* (Ithaca, NY: Cornell University Press, 2003), 140.

20. Stephen G. Brooks and William C. Wohlforth, *America Abroad: The United States' Global Role in the 21ˢᵗ Century* (Oxford: Oxford University Press, 2016), 100.

21. Victor D. Cha, "Powerplay: Origins of the U.S. Alliance System in Asia," *International Security* 34, no. 3 (Winter 2009/2010): 158–96.

22. Songying Fang, Jesse C. Johnson, and Brett Ashley Leeds, "To Concede or Resist? The Restraining Effect of Military Alliances," *International Organization* 68 (Fall 2014): 775–809.

23. Paul Schroeder, "Alliances, 1815-1945: Weapons of Power and Tools of Management," in Klaus Knorr, ed., *Historical Dimensions of National Security Problems* (Lawrence: University Press of Kansas, 1976), 242. See also Cha, "Powerplay," 164.

24. Thomas J. Christensen and Jack Snyder, "Chain Gangs and Passed Bucks: Predicting Alliance Patterns in Multipolarity," *International Organization* 44, no. 2 (Spring 1990): 140–41.

25. Sayle, *Enduring Alliance,* 16–17.

26. Barry R. Posen, *Restraint: A New Foundation for U.S. Grand Strategy* (Ithaca, NY: Cornell University Press, 2014)*,* 33–50.

27. Sayle, *Enduring Alliance,* 20.

28. Michael A. Allen, Julie VanDusky-Allen, and Michael E. Flynn, "The Localized and Spatial Effects of US Troop Deployments on Host-State Defense Spending," *Foreign Policy Analysis* 12, no. 4 (2016): 674–94.

29. Michael Beckley, "The Myth of Entangling Alliances: Reassessing the Security Risks of U.S. Defense Pacts," *International Security* 39, no. 4 (Spring 2015): 7–48.

30. Stacie L. Pettyjohn and Jennifer Kavanaugh, *Access Granted: Political Challenges to the U.S. Overseas Military Presence, 1945-2014* (Santa Monica, CA: RAND, 2014), 3–4.

31. David Vine, *Base Nation: How U.S. Military Bases Abroad Harm America and the World* (New York, NY: Metropolitan Books, 2015), 6–7.

32. Robert Art, *A Grand Strategy for America,* 145.

33. "Army Prepositioned Stock – Europe," *US Army Online,* August 3, 2017, https://www.army.mil/standto/archive_2017-08-03/. See also Michelle Shevin-Coetzee, "The European Deterrence Initiative," *Center for Strategic and Budgetary Assessments,* January 25, 2019, https://csbaonline.org/research/publications/the-european-deterrence-initiative, 9–10.

34. *Joint Operations*, Joint Publication 3-0, Change 1 (Washington, DC: Government Printing Office, 2018), GL-13.

35. Stacie L. Pettyjohn and Jennifer Kavanaugh, *Access Granted: Political Challenges to the U.S. Overseas Military Presence, 1945-2014* (Santa Monica, CA: RAND, 2014), 78–80.

36. Pettyjohn and Kavanaugh, *Access Granted: Political Challenges to the U.S. Overseas Military Presence, 1945-2014*, 80–83, 89–106, 110–14.

37. Pettyjohn and Kavanaugh, *Access Granted: Political Challenges to the U.S. Overseas Military Presence, 1945-2014*, 110–14.

38. Stephan Frühling and Guillaume Lasconjarias, "NATO, A2/AD and the Kaliningrad Challenge," *Survival* 58, no. 2 (2016): 95–96.

39. Sayle, *Enduring Alliance: A History of NATO and the Postwar Global Order*, 11–14.

40. Elizabeth Piper, "Special Report: Why Ukraine Spurned the EU and Embraced Russia," *Reuters,* December 19, 2013, https://www.reuters.com/article/us-ukraine-russia-deal-special-report-idUSBRE9BI0DZ20131219.

41. "Huge Ukraine Rally over EU Agreement Delay," *BBC News*, November 24, 2013, https://www.bbc.com/news/world-europe-25078952.

42. "Ukraine Protests: 'Fringe' Demonstrators Storm Council," *BBC News,* December 1, 2013, https://www.bbc.com/news/av/world-europe-25177679/ukraine-protests-fringe-demonstrators-storm-council.

43.  "Ukraine Crisis: Timeline," *BBC News,* November 13, 2014, https://www
.bbc.com/news/world-middle-east-26248275.

44.  Tim Sullivan, "Russian Troops Take Over Ukraine's Crimea Region," *The
Associated Press,* March 1, 2014, Nexi Uni.

45.  Dalton Bennett, "Russia Reinforces Military Presence in Crimea," *Associated
Press,* March 8, 2014, Nexi Uni.

46.  Lionel M. Beehner, Colonel Liam S. Collins, and Robert T. Person, "The Fog
of Russian Information Warfare," in *Perceptions are Reality: Historical Case Studies
of Information Operations in Large-Scale Combat Operations*, eds. Colonel Mark D.
Vertuli and Lieutenant Colonel Bradley S. Loudon (Fort Leavenworth, KS: Army
University Press, 2018), 40.

47.  "Crimea Declares Independence, Seeks UN Recognition," *RT,* March 17,
2014, https://www.rt.com/news/crimea-referendum-results-official-250/.

48.  "Russian Lawmakers Welcome Separatist Steps by Crimea," *NPR Public
Broadcasting,* March 7, 2014, https://www.npr.org/blogs/thetwo-way/2014/03/07
/287141109/russian-lawmakers-welcome-separatist-steps-by-crimea

49.  "Obama Condemns Russian 'Intervention' in Ukraine," *NPR Public
Broadcasting,* March 6, 2014, https://www.npr.org/sections/thetwo-way/2014/03/06
/286847526/obama-condemns-russian-intervention-in-ukraine.

50.  Vladimir Isachenkov, "Putin Visits Crimea to Mark 5th Annivesrity of
Annexation," *Associated Press,* March 18, 2019, https://apnews.com/e40386d
7452749a8886d9196751f66c4. Damien Sharkov, "Putin Claims Russia 'Forced to
Defend' Ukraine Separatists," *Newsweek*, October 12, 2016, https://www.newsweek
.com/putin-claims-russia-forced-defend-ukraine-separatists-509281.

51.  Luke Harding, "Georgia Angered by Russia-Abkhazia Military Agreement,"
*The Guardian,* November 25, 2014, https://www.theguardian.com/world/2014/
nov/25/georgia-russia-abkhazia-military-agreement-putin; "U.S. Condemns Russian
Military Deal with Georgian Breakaway Region," *Radio Free Europe/Radio Liberty,*
January 26, 2018, https://www.rferl.org/a/u-s-condemns-russian-ossetia-military-deal
-georgia/29000754.html.

52.  "Face the Nation Transcripts: Kerry, Hagel," *CBS Face the Nation,* March
2, 2014, https://www.cbsnews.com/news/face-the-nation-transcripts-march-2-2014
-kerry-hagel/.

53.  Deborah Seward, "Russians in Crimea Seek Independence from Ukraine,"
*The Associated Press,* April 25, 1992, Nexis Uni.

54.  Deborah Seward, "Russians in Crimea Seek Independence from Ukraine,"
*The Associated Press,* April 25, 1992, Nexis Uni.

55.  "Ukrainian President Reins in Crimea Referendum Plan," *Agence France
Presse,* March 16, 1994, Nexi Uni.

56.  Frühling and Lasconjarias, "NATO, A2/AD and the Kaliningrad Challenge," 103.

57.  Robbie Gramer, "Operation Dragoon Ride," *Foreign Affairs*, May 13, 2015,
https://www.foreignaffairs.com/articles/baltics/2015-05-13/operation-dragoon-ride.

58.  Lionel M. Beehner, Colonel Liam S. Collins, and Robert T. Person, "The Fog
of Russian Information Warfare," in *Perceptions are Reality: Historical Case Studies
of Information Operations in Large-Scale Combat Operations*, eds. Colonel Mark D.

Vertuli and Lieutenant Colonel Bradley S. Loudon (Fort Leavenworth, KS: Army University Press, 2018), 31–32.

59. Alexander Lanoszka, "Russian Hybrid Warfare and Extended Deterrence in Eastern Europe," *International Affairs* 92, no. 1 (2016): 177–80.

60. Lanoszka, "Russian Hybrid Warfare and Extended Deterrence in Eastern Europe," 182.

61. "Latvian Union of Russians Sign Cooperation Agreement with Crimean PM's Political Party," *LETA,* August 12, 2014, Nexi Uni.

62. Ioana Popa, "Russia's Double-Edged Separatism," April 7, 2015, *ETH Zurich Center for Security Studies,* https://www.files.ethz.ch/isn/189833/9bc6fc7 4a41433d218dbeb91a89dc2e2.pdf, 1–3.

63. "Russia 'Danger' to Latvia, Lithuania, and Estonia," *BBC News Online,* February 19, 2015, https://www.bbc.com/news/uk-31528981.

64. "The European Activity Set," *US Army Online,* January 27, 2014, https:// www.army.mil/standto/archive_2014-01-27/.

65. Michelle Shevin-Coetzee, "The European Deterrence Initiative," *Center for Strategic and Budgetary Assessments,* January 25, 2019, https://csbaonline.org/ research/publications/the-european-deterrence-initiative,3–5.

66. Office of the Press Secretary, "Remarks by President Obama and President Komorowski of Poland in a Joint Press Conference," The White House, June 3, 2014, https://obamawhitehouse.archives.gov/the-press-office/2014/06/03/remarks -president-obama-and-president-komorowski-poland-joint-press-conf; "European Reassurance Initiative: Obama Announces $1 bn Fund," *BBC World News,* June 3, 2014, https://www.bbc.com/news/world-europe-27671691.

67. Funding would grow to over $6.5 billion for FY 2019. Michelle Shevin-Coetzee, "The European Deterrence Initiative," 4.

68. "Atlantic Resolve Fact Sheet," *U.S. Army Europe Online,* June 6, 2018, https://www.eur.army.mil/Newsroom/Fact-Sheets-Infographics/Fact-Sheet-Article -View/Article/1451471/atlantic-resolve-fact-sheet/.

69. "NATO's Readiness Action Plan Fact Sheet," *NATO Online,* December 2014, https://www.nato.int/nato_static_fl2014/assets/pdf/pdf_2014_12/20141202 _141202-facstsheet-rap-en.pdf.

70. Robbie Gramer, "Operation Dragoon Ride," *Foreign Affairs*, May 13, 2015, https://www.foreignaffairs.com/articles/baltics/2015-05-13/operation-dra-goon-ride.

71. Robbie Gramer, "Operation Dragoon Ride," *Foreign Affairs*, May 13, 2015, https://www.foreignaffairs.com/articles/baltics/2015-05-13/operation-dragoon-ride.

72. Rick Lyman, "To Reassure Europe," *New York Times (International),* March 30, 2015, LexisNexis Academic.

73. Ben Hodges, Janusz Bugajksi, and Peter B. Doran, *Securing the Suwalki Corridor: Strategy, Statecraft, Deterrence, and Defense* (Washington, DC: Center for European Analysis, July 2018), 25–31, quotation on 28.

74. Michelle Tan, "Strykers Begin 'Road March,'" *Army Times,* March 21, 2015, https://www.armytimes.com/news/your-army/2015/03/21/strykers-begin-road-march -across-eastern-europe/.

75. Robbie Gramer, "Operation Dragoon Ride," *Foreign Affairs*, May 13, 2015, https://www.foreignaffairs.com/articles/baltics/2015-05-13/operation-dragoon-ride.

76. "Operation Dragoon Ride: 'Lightning' VLOG Part 2," Video hosted by the 2nd Calvary Regiment, https://www.youtube.com/watch?v=gBxkKOmnX2.

77. John Vandiver, "Grateful Lithuanians Greet US Troops as Operation Dragoon Ride Gets Underway," *Stars and Stripes,* March 24, 2015, https://www.stripes.com/news/europe/grateful-lithuanians-greet-us-troops-as-operation-dragoon-ride-gets-underway-1.336207.

78. Rick Lyman, "To Reassure Europe," *New York Times (International),* March 30, 2015, LexisNexis Academic.

79. Paula Kennedy and Simona Kralova, "Russian Bid for Czech Hearts and Minds," *BBC News,* April 2, 2015, https://www.bbc.com/news/world-europe-32070184.

80. Paula Kennedy and Simona Kralova, "Russian Bid for Czech Hearts and Minds," *BBC News,* April 2, 2015, https://www.bbc.com/news/world-europe-32070184.

81. "Tank? No thanks!: Czechs Unhappy about US Military Convoy Crossing Country," *RT Online.* March 22, 2015, https://www.rt.com/news/243073-czech-protest-us-tanks/.

82. Daisy Sindelar, "U.S. Convoy: In Czech Republic, Real-Life Supporters Outnumber Virtual Opponents," *Radio Free Europe*, March 30, 2015, https://www.rferl.org/a/us-convoy-czech-republic-supporters-virtual-opponents/26928346.html.

83. Dan Lamothe, "In Show of Force, the Army's Operation Dragoon Ride Rolls through Europe," *The Washington Post,* March 24, 2015, https://www.washingtonpost.com/news/checkpoint/wp/2015/03/24/in-show-of-force-the-armys-operation-dragoon-ride-rolls-through-europe/.

84. "Calvary Ride," *The Economist,* April 1, 2015, https://www.economist.com/europe/2015/04/01/cavalry-ride.

85. "Most Czechs Do Not Mind *the 'Dragoon Ride,' Expresses an Alliance with NATO,"* O24 *Česká televise,* March 25, 2015, https://ct24.ceskatelevize.cz/domaci/1514904-jizda-dragounu-vetsine-cechu-nevadi-vyjadruje-spojenectvi-s-nato.

86. Rick Lyman, "To Reassure Europe," *New York Times (International),* March 30, 2015, LexisNexis Academic. See also

87. Robbie Gramer, "Operation Dragoon Ride," *Foreign Affairs*, May 13, 2015, https://www.foreignaffairs.com/articles/baltics/2015-05-13/operation-dragoon-ride.

88. David A. Shlapak and Michael W. Johnson, *Reinforcing Deterrence on NATO's Eastern Flank* (Santa Monica, CA: RAND, 2016), https://www.rand.org/pubs/research_reports/RR1253.html.

89. Statement by Major General David Allvin before the House Committee on Armed Services, Subcommittee on Oversight and Investigations, on European Reassurance Initiative Oversight, *Political Transcript Wire,* July 15, 2016.

90. Shevin-Coetzee, "The European Deterrence Initiative," 3.

91. "NATO's Enhanced Forward Presence Fact Sheet," *NATO Factsheets,* March 2019, https://www.nato.int/nato_static_fl2014/assets/pdf/pdf_2019_04/20190402_1904-factsheet_efp_en.pdf.

92.    Cristina Maza, "Vladimir Putin's Adviser Tells Americans: 'Russia Interferes in Your Brains, We Change Your Conscience'," *Newsweek,* February 12, 2019, https://www .newsweek.com/russia-president-vladimir-putin-election-americans-1327793.

93.    Heather A. Conley and Matthew Melino, "Russian Malign Influence in Montenegro," *CSIS Briefs, Center for Strategic and International Studies,* May 2019, https://www.csis.org/analysis/russian-malign-influence-montenegro#:~:text =Russian%20malign%20influence%20in%20the%20Western%20Balkans%20is ,from%20joining%20the%20North%20Atlantic%20Treaty%20Organization%20 %28NATO%29.

94.    "Video: EFP Battlegroup Lithuania- Education Story," *NATO Supreme Headquarters Allied Powers Europe Public Affairs,* January 30, 2020, https://shape .nato.int/efp/latest-news/video-efp-battlegroup-lithuania-education-story.

95.    Angela O'Mahony, Miranda Priebe, Bryan Frederick, Jennifer Kavanagh, Matthew Lane, Trevor Johnston, Thomas S. Szayna, Jakub P. Hlávka, Stephen Watts, Matthew Povlock, *U.S. Presence and the Incidence of Conflict* (Santa Monica, CA: RAND Corporation, 2018), 44–51.

96.    Posen, *Restraint,* 27.

# CHAPTER 8

1.    Roger McDermott, "Gerasimov Calls for New Strategy to Counter Color Revolution," *Eurasia Daily Monitor* 13, no. 46 (March 8, 2016), https://jamestown .org/program/gerasimov-calls-for-new-strategy-to-counter-color-revolution/.

2.    Dmitry Adamsky, "Cross-Domain Coercion: The Current Russian Art of Strategy," *Proliferation Papers,* no. 54 (November 2015): 21–26.

3.    Daniel W. Drezner, Ronald R. Krebs, and Randall Schweller, "The End of Grand Strategy," *Foreign Affairs* 99, no. 3 (May/June 2020), 107.

4.    Nina Silove, "Beyond the Buzzword: The Three Meanings of 'Grand Strategy'," *Security Studies* 27, no. 1 (2018): 27–57.

5.    Barry R. Posen, *Restraint: A New Foundation for U.S. Grand Strategy* (Ithaca, NY: Cornell University Press, 2014), 1.

6.    Paul C. Avey, Jonathan N. Markowitz, and Robert J. Reardon, "Disentangling Grand Strategy: International Relations Theory and U.S. Grand Strategy," *Texas National Security Review* 2, no. 1 (November 2018), 35.

7.    Avey, Markowitz, and Reardon, "Disentangling Grand Strategy: International Relations Theory and U.S. Grand Strategy," 35–41.

8.    Stephen G. Brooks and William C. Wohlforth, *America Abroad: The United States' Global Role in the 21st Century* (Oxford: Oxford University Press, 2016), 98–101.

9.    The grand strategy of "liberal internationalism" is best articulated by G. John Ikenberry, though through his book *Liberal Leviathan,* not his contribution to the article "Don't Come Home America," the latter of which advocates for deep engagement, but not necessarily democracy promotion, human rights, and humanitarian

intervention. See G. John Ikenberry, *Liberal Leviathan* (Princeton, NJ: Princeton University Press, 2011); Stephen G. Brooks, G. John Ikenberry, and William C. Wohlforth, "Don"t Come Home America: The Case Against Retrenchment." *International Security* 37, no. 3 (2012): 13–14.

10. John J. Mearsheimer and Stephen M. Walt, "The Case for Offshore Balancing: A Superior U.S. Grand Strategy," *Foreign Affairs* 95, no. 4 (July/August 2016): 73–74.

11. Barry R. Posen, *Restraint: A New Foundation for U.S. Grand Strategy* (Ithaca, NY: Cornell University Press, 2014), 33–50.

12. Robert A. Pape and James K. Feldman, *Cutting the Fuse: The Explosion of Global Suicide Terrorism and How to Stop It* (Chicago, IL: University of Chicago Press, 2010).

13. Posen, *Restraint,* 135–63, quote on 161.

14. The best representation of this debate is Barry R. Posen and Andrew L. Ross, "Competing Visions for U.S. Grand Strategy," *International Security* 21, no. 3 (Winter 1996/1997): 5–53.

15. For the former, see Drezner, Krebs, and Schweller, "The End of Grand Strategy," 107–17; for the latter, see David M. Edelstein and Ronald R. Krebs, "The Delusion of Grand Strategy," *Foreign Affairs*, November/December 94, no. 6 (2015), 109–16.

16. See, for instance, Carl Boggs ed., *Masters of War: Militarism and Blowback in the Era of American Empire* (New York: Routledge, 2003); Melvin A. Goodman, *National Insecurity: The Cost of American Militarism* (San Francisco: City Light Books, 2013); Gordon Adams, "The Militarization of U.S. Foreign Policy: Reversing the Trend," *Huffington Post Blog,* April 7, 2010, accessed December 2, 2017, accessible at https://www.huffingtonpost.com/gordon-adams/the-militarization-of-us_b_451435.html.

17. Rachel Maddow, *Drift: The Unmooring of American Military Power* (New York: Crown Publishers, 2012), 251.

18. Brett Rosenberg and Jake Sullivan, "The Case for a National Security Budget," *Foreign Affairs,* November 19, 2019, https://www.foreignaffairs.com/articles/2019-11-19/case-national-security-budget.

19. Jon Greenberg reveals this is not exactly true, but close: 6,500 military musicians to 8,100 diplomats. Jon Greenberg, "Does the U.S. Have About as Many Military Band Members as Diplomats?" *Politifact*, March 31, 2017, accessed January 8, 2018, www.politifact.com/global-news/statements/2017/mar/31/nicholas-burns/are-there-more-military-band-members-diplomats/.

20. A statement after which General Powell wrote, "I thought I would have an aneurysm." Colin Powell and Joseph E. Persico, *My American Journey* (New York: Random House, 1995), 576.

21. Andrew J. Bacevich, *The New American Militarism: How Americans Are Seduced by War* (Oxford, UK: Oxford University Press, 2005), 18.

22. Andrew J. Bacevich, *The New American* Militarism, Chapters 6 and 7.

23. Brooks, *How Everything Became War and the Military Became Everything*, 13.

24. Original emphasis. Ibid., 8.

25. Ibid., 261–67.

26.    Robert M. Gates, "The Overmilitarization of American Foreign Policy," *Foreign Affairs* 99, no. 4 (July/August 2020): 121–32, quotes on 128–29.

27.    Reveron, *Exporting Security,* 72–77.

28.    Fred Kaplan, *The Insurgents: David Petraeus and the Plot to Change the American Way of War* (New York: Simon and Schuster, 2013), 71–72.

29.    Thomas Gibbons-Neff, "U.S., NATO Countries Begin Largest Military Exercise in Eastern Europe since Cold War," *The Washington Post,* accessed August 7, 2016, https://www.washingtonpost.com/news/checkpoint/wp/2016/06/07/u-s-nato-countries -begin-largest-military-exercise-in-europe-since-cold-war/?utm_term=.bf662ba04d55.

30.    Ian J. Brzezinski and Nicholas Varangis, "The NATO-Russia Exercise Gap," *The Atlantic Council NATO Source.* February 23, 2015. Accessed September 27, 2017. http://www.atlanticcouncil.org/blogs/natosource/the-nato-russia-exercise-gap.

31.    Andrea Shalal, "Eyeing Russia, U.S. Military Shifts Toward More Global War Games," *Reuters,* August 3, 2017.

32.    Lieutenant General Mike Lundy and Colonel Rich Creed, "The Return of U.S. Army Field Manual 3-0, *Operations,*" *Military Review* (November-December 2017): 14–21, quotation on 14.

33.    Ibid.

34.    Ibid., 21.

## APPENDIX

1.    This chapter is adapted from Kyle J. Wolfley, "Military Statecraft and the Use of Multinational Exercises in World Politics," *Foreign Policy Analysis,* 17, no. 2 (2021), oraa022, https://doi.org/10.1093/fpa/oraa022.

2.    For instance, according to the Military Balance, out of forty-eight states in Sub-Saharan Africa, only forty states have an "air force" or "air wing" and only 26 states have a "navy" or "maritime wing". See "Chapter Nine: Sub-Saharan Africa," *The Military Balance* 118, no. 2 (2018): 429–98.

3.    For instance, the Indian military announced that the Indian and Indonesian navies were simultaneously conducting a "coordinated patrol" to maintain open ship-ping lanes as well as a "bilateral maritime exercise," both in the Andaman Sea. See "Coordinated Patrol and India-Indonesia Bilateral Maritime Exercise Commence at Belawan, Indonesia," *Ministry of Defence, Government of India,* Accessed October, 14, 2018, HYPERLINK "https://www.indiannavy.nic.in/content/coordinated-patrol -and-india-indonesia-bilateral-maritime-exercise-commence-belawan" https://www .indiannavy.nic.in/content/coordinated-patrol-and-india-indonesia-bilateral-maritime -exercise-commence-belawan.

4.    Vito D'Orazio, "Joint Military Exercises: 1970-2010 [dataset]," HYPERLINK "http://www.vitodorazio.com/data.html" http://www.vitodorazio.com/data.html. D'Orazio's data was originally collected as part of his dissertation project; see Vito D'Orazio, "International Military Cooperation: From Concepts to Constructs" PhD dissertation, Pennsylvania State University, 2013.

5.     Note: Building Partner-Capacity training programs are unique among military exercises in the long-term nature of these training efforts as well as the holistic approach to building capacity (involving not only the military but other ministries as well). Thus, I only code BPC exercises in the dataset which were reported in the news or other scholarly works and contain discrete training events, such as the UK's *Operation Palliser,* France's RECAMP exercises in Africa, and certain US exercises in the Philippines.

6.     For instance, see D'Orazio (2013) and Roseanne W. McManus and Mark David Nieman, "Identifying the Level of Major Power Support Signaled for Protégés: A Latent Measure Approach," *Journal of Peace Research* 56, no. 3 (2019): 364–78.

7.     Although the use of dyads in political science has come under recent scrutiny, I argue that my use of dyad-years is valid for two reasons. First, because I only include directed-dyads between seven major powers and the other states in the international system, I avoid issues concerned with interdependence between states commonly found in regular dyad datasets. In other words, the variation is largely with the partner, not the entire major power-partner dyad. Although I group all major powers together for most of my tests in this chapter, the appendix provides robustness checks for each individual major power. Second, although splitting multilateral events into bilateral events could be problematic, I argue that exercises are different from other major multinational events, such as wars or treaties. That is, I believe there is little difference between bilateral and multilateral exercises: an exercise between the United States and Ghana or one between the United States, Ghana, and other Asian and European partners are largely similar. Moreover, these exercises are not as costly as war or treaties: militaries look forward to opportunities to send troops for training, even among rival countries. More importantly, without the use of partner-years, I would be consciously selecting on the dependent variable (exercises that actually occur) and unable to observe the variation between partners that are chosen for exercises and those that are not; thus, I would not be able to capture the counterfactual "non-exercise" and would consequently lose leverage over my argument. For a major critique of the use of dyads (which guides my two points in defense), see Paul Poast, "Dyads Are Dead, Long Live Dyads! The Limits of Dyadic Designs in International Relations Research," *International Studies Quarterly* 60 (2016): 369–74.

8.     Scott D. Bennett and Allan Stam, "*EUGene*: A Conceptual Manual," *International Interactions* 26 (2000): 179–204. Version 3.212. EUGene software can be accessed at http://www.eugenesoftware.la.psu.edu/.

9.     If Japan is constitutionally unable to deploy military power, then the country's armed forces would not conduct "rehearsals," but only "deterrence" in self-defense. Thus, the case of Japan may be partly biased away from traditional explanations. Moreover, according to my data, Japan has only conducted exercises with the United States as a participant, as opposed to the other major power that conducted (at least some), exercises without the United States. Japan's military reliance on the United States calls into question its independence in military doctrine.

10.     Correlates of War Project. 2017. "National Military Capabilities, v5.0." Online, HYPERLINK "http://correlatesofwar.org" \h http://correlatesofwar.org. See also Singer, J. David, Stuart Bremer, and John Stuckey, "Capability Distribution,

Uncertainty, and Major Power War, 1820-1965," in Bruce Russett ed., *Peace, War, and Numbers* (Beverly Hills: Sage Publication, 1972), 19–48. For a discussion of whether India should be included as a great or major power, see Manjeet S. Pardesi, "Is India a Great Power? Understanding Great Power Status in Contemporary International Relations," *Asian Security* 11, no. 1 (2015): 1–30.

11. I gleaned troop-level data from the Correlates of War Project, "National Military Capabilities, v5.0."

12. I used the textual analysis software Wordstat from Provalis Research to search for the frequency of the following words that describe strategic uncertainty: "ambiguous, ambiguity, instability, predict, predictability, prediction, uncertain, uncertainty, unpredictable, unpredictability, unstable, volatile, volatility." This is a similar approach to Loughran and McDonald (2011) who created an "uncertainty" dictionary for analysis of financial planning documents. Tim Loughran and Bill McDonald, "When is a Liability not a Liability? Textual Analysis, Dictionaries, and 10-Ks," *The Journal of Finance* 66, no. 1 (2011): 35–65.

13. Benjamin M. Jensen, *Forging the Sword: Doctrinal Change in the U.S. Army* (Stanford: Stanford University Press, 2016), 5–7.

14. Snyder, *The Ideology of the Offensive,* 24–34; Stephen Van Evera, "The Cult of the Offensive and the Origins of the First World War," *International Security* 9, no. 1 (Summer 1984): 61–63; Posen, *The Sources of Military Doctrine,* 41–51.

15. Posen, *The Sources of Military Doctrine,* 51–54.

16. Stephen Van Evera, "The Cult of the Offensive and the Origins of the First World War," 58–107; Jack Snyder, "Civil-Military Relations and the Cult of the Offensive, 1914 and 1984," *International Security* 9, no. 1 (Summer 1984): 109–10.

17. The original organizational and bureaucratic politics models are described in Graham T. Allison, *Essence of Decision: Explaining the Cuban Missile Crisis* (Boston: Little, Brown, 1971); see also Morton H. Halperin, Priscilla A. Clapp, and Arnold Kantor, *Bureaucratic Politics and Foreign Policy* (Washington, DC: Brookings Institution Press, 2006). In terms of Allison's models, there is considerable overlap between the organizational and bureaucratic models' expectations of organizational behavior: see Jonathan Bendor and Thomas H. Hammond, "Rethinking Allison's Models," *American Political Science Review* 86, no. 2 (June 1992): 301–22. The traditional works tend to include expectations from both models when explaining parochial military behavior.

18. Celeste Wallander, "Institutional Assets and Adaptability: NATO after the Cold War," *International Organization* 54, no. 4 (Autumn 2000): 714.

19. Military spending is for the entire state military as land-based expenditures is unavailable. Military spending was derived from the Stockholm International Peace Research Institute, "SIPRI Military Expenditure Database," https://www.sipri .org/databases/milex. Russian and Chinese military expenditures were missing from the SIPRI dataset during the 1980s; thus, the Correlates of War's National Military Capabilities (NMC) Index provides expenditures for Russia from 1980 to 1991 and China from 1980 to 1989.

20. Morton H. Halperin and Priscilla A. Clapp, *Bureaucratic Politics and Foreign Policy* (Washington, DC: Brookings Institution Press, 2006), 32–33.

21. For defense-pact signatories, I use "Type I" formal defense pacts according to the Correlates of War typology; see Gibler (2009). A list of ground-based multilateral coalitions that I apply in my dataset from 1980 to 2016 are available in Figures A.9 and A.10. Russia and members of the Collective Security Treaty Organization (CSTO) are considered non-allies since the CSTO represents more of a security organization intended to regulate member behavior and respond to non-state threats, there have been no CSTO deployments since the organization's inception, and the Central Asian states are of little use for deterrence against NATO. See Gregory Gleason and Marat E. Shaihutdinov, "Collective Security and Non-State Actors in Eurasia," *International Studies Perspectives* 6 (2005): 274–84.

22. Colonial and sovereign history was determined using the Correlates of War Project's Colonial/Dependency Contiguity dataset. See *Correlates of War Project. 2017, "*Colonial Contiguity Data, 1816-2016. Version 3.1." *Online,* http://www.correlatesofwar.org/data-sets/colonial-dependency-contiguity.

23. Nathaniel Beck and Jonathan N. Katz, "Nuisance vs. Substance: Specifying and Estimating Time-Series-Cross-Section Models," *Political Analysis* 6 (2006): 1–36.

24. Because the Time-Series Cross-Sectional (TSCS) data include serially correlated errors, clustered robust standard errors are included for all models that do not include a lagged dependent variable as an independent variable. The explanatory variable in Model 2 loses its significance when a lagged dependent variable is included in the model, which is not surprising given how many exercise programs are conducted on a regular basis (as previously mentioned) and the small number of observations in the model (36).

25. Because China and India conducted no major multinational exercises during the Cold War, the independent variable does not vary for these countries. However, Russia serves as an important case beyond the West.

26. These marginal change plots were developed in J. Scott Long and Jeremy Freese, *Regression Models for Categorical Dependent Variables Using Stata* (College Station, TX: Stata Press, 2014), 415–20.

# Selected Bibliography

Adams, Gordon and Shoon Murray, eds. *Mission Creep: The Militarization of US Foreign Policy?* Washington, DC: Georgetown University Press, 2014.

Adamsky, Dmitry. "The Revolution in Military Affairs." In *Net Assessment and Military Strategy: Retrospective and Prospective Essays,* edited by Thomas G. Mahnken, 153–74. Amherst: Cambria Press, 2020.

"Agreement Between the Government of the Republic of India and the Government of the People's Republic of China on Confidence Building Measures in the Military Field Along the Line of Actual Control." *United Nations Peacemaker Online.* September 7, 1993. http://peacemaker.un.org/sites/peacemaker.un.org/files/CN%20IN_930907_Agreement%20on%20India-China%20Border%20Areas.pdf.

"Agreement Between the Government of the Republic of India and the Government of the People's Republic of China on Confidence Building Measures in the Military Field Along the Line of Actual Control in the India-China Border Areas." First Published May 1, 1997. *China Report* 33, no. 2 (1997): 241–47.

Albrecht, Peter and Paul Jackson. *Securing Sierra Leone, 1997-2013: Defence, Diplomacy, and Development in Action.* Royal United Services Institute for Defence and Security Studies. Abingdon: Routledge Journals, 2014.

Alexander, Martin S. and William J. Philpott. "The Entente Cordiale and the Next War: Anglo-French Views on Future Military Cooperation, 1928-1939." *Intelligence and National Security* 13, no. 1 (1998): 53–84.

Allen, Kenneth, Phillip C. Saunders, and John Chen. *Chinese Military Diplomacy, 2003-2016: Trends and Implications.* Washington, D.C.: National Defense University Press, 2017.

Allen, Michael A., Julie Van Dusky-Allen, and Michael E. Flynn. "The Localized and Spatial Effects of US Troop Deployments on Host-State Defense Spending." *Foreign Policy Analysis* (October 2014): 674–94.

Allison, Graham T. *Essence of Decision: Explaining the Cuban Missile Crisis.* Boston: Little, Brown, 1971.

Allison, Paul D. *Fixed Effects Regression Models.* Thousand Oaks: Sage, 2009.

Allison, Roy. *Russia, the West, and Military Intervention.* Oxford: Oxford University Press, 2013.

———. "Russian 'Deniable' Intervention in Ukraine: How and Why Russia Broke the Rules." *International Affairs* 90, no. 6 (November 2014): 1255–97.

———. "Virtual Regionalism, Regional Structures and Regime Security in Central Asia." *Central Asian Survey* 27, no. 2 (June 2008): 185–202.

Ambrosio, Thomas. "Beyond the Transition Paradigm: A Research Agenda for Authoritarian Consolidation." *Demokratizatsiya* 22, no. 3 (2014): 471–94.

———. "Insulating Russia from a Colour Revolution: How the Kremlin Resists Regional Democratic Trends." *Democratization* 14, no. 2 (April 2007): 232–52.

Andreß, Hans-Jürgen, Katrin Golsch, and Alexander W. Schmidt. *Applied Panel Data Analysis for Economic and Social Surveys.* Heidelberg: Springer, 2013.

*Army Exercises.* US Army Regulation 350-28. Washington, DC: Government Printing Office, December 9, 1997.

*Army Training and Leader Development.* Army Regulation 350-1. Washington, DC: Government Printing Office, 2014.

*Army Vision 2010.* Washington, DC: The Joint Chiefs of Staff, 1996.

Art, Robert J. *A Grand Strategy for America.* Ithaca, NY: Cornell University Press, 2003.

———. "American Foreign Policy and the Fungibility of Force." *Security Studies* 5, no. 4 (June 1996): 7–42.

———. "To What Ends Military Power?" *International Security* 4, no. 4 (Spring 1980): 3–35.

———. and Kelly M. Greenhill. "Coercion: An Analytical Overview." In *Coercion: The Power to Hurt in International Politics.* Oxford: Oxford University Press, 2018.

Asmus, Ronald D. *Opening NATO's Door: How the Alliance Remade Itself for a New Era.* Columbia University Press, 2012.

"Aspin's News Conference of October 20, 1993." United States Information Agency Wireless

Atkinson, Carol. "Constructivist Implications of Material Power: Military Engagement and the Socialization of States, 1972?2000." *International Studies Quarterly* 50, no. 3 (September 2006): 509–37.

———. "Does Soft Power Matter? A Comparative Analysis of Student Exchange Programs 1980–2006." *Foreign Policy Analysis* 6, no. 1 (2010): 1–22.

———. *Military Soft Power: Public Diplomacy through Military Educational Exchange.* Lanham, MD: Rowman & Littlefield, 2014.

Avey, Paul C., Jonathan N. Markowitz, and Robert J. Reardon. "Disentangling Grand Strategy: International Relations Theory and U.S. Grand Strategy." *Texas National Security Review* 2, no. 1 (November 2018): 29–50.

Bacevich, Andrew. *The New American Militarism: How Americans are Seduced by War.* Oxford: Oxford University Press, 2005.

Baker, James H. Testimony Before the Senate Finance Subcommittee on International Trade, February 19, 1987.

Baldwin, David A. *Economic Statecraft.* Princeton: Princeton University Press, 1985.

———. *Power and International Relations*. Princeton: Princeton University Press, 2016.

Bartholomees, J. Boone, Army War College (U.S.), and Army War College (U.S.), eds. *U.S. Army War College Guide to National Security Issues*, 5ᵗʰ Edition. Carlisle, PA: Strategic Studies Institute, U.S. Army War College, 2012.

Beck, Nathaniel and Jonathan N. Katz. "Nuisance vs. Substance: Specifying and Estimating Time-Series-Cross-Section Models." *Political Analysis* 6 (2006): 1–36.

Beckley, Michael. "The Myth of Entangling Alliances: Reassessing the Security Risks of U.S. Defense Pacts." *International Security* 39, no. 4 (Spring 2015): 7–48.

———. "The Power of Nations: Measuring What Matters." *International Security* 43, no. 2 (Fall 2018): 7–44.

Beehner, Lionel M., Colonel Liam S. Collins, and Robert T. Person. "The Fog of Russian Information Warfare." In *Perceptions are Reality: Historical Case Studies of Information Operations in Large-Scale Combat Operations*, edited by Colonel Mark D. Vertuli and Lieutenant Colonel Bradley S. Loudon, 31–50. Fort Leavenworth, KS: Army University Press, 2018.

Bellin, Eva. "Reconsidering the Robustness of Authoritarianism in the Middle East: Lessons from the Arab Spring." *Comparative Politics* 44, no. 2 (January 2012): 127–49.

Bennett, Scott D. and Allan Stam. "*EUGene*: A Conceptual Manual." *International Interactions* 26 (2000): 179–204. Version 3.212.

Bensten, Lloyd M. Statement Before the Senate Finance Subcommittee on International Trade, February 19, 1987.

Berman, Eric G. "The Provision of Lethal Military Equipment: French, UK, and US Peacekeeping Policies Toward Africa." *Security Dialogue* 34, no. 2 (2003): 199–214.

Bescht, Volker. "To Reach the Common Goal." *NATO's Nations and Partners for Peace* (January 2000): 93–95.

Betts, Richard K. "Nuclear Peace and Conventional War." *Journal of Strategic Studies* 11, no. 1 (March 1988): 79–95.

Biddle, Stephen D. *Military Power: Explaining Victory and Defeat in Modern Battle*. Princeton: Princeton University Press, 2004.

Biddle, Stephen, Julia Macdonald, and Ryan Baker. "Small Footprint, Small Payoff: The Military Effectiveness of Security Force Assistance." *Journal of Strategic Studies* 41, no. 1–2 (February 23, 2018): 89–142.

Black, Jeremy. *Western Warfare: 1775-1882*. New York: Routledge, 2014.

Blackwill, Robert D., and Jeffrey W. Legro. "Constraining Ground Force Exercises of NATO and the Warsaw Pact." *International Security* 14, no. 3 (1989): 68.

Blank, Stephen. "What Do the Zapad 2013 Exercises Reveal?" In *Russia's Zapad 2013 Military Exercise: Lessons for Baltic Regional Security,* edited by Liudas Zdanavičius and Matthew Czekaj, 8–13. Washington, DC: The Jamestown Foundation, 2015.

Blankenship, Brian. "Promises under Pressure: Statements of Reassurance in U.S. Alliances," *International Studies Quarterly* 64, no. 4 (2020): 1017–1030.

Blanning, Tim. *Frederick the Great: King of Prussia.* New York: Random House, 2016.

Blasko, Dennis J. "Integrating the Services and Harnessing the Military Area Commands." *Journal of Strategic Studies* 39, no. 5–6 (September 18, 2016): 685–708.

Blumenson, Martin. "Kasserine Pass, 30 January – 22 February 1943." In *America's First Battles: 1776-1965,* edited by Charles E. Heller and William A. Stofft. Kansas: University Press of Kansas, 1986.

Boggs, Carl, ed. *Masters of War: Militarism and Blowback in the Era of American Empire.* New York: Routledge, 2003.

Bordiuzha, Nikolay. "Channel, Arsenal, Proxy and Other CSTO Operations." *International Affairs (Moscow)* 3 (2009): 147–52.

Boyle, Michael J. "Do Counterterrorism and Counterinsurgency Go Together?" *International Affairs* 86, no. 2 (March 2010): 333–53.

Brands, Hal. *Making the Unipolar Moment: US Foreign Policy and the Rise of the Post-Cold War Order.* Ithaca, NY: Cornell University Press, 2016.

———. *What Good is Grand Strategy? Power and Purpose in American Statecraft from Harry S. Truman to George W. Bush.* Ithaca: Cornell University Press, 2014.

Brinkley, Douglas. "Democratic Enlargement: The Clinton Doctrine." *Foreign Policy*, no. 106 (1997): 110–27.

Brooks, Rosa. *How Everything Became War and the Military Became Everything: Tales from the Pentagon.* New York: Simon and Schuster, 2016.

Brooks, Stephen G. and William C. Wohlforth. *America Abroad: The United States' Global Role in the 21ˢᵗ Century.* Oxford: Oxford University Press, 2016.

———.and *World Out of Balance: International Relations and the Challenge of American Primacy.* Princeton: Princeton University Press, 2008.

Brooks, Stephen G., William C. Wohlforth, and G. John Ikenberry. "Don't Come Home, America: The Case Against Retrenchment." *International Security* 37, no. 3 (Winter 2012/13): 7–51.

Brzezinski, Ian J. and Nicholas Varangis. "The NATO-Russia Exercise Gap." *The Atlantic Council NATO Source.* February 23, 2015. Accessed September 27, 2017. http://www.atlanticcouncil.org/blogs/natosource/the-nato-russia-exercise-gap.

Bueno de Mesquita, Bruce, James Morrow, Randolph Siverson, and Alaister Smith. "An Institutional Explanation of the Democratic Peace." *American Political Science Review* 93, no. 4 (1999): 791–807.

Bukenya, Badru and Pablo Yanguas. "Building State Capacity for Inclusive Development: The Politics of Public Sector Reform." *Effective States and Inclusive Development (ESID) Working Paper*, no. 25. October 2013.

Bush, George H.W. and Brent Scowcroft. *A World Transformed.* New York: Alfred Knopf, 1999.

*Capstone Concept for Joint Operations.* Version 2.0. Washington, DC: Joint Chiefs of Staff, 2005.

Caravelli, John M. "Soviet and Joint Warsaw Pact Exercises: Functions and Utility." *Armed Forces and Society* 9, no. 3 (Spring 1983): 393–426.

Carney, Stephen A. *Allied Participation in Operation Iraqi Freedom.* Washington, DC: United States Army Center of Military History, 2011.

Carr, E.H. *The Twenty Years' Crisis: 1919-1938,* 2nd Edition. London: The MacMillan Press, 1981.

Cha, Victor D. "Powerplay: Origins of the U.S. Alliance System in Asia." *International Security* 34, no. 3 (Winter 2009/2010): 158–96.

Charap, Samuel. "The Ghost of Hybrid War." *Survival* 57, no. 6 (November 2, 2015): 51–58.

Cheyre, Emilio. "Defence Diplomacy." In *The Oxford Handbook of Modern Diplomacy,* edited by Andrew F. Cooper, Jorge Heine, and Ramesh Thakur, 369–81. Oxford: Oxford University Press, 2013.

Chiba, Daina, Carla Martinez Machain, and William Reed. "Major Powers and Militarized Conflict." *Journal of Conflict Resolution* 58, no. 6 (2014): 976–1002.

Christensen, Thomas and Jack Snyder. "Chain Gangs and Passed Bucks: Predicting Alliance Patterns in Multipolarity." *International Organization* 44, no. 2 (Spring 1990): 137–68.

Christopher, Warren. US Department of State Dispatch, 4.9, U.S. Government Printing Office. March 1, 1993.

Clausewitz, Carl von. *On War.* Edited by Michael Howard and Peter Paret. Indexed Edition. Princeton: Princeton University Press, 1976.

Clinton, William. *A National Security Strategy of Engagement and Enlargement.* Washington, DC: The White House, 1995.

Coatsworth, John H. "The Cold War in Central America, 1975–1991." In *The Cambridge History of the Cold War,* edited by Melvyn P. Leffler and Odd Arne Westad, 201–21. Cambridge: Cambridge University Press, 2010.

Cohen, William S. *Report of the Quadrennial Defense Review.* Washington, DC: Government Printing Office, 1997.

Collective Security Treaty Organization. "Tashkent Treaty." Original publication 1992, Accessed January 8, 2017. http://odkb-csto.org/documents/detail.php?ELEMENT_ID=1897.

Collins, Kathleen. "Kyrgyzstan's Latest Revolution." *Journal of Democracy* 22, no. 3 (July 2011): 150–64.

*Concept for Future Joint Operations: Expanding Joint Vision 2010.* Washington, DC: Government Printing Office, May 1997.

Correlates of War Project. 2017. "Colonial Contiguity Data, 1816-2016. Version 3.1." *Online,* http://www.correlatesofwar.org/data-sets/colonial-dependency-contiguity.

———. "National Military Capabilities, v5.0." *Online,* http://correlatesofwar.org.

———. "State System Membership List, v2016." Online, http://correlatesofwar.org.

Cottey, Andrew, and Anthony Forster. *Reshaping Defence Diplomacy: New Roles for Military Cooperation and Assistance. The Adelphi Papers* 44, no. 365 (May 2004): 1–84.

Crackel, Theodore J. "The Battle of Queenston Heights, 13 October 1812." In *America's First Battles: 1776-1965,* edited by Charles E. Heller and William A. Stofft, 35. Kansas: University Press of Kansas, 1986.

Crawford, Timothy W. "Preventing Enemy Coalitions: How Wedge Strategies Shape Power Politics." *International Security* 35, no. 4 (April 2011): 155–89.

Creveld, Martin van. *The Transformation of War*. New York: The Free Press, 1991.

Cronin, Audrey Kurth. "Behind the Curve: Globalization and International Terrorism." *International Security* 27, no. 3 (Winter 2002/2003): 30–58.

D'Orazio, Vito. "Constraining Cooperation: Military Relations and Government Repression." Unpublished Manuscript, September 30, 2016, accessible at http://www.vitodorazio.com/uploads/1/3/0/2/13026085/constraining_cooperation_24.pdf.

"International Military Cooperation: from Concepts to Constructs." Ph.D. dissertation, Pennsylvania State University, 2013.

———. "JME Data V.3". http://www.vitodorazio.com/data.html.

———. "War Games: North Korea's Reaction to US and South Korean Military Exercises." *Journal of East Asian Studies* 12 (2012): 275–94.

"NATO: U.S. Assistance to the Partnership for Peace." GAO-01-734. July 2001.

Dahl, Robert A. "The Concept of Power," *Behavioral Science* 2, no. 3 (1957): 201–15.

Das, Rup Narayan. *India-China Relations: A New Paradigm*. New Delhi: The Institute for Defence Studies and Analysis Monograph Series, no. 19, May 2013.

De Haas, Marcel. "War Games of the Shanghai Cooperation Organization and the Collective Security Treaty Organization: Drills on the Move!" *The Journal of Slavic Military Studies* 29, no. 3 (July 2, 2016): 378–406.

De Santis, Hugh. "Romancing NATO: Partnership for Peace and East European Stability." *The Journal of Strategic Studies* 17, no. 4 (1994): 61–81.

Depak, B.R. *India & China, 1904-2004: A Century of Peace and Conflict*. New Delhi: Manak Publications, 2005.

Department of Public Information, United Nations. "Somalia- UNOSOM I." March 21, 1997. https://www.un.org/Depts/DPKO/Missions/unosomi.htm.

*Doctrine for the Armed Forces of the United States*. Joint Publication 1. Change 1. Washington, DC: Department of Defense, 12 July 2017.

Dodd, Tom and Mark Oakes. *The Strategic Defence Review White Paper*, Research Paper 98/91. UK House of Commons Library. October 15, 1998. http://research-briefings.files.parliament.uk/documents/RP98-91/RP98-91.pdf.

Dombrowski, Peter and Simon Reich. "The Strategy of Sponsorship." *Survival* 57, no. 5 (September 3, 2015): 121–48.

Dorman, Andrew M. *Blair's Successful War: British Military Intervention in Sierra Leone*. Farnham: Ashgate, 2009.

Doughty, Robert A. Ira D. Gruber, Roy K. Flint, Mark Grimsley, George C. Herring, Donald H. Howard, John A. Lynn, Williamson Murray. *Warfare in the Western World: Military Operations Since 1871,* Volume 2. Boston: Houghton Mifflin Company, 2008.

Doyle, Michael W. and Nicholas Sambanis. *Making War and Building Peace: United Nations Peace Operations*. Princeton: Princeton University Press, 2006.

Drezner, Daniel W., Ronald R. Krebs, and Randall Schweller. "The End of Grand Strategy." *Foreign Affairs* 99, no. 3 (May/June 2020), 107–17.

Dyson, Major General Karen E. and Davis S. Welch. "Army FY 2015 Budget Overview." *US Army Financial Management and Comptroller.* March 2014. https://www.asafm.army.mil/documents/BudgetMaterial/fy2015/overview.pdf.

Edmunds, Timothy, Anthony Forster, and Andrew Cottey. "Armed Forces and Society: A Framework for Analysis." In *Soldiers and Societies in Postcommunist Europe,* edited by Timothy Edmunds, Anthony Forster, and Andrew Cottey, 1–24. Basingstoke: Palgrave MacMillan, 2003.

Fang, Songying, Jesse C. Johnson, and Brett Ashley Leeds. "To Concede or to Resist? The Restraining Effect of Military Alliances." *International Organization* 68, no. 4 (2014): 775–809.

Farrell, John F. "Team Spirit: A Case Study on the Value of Military Exercises as a Show of Force in the Aftermath of Combat Operations." *Air & Space Power Journal* (Fall 2009): 95–106.

Fearon, James. "Domestic Political Audiences and the Escalation of International Disputes." *American Political Science Review* 88, no. 3 (1994): 577–92.

———. "Rationalist Explanations for War." *International Organization* 49, no. 3 (1995): 379–414.

———. and David Laitin. "Ethnicity, Insurgency and Civil War." *American Political Science Review* 97, no. 1 (2003): 75–86.

Feaver, Peter D. *Armed Servants: Agency, Oversight, and Civil-Military Relations.* Cambridge: Harvard University Press, 2003.

Federation of American Scientists. "PRC: 2004 White Paper on National Defense Published." December 27, 2004, translated by the Federation of American Scientists. https://fas.org/nuke/guide/china/doctrine/natdef2004.html.

Finnemore, Martha. *The Purpose of Intervention: Changing Beliefs of Intervention.* Ithaca: Cornell University Press, 2003.

*Foreign Humanitarian Assistance,* US Military Joint Publication 3-29. Washington, DC: Government Printing Office, January 2014.

Forest, James J.F., and Rebecca Crispin. "AFRICOM: Troubled Infancy, Promising Future." *Contemporary Security Policy* 30, no. 1 (April 2009): 5–27.

Forrest, Alan. *Napoleon's Men: The Soldiers of the Revolution and Empire.* London: Hambledon and London, 2002.

Fravel, M. Taylor. *Strong Borders, Secure Nation: Cooperation and Conflict in China's Territorial Disputes.* Princeton: Princeton University Press, 2008.

Freedman, Lawrence. *Strategy: A History.* Oxford: Oxford University Press, 2013.

French Ministry of Defense. *French White Paper: Defence and National Security 2013.* https://www.defense.gouv.fr/english/dgris/defence-policy/white-paper-2013/white-paper-2013.

Frühling, Stephan, and Guillaume Lasconjarias. "NATO, A2/AD and the Kaliningrad Challenge." *Survival* 58, no. 2 (March 3, 2016): 95–116.

Gaddis, John Lewis. *The Cold War: A New History.* New York: Penguin Books, 2005.

Gates, Robert M. *Duty: Memoirs of a Secretary at War.* New York: Alfred A. Knopf, 2014.

"Helping Others Defend Themselves: The Future of U.S. Security Assistance." *Foreign Affairs* 89, no. 3 (May/June 2010): 2–6.

———. "The Overmilitarization of American Foreign Policy." *Foreign Affairs* 99, no. 4 (July/August 2020): 121–32.

Gavin, Francis J. "Strategies of Inhibition: U.S. Grand Strategy, the Nuclear Revolution, and Nonproliferation." *International Security* 40, no. 1 (2015): 9–46.

Gelpi, Christopher, Peter D. Feaver, and Jason Reifler. *Paying the Human Costs of War: American Public Opinion and Casualties in Military Conflicts.* Princeton: Princeton University Press, 2009.

Gerring, John. "Causal Mechanisms, Yes But…" *Comparative Politics Studies* 43, no. 11 (2010): 1499–526.

Gheciu, Alexandra. *NATO in the "New Europe": The Politics of International Socialization After the Cold War.* Stanford: Stanford University Press, 2005.

———. "Security Institutions as Agents of Socialization? NATO and the 'New Europe.'" *International Organization* 59, no. 4 (October 2005): 973–1012.

Gibler, Douglas M. *International Military Alliances, 1648-2008.* Volume 2. Washington, DC: CQ Press, 2009.

Gill, Lesley. *The School of the Americas: Military Training and Political Violence in the Americas.* Durham: Duke University Press, 2004.

Giragosian, Richard. "The US Military Engagement in Central Asia and the Southern Caucasus: An Overview." *The Journal of Slavic Military Studies* 17, no. 1 (March 2004): 43–77.

Glaser, Charles L., and Chaim Kaufmann. "What Is the Offense-Defense Balance and Can We Measure It?" *International Security* 22, no. 4 (1998): 44–82.

Gleason, Gregory and Marat E. Shaihutdinov. "Collective Security and Non-State Actors in Eurasia." *International Studies Perspectives* 6 (2005): 274–84.

Goddard, Stacie. *When Right Makes Might: Rising Powers and World Order.* Ithaca, NY: Cornell University Press, 2018.

———. and Daniel H. Nexon. "The Dynamics of Global Power Politics: A Framework for Analysis." *Journal of Global Security Studies* 1, no. 1 (2016): 4–18.

Goldgeier, James. *Not Whether but When: The U.S. Decision to Enlarge NATO.* Washington, DC: Brookings Institution Press, 1999.

Goldstein, Lyle. "Beyond the Steppe: Projecting Power into the New Central Asia." *The Journal of Slavic Military Studies* 17, no. 2 (2004): 183–213.

Goodman, Melvin A. *National Insecurity: The Cost of American Militarism.* San Francisco: City Light Books, 2013.

Government Accountability Office. "Army Pacific Pathways: Comprehensive Assessment and Planning Needed to Capture Benefits Relative to Costs and Enhance Value for Participating Units." Highlights of GAO-17-126. November 2016.

"The Government's Expenditure Plans, 2006-07 to 2007-08," July 2006. http://webarchive.nationalarchives.gov.uk/20070305140626/http://www.mod.uk/NR/rdonlyres/A556F11A-E9A4-4330-A96A-898A0B760808/0/MODExpenditurePlan200607to200708.pdf.

Gramer, Robbie. "Operation Dragoon Ride," *Foreign Affairs*, May 13, 2015, https://www.foreignaffairs.com/articles/baltics/2015-05-13/operation-dragoon-ride.

Granger, Jesse. "Operation Atlantic Resolve: A Case Study in Effective Communication Strategy." *Military Review* (January/February 2015):116–23.

Guifang, Wang, Senior Colonel. "Viewpoints on Enhancing Military CBMs Along the China-India Border." In *Military Confidence-Building and India-China Relations: Fighting Distrust,* edited by Dipankar Banerjee and Jabin T. Jacob, 55–60. New Delhi: Pentagon Press, 2013.

Guyot-Réchard, Bérénice. *Shadow States: India, China and the Himalayas, 1910-1962.* Cambridge: Cambridge University Press, 2017.

Halperin, Morton H., Priscilla A. Clapp, and Arnold Kantor, *Bureaucratic Politics and Foreign Policy.* Washington, DC: Brookings Institution Press, 2006.

Hart, B.H. Liddell. *Strategy,* 2nd Revised Edition. New York: Frederick A. Praeger, 1967.

———. *The British Way in Warfare.* New York: Macmillan, 1933.

Held, David and Anthony McGrew, David Goldblatt and Jonathan Perraton. *Global Transformations: Politics, Economic and Culture.* Stanford, CA: Stanford University Press, 1999.

Herspring, Dale R. and Roger N. McDermott. "Serdyukov Promotes Systemic Russian Military Reform." *Orbis* 54, no. 2 (Spring 2010): 284–301.

Hodges, Ben, Janusz Bugajksi, and Peter B. Doran, *Securing the Suwalki Corridor: Strategy, Statecraft, Deterrence, and Defense.* Washington, DC: Center for European Analysis, July 2018.

Reid, Brian Holden. "The British Way in Warfare: Liddell Hart's Idea and Its Legacy." *The RUSI Journal* 156, no. 6 (December 2011): 70–76.

Holslag, Jonathan. "The Persistent Military Security Dilemma Between China and India." *The Journal of Strategic Studies* 32, no. 6 (December 2009): 811–40.

Hopf, Ted. "Identity, Legitimacy, and the Use of Military Force: Russia's Great Power Identities and Military Intervention in Abkhazia." *Review of International Studies* 31 (December 2005): 225–43.

House of Commons. Debate. 23 May 2000. Vol. 350 cc864. https://publications.parliament.uk/pa/cm199900/cmhansrd/vo000523/debtext/00523-06.htm.

Human Rights Watch. "Bullets Were Falling Like Rain: The Andijan Massacre, May, 13, 2005." Accessed January 16, 2017. https://www.hrw.org/report/2005/06/06/bullets-were-falling-rain/andijan-massacre-may-13-2005.

Huth, Paul. "Deterrence and International Conflict: Empirical Findings and Theoretical Debates." *Annual Review of Political Science* 2 (1999): 25–48.

———. "Extended Deterrence and the Outbreak of War." *American Political Science Review* 82, no. 2 (Jun. 1988): 423–43.

Illarionov, Andrei. "The Russian Leadership's Preparation for War, 1999-2008." In *The Guns of August 2008: Russia's War in Georgia,* edited by Svante E. Cornell and Frederick Starr, 49–84. New York: Routledge, 2015.

Information Office of the State Council of the People's Republic of China. *China's National Defense in 2006.* December 2006. http://www.china.org.cn/english/features/book/194421.htm;

Ismay, Lord. *NATO: The First Five Years, 1949-1954.* Paris: North Atlantic Treaty Organization, 1954.

Izumikawa, Yasuhiro. "Binding Strategies in Alliance Politics: The Soviet-Japanese-US Diplomatic Tug of War in the Mid-1950s." *International Studies Quarterly* 62, no. 1 (March 1, 2018): 108–20.

Jackson, Ashley. "British-African Defence and Security Connections." *Defence Studies* 6, no. 3 (September 2006): 351–76.

Jackson, Nicole J. "The Role of External Factors in Advancing Non-Liberal Democratic Forms of Political Rule: A Case Study of Russia's Influence on Central Asian Regimes." *Contemporary Politics* 16, no. 1 (March 2010): 101–18.

Jackson, Paul. "Security Sector Reform and State Building." *Third World Quarterly* 32, no. 10 (November 2011): 1803–22.

Järvenpää, Pauli. "Zapad 2013: A View from Helsinki." In *Russia's Zapad 2013 Military Exercise: Lessons for Baltic Regional Security,* edited by Liudas Zdanavičius and Matthew Czekaj, 43–57. Washington, DC: The Jamestown Foundation, 2015.

Jensen, Benjamin M. *Forging the Sword: Doctrinal Change in the U.S. Army.* Stanford: Stanford University Press, 2016.

Jervis, Robert. "Cooperation Under the Security Dilemma." *World Politics* 30, no. 2 (Jan. 1978): 167–214.

———. *The Meaning of the Nuclear Revolution: Statecraft and the Prospect of Armageddon.* Ithaca: Cornell University Press, 1989.

———. *System Effects: Complexity in Political and Social Life.* Princeton: Princeton University Press, 1997.

Johnson, Chalmers. "American Militarism and Blowback: The Costs of Letting the Pentagon Dominate Foreign Policy." *New Political Science* 24, no. 1 (2002): 21–38.

Johnson, Jesse C., Brett Ashley Leeds, and Ahra Wu. "Capability, Credibility, and Extended General Deterrence." *International Interactions* 41, no. 2 (March 15, 2015): 309–36.

*Joint Operations,* US Joint Publication 3-0. Washington, DC: Government Printing Office, 1993.

*Joint Operations,* US Joint Publication 3-0. Washington, DC: Government Printing Office, 1995.

*Joint Operations,* US Joint Publication 3-0. Washington, DC: Government Printing Office, 2001.

*Joint Operations,* US Joint Publication 3-0. Washington, DC: Government Printing Office, 2006.

*Joint Operations,* US Joint Publication 3-0. Washington, DC: Government Printing Office, January 17, 2017.

*Joint Operations,* US Joint Publication 3-0. Change 1. Washington, DC: Government Printing Office, October 22, 2018.

*Joint Planning,* US Joint Publication 5-0. Washington, DC: Government Printing Office, June 16, 2017.

*Joint Vision 2010.* Washington, DC: The Joint Chiefs of Staff, 1996.

Kaldor, Mary. *New and Old Wars: Organized Violence in a Global Era.* Stanford: Stanford University Press, 2012.

Kalyvas, Stathis N. and Laia Balcells. "International System and Technologies of Rebellion: How the End of the Cold War Shaped Internal Conflict." *American Political Science Review* 104, no. 3 (August 2010): 415–29.

Kamphausen, Roy, David Lai, Andrew Scobell, eds. *The PLA at Home and Abroad: Assessing the Operational Capabilities of China's Military.* Carlisle, PA: Strategic Studies Institute, U.S. Army War College, 2010.

Kaplan, Fred. *The Insurgents: David Petraeus and the Plot to Change the American Way of War.* New York: Simon and Schuster, 2013.

Kearn, David W. "The Hard Truths about Soft Power." *Journal of Political Power* 4, no. 1 (April 2011): 65–85.

Keele, Luke and Nathan J. Kelly. "Dynamic Models for Dynamic Theories: The Inns and Outs of Lagged Dependent Variables." *Political Analysis* 14, no. 2 (Spring 2006): 186–205.

Kennan, George. *The Fateful Alliance: France, Russia, and the Coming of the First World War.* New York: Pantheon Books, 1984.

Kennedy, Paul. "Military Coalitions and Coalition Warfare over the Past Century." In *Coalition Warfare: An Uneasy Accord,* edited by Keith Neilson and Roy A. Prete. Ontario, Canada: Wilfrid Laurier University Press, 1981.

Keohane, Robert O. "The Globalization of Informal Violence, Theories of World Politics, and the 'Liberalism of Fear'." *Dialog-International Organization* (Spring 2002): 29–43.

Kerr, David and Laura C. Swinton. "China, Xinjiang, and the Transnational Security of Central Asia." *Critical Asian Studies* 40, no. 1 (2008): 89–112.

Kier, Elizabeth. *Imagining War: French and British Military Doctrine Between the Wars.* Princeton: Princeton University Press, 1997.

Kimball, Warren F. *The Most Unsordid Act: Lend-Lease, 1939-1941.* Baltimore: Johns Hopkins Press, 1969.

King, Anthony. "On Combat Effectiveness in the Infantry Platoon: Beyond the Primary Group Thesis." *Security Studies* 25, no. 4 (2016): 699–728.

Kirkpatrick, Jeane. "A Normal Country in a Normal Time." *National Interest* (Fall 1990).

Kirshner, Jonathan. "The Changing Calculus of Conflict?" *Security Studies* 16, no. 4 (December 6, 2007): 583–97.

———. ed. *Globalization and National Security.* New York: Routledge, 2006.

———. "The Economic Sins of Modern IR Theory and the Classical Realist Alternative." *World Politics* 67, no. 1 (January 2015): 155–83.

Knight, Frank. *Risk, Uncertainty, and Profit.* Ithaca: Cornell University Press, 1921.

Knopf, Jeffrey W. "Varieties of Assurance," *Journal of Strategic Studies* 35, no. 3 (2012): 375–99.

Kokoshin, Andrei A. *Soviet Strategic Thought, 1917-1991.* Cambridge, MA: The MIT Press, 1998.

Kollars, Nina. "Genius and Mastery in Military Innovation." *Survival* 59, no. 2 (March 4, 2017): 125–38.

Kovacs, Mimmi Söderberg. "Bringing the Good, the Bad, and the Ugly into the Peace Fold: the Republic of Sierra Leone's Armed Forces After the Lomé Peace

Agreement." In *New Armies from Old: Merging Competing Military Forces After Civil Wars,* edited by Roy Licklider. Washington, DC: Georgetown University Press, 2014.

Krasner, Stephen D. *Defending the National Interest: Raw Materials Investments and U.S. Foreign Policy.* Princeton: Princeton University Press, 1978.

Kreps, Sarah E. *Coalitions of Convenience: United States Military Interventions After the Cold War.* Oxford, UK: Oxford University Press, 2011.

Kydd, Andrew H. *Trust and Mistrust in International Relations.* Princeton: Princeton University Press, 2005.

Kydd, Andrew. "Trust, Reassurance, and Cooperation." *International Organization* 54, no. 2 (2000): 325–57.

Lai, David. *Learning from the Stones: A Go Approach to Mastering China's Strategic Concept, Shi.* Carlisle: Army War College, Strategic Studies Institute. May 1, 2004.

Lal, Rollie. *Understanding India and China: Security Implications for the United States and the World.* Westport: Praeger Security International, 2006.

Langer, William L. "The Franco-Russian Alliance (1890-1894)." *The Slavonic Review* 3, no. 9 (March 1925): 554–75.

Lanoszka, Alexander. "Russian Hybrid Warfare and Extended Deterrence in Eastern Europe." *International Affairs* 92, no. 1 (2016): 175–95.

Larson, Deborah Welch and Alexei Shevchenko. "Status Seekers: Chinese and Russian Responses to U.S. Primacy." *International Security* 34, no. 4 (Spring 2010): 63–95.

Larson, Eric V., David T. Orletsky, and Kristin Leuschner, *Defense Planning in a Decade of Change: Lessons from the Base Force, Bottom-Up Review, and Quadrennial Defense Review.* Santa Monica, CA: Project Air Force RAND, 2001.

Laswell, Harold. *Politics: Who Gets What, When, and How.* New York: Meridian Books, 1958.

Latham, Michael E. "The Cold War in the Third World, 1963-1975." In *The Cambridge History of the Cold War, Volume 2,* edited by Melvyn P. Leffler and Odd Arne Westad. Cambridge: Cambridge University Press, 2010.

Latimer, Jon. *Deception in War: The Art of the Bluff, the Value of Deceit, and the Most Thrilling Episodes of Cunning in Military History, from the Trojan Horse to the Gulf War.* New York: Overlook Press, 2001.

Lauren, Paul Gordon, Gordon A. Craig, and Alexander L. George. *Force and Statecraft: Diplomatic Challenges of our Time.* Oxford: Oxford University Press, 2014.

Lawrence, Susan V. and Michael E. Martin. "Understanding China's Political System." *Congressional Research Service.* March 20, 2013. https://fas.org/sgp/crs/row/R41007.pdf.

Le Grys, Barry J. "British Military Involvement in Sierra Leone, 2001-2006." In *Security Sector Reform in Sierra Leone 1997-2007: Views from the Front Line,* edited by Peter Albrecht and Paul Jackson, 39–60. Berlin: Lit Verlag, 2010.

Leeds, Brett Ashley, "Do Alliances Deter? The Influence of Military Alliances on the Initiation of Militarized Interstate Disputes." *American Journal of Political Science* 47, no. 3 (Jul 2003): 427–39.

————. and Jesse C. Johnson. "Theory, Data, and Deterrence: A Response to Kenwick, Vasquez, and Powers." *The Journal of Politics* 79, no. 1 (January 2017): 335–40.

Leffler, Melvyn P. "The Emergence of an American Grand Strategy, 1945-1952." In *The Cambridge History of the Cold War, Volume 1*, edited by Melvyn P. Leffler and Odd Arne Westad. Cambridge, UK: Cambridge University Press, 2010.

Levitsky, Steven and Lucan Way. *Competitive Authoritarianism: Hybrid Regimes after the Cold War*. Cambridge: Cambridge University Press, 2010.

Levy, Jack S. "Case Studies: Types, Designs, and Logics of Inference." *Conflict Management and Peace Science* 25, no. 1 (February 2008): 1–18.

Long, J. Scott, and Jeremy Freese. *Regression Models for Categorical Dependent Variables Using Stata*. College Station, TX: Stata Press, 2014.

Loughran, Tim and Bill McDonald. "When Is a Liability not a Liability? Textual Analysis, Dictionaries, and 10-Ks." *The Journal of Finance* 66, no. 1 (2011): 35–65.

Lucas, Nathan J. and Kathleen J. McInnis. "The 2015 National Security Strategy: Authorities, Changes, Issues for Congress." *Congressional Research Service*. April 5, 2016. https://fas.org/sgp/crs/natsec/R44023.pdf.

————. "What Is 'Building Partner Capacity?' Issues for Congress." *Congressional Research Service*. December 18, 2015, https://fas.org/sgp/crs/natsec/R44313.pdf.

Lundy, Lieutenant General Mike, and Colonel Rich Creed. "The Return of U.S. Army Field Manual 3-0, Operations." *Military Review* (November/December 2017): 14–21.

Lyall, Jason, and Isaiah Wilson III. "Rage against the Machines: Explaining Outcomes in Counterinsurgency Wars." *International Organization* 63, no. 1 (2009): 67–106.

MacDonald, Paul K. "'Retribution Must Succeed Rebellion': The Colonial Origins of Counterinsurgency Failure." *International Organization* 67, no. 2 (April 2013): 253–86.

Mack, Andrew. "Global Political Violence: Explaining the Post-Cold War Decline." *Coping with Crisis Working Paper Series*. International Peace Academy Publications, 2007.

Maddow, Rachel. *Drift: The Unmooring of American Military Power*. New York: Crown Publishers, 2012.

Malik, V.P. *India's Military Conflicts and Diplomacy: An Inside View of Decision Making*. Uttar Pradesh, India: Harper Collins, 2013.

Maoz, Zeev and Bruce Russett. "Normative and Structural Causes of Democratic Peace, 1946-1986." *American Political Science Review* 87, no. 3 (September 1993): 624–38.

Marat, Erica. *The Military and the State in Central Asia: From Red Army to Independence*. New York: Routledge, 2010.

March, James G. and Herbert A. Simon. *Organizations*. New York: John Wiley & Sons, 1958.

Marshall, Monty G. "Major Episodes of Political Violence: 1946-2016." *Center for Systemic Peace*. June 15, 2017. http://www.systemicpeace.org/warlist/warlist.htm.

Mastny, Vojtech. "Imagining War in Europe: Soviet Strategic Planning." In *War Plans and Alliances in the Cold War: Threat Perceptions in the East and West,* edited by Vojtech Mastny, Sven G. Holtsmark, and Andreas Wenger. London, UK: Routledge, 2006.

Mazarr, Michael, Arthur Chan, Alyssa Demus, Bryan Frederick, Alireza Nader, Stephanie Pezard, Julia Thompson, and Elina Treyger. *What Deters and Why: Exploring Requirements for Effective Deterrence of Interstate Aggression.* RAND Corporation, 2018.

McCarthy, Michael J. *The Limits of Friendship: US Security Cooperation in Central Asia.* Maxwell Air Force Base, Alabama: Air University Press, 2007.

McInnis, Kathleen J. "Coalition Contributions to Countering the Islamic State." *Congressional Research Service.* August 24, 2016. https://fas.org/sgp/crs/natsec/R44135.pdf.

McManus, Roseanne W. and Mark David Nieman. "Identifying the Level of Major Power Support Signaled for Protégés: A Latent Measure Approach." *Journal of Peace Research* 56, no. 3 (2019): 364–78.

Mearsheimer, John J. *Liddell Hart and the Weight of History.* Ithaca: Cornell University Press, 1988.

———. *The Tragedy of Great Power Competition.* New York: W.W. Norton, 2014.

———. and Stephen M Walt. "The Case for Offshore Balancing: A Superior U.S. Grand Strategy," *Foreign Affairs* 95, no. 4 (July/August 2016): 70–83.

———., Barry R. Posen, Eliot A. Cohen, Steven J. Zologa, Malcom Chalmers, and Lutz Unterseher. "Correspondence: Reassessing Net Assessment and the Tank Gap Data Flap." *International Security* 13, no. 4 (Spring 1989): 128–79.

*Military Contribution to Cooperative Security (CS) Joint Operating Concept,* version 1.0. Washington, DC: Joint Chiefs of Staff, 2008.

*Military Operations Other Than War,* Joint Publication 3-07. Washington, DC: Government Printing Office, June 1995.

Ministry of Defence, Government of India, *Annual Report 2018-2019,* https://mod.gov.in/sites/default/files/MOD-English2004.pdf.

Monteiro, Nuno. "Unrest Assured: Why Unipolarity Is Not Peaceful." *International Security* 36, no. 3 (Winter 2011/2012): 9–40.

Moore, Rebecca. *NATO's New Mission: Projecting Stability in a Post-Cold War World.* Connecticut: Praeger, 2007.

Morgan, Patrick M. *Deterrence: A Conceptual Analysis.* Beverly Hills: Sage Publications, 1983.

———. *Deterrence Now.* Cambridge: Cambridge University Press, 2003.

Morgenthau, Hans J. *In Defense of the National Interest.* New York: Knopf, 1951.

———. *Politics Among Nations: The Struggle for Power and Peace,* 5th Edition. Knopf: New York, 1973.

Morrow, James D. "Alliances and Asymmetry: An Alternative to the Capability Aggregation Model of Alliances." *American Journal of Political Science* 35, no. 4 (November 1991): 904–33.

———. "Alliances: Why Write Them Down?" *Annual Review of Political Science* 3, no. 1 (June 2000): 63–83.

Mueller, John. "War Has Almost Ceased to Exist: An Assessment." *Political Science Quarterly* 124, no. 2 (Summer 2009): 297–321.

*Multinational Operations.* US Joint Publication 3-16. Washington, DC: Government Printing Office, July 16, 2013.

Nathan, Andrew J. and Andrew Scobell. *China's Search for Security.* New York: Columbia University Press, 2012.

*NATO Handbook,* North Atlantic Treaty Organization. Brussels: NATO Office of Information and Press, 1995.

Nelson, Stephen C., and Peter J. Katzenstein. "Uncertainty, Risk, and the Financial Crisis of 2008." *International Organization* 68, no. 2 (2014): 361–92.

Nikitina, Yulia. "The Collective Security Treaty Organization Through the Looking Glass." *Problems of Post-Communism* 59, no. 3 (May 1, 2012): 41–52.

Nolushingu, Sam C. *Limits of Anarchy: Intervention and State Formation in Chad.* Charlottesville: University Press of Virginia, 1996.

Nye, Joseph S. *The Future of Power.* New York: Public Affairs, 2011.

———. "Public Diplomacy and Soft Power." *The Annals of the American Academy of Political and Social Science* 616, no. 1 (March 2008): 94–109.

———. *Soft Power: The Means to Success in World Politics.* New York: Public Affairs, 2004.

O'Shaughnessy, Terrence J., Matthew D. Strohmeyer, and Christopher D. Forrest. "Strategic Shaping: Expanding the Competitive Space." *Joint Forces Quarterly* 90, no. 3 (2018): 10–15.

O'Mahony, Angela, Miranda Priebe, Bryan Frederick, Jennifer Kavanagh, Matthew Lane, Trevor Johnston, Thomas Szayna, Jakub Hlavka, Stephen Watts, and Matthew Povlock. *U.S. Presence and the Incidence of Conflict.* RAND Corporation, 2018.

Odgaard, Liselotte and Thomas Galasz Nielsen. "China's Counterinsurgency Strategy in Tibet and Xinjiang." *Journal of Contemporary China* 23, no. 87 (2014): 535–55.

Office of the Under Secretary of Defense (Comptroller). "National Defense Budget Estimates for FY 2000." March 1999. http://comptroller.defense.gov/Portals/45/Documents/defbudget/Docs/fy2000_greenbook.pdf.

*Operations,* US Army Field Manual 100-5. Washington, DC: Government Printing Office, 1986.

Organization for Security and Co-Operation in Europe, "Vienna Document 2011 on Confidence- and Security-Building Measures," November 30, 2011, http://www.osce.org/fsc/86597?download=true.

Owen, John M. "How Liberalism Produces the Democratic Peace." *International Security* 19, no. 2 (Autumn 1994): 87–125.

Pardesi, Manjeet S. "Is India a Great Power? Understanding Great Power Status in Contemporary International Relations." *Asian Security* 11, no. 1 (2015): 1–30.

Parker, Geoffrey. *The Military Revolution: Military Innovation and the Rise of the West, 1500-1800.* Cambridge: Cambridge University Press, 1988.

Pape, Robert A. *Bombing to Win: Air Power and Coercion in War.* Ithaca: Cornell University Press, 1996.

Paret, Peter, Gordon A. Craig, and Felix Gilbert, eds. *Makers of Modern Strategy: From Machiavelli to the Nuclear Age.* Princeton: Princeton University Press, 1986.

Perkins, David G. "Multi-Domain Battle: The Advent of Twenty-First Century War." *Military Review* (November/December 2017): 8–13.

Pettyjohn, Stacie L., and Jennifer Kavanagh. *Access Granted: Political Challenges to the U.S. Overseas Military Presence, 1945-2014*. Research Report, RR-1339-AF. Santa Monica: RAND Corporation, 2016.

Pevehouse, Jon C. "Democracy from the Outside-in? International Organizations and Democratization." *International Organization* 56, no. 3 (2002): 515–49.

Poast, Paul. "Dyads Are Dead, Long Live Dyads! The Limits of Dyadic Designs in International Relations Research." *International Studies Quarterly* 60 (2016): 369–74.

Porter, Patrick. *The Global Village Myth*. Washington, DC: Georgetown University Press, 2015.

Posen, Barry R. "Command of the Commons: The Military Foundation of U.S. Hegemony." *International Security* 28, no. 1 (July 2003): 5–46.

———. "Foreword: Military Doctrine and the Management of Uncertainty." *Journal of Strategic Studies* 39, no. 2 (February 23, 2016): 159–73.

———. *Restraint: A New Foundation for U.S. Grand Strategy*. Ithaca, NY: Cornell University Press, 2014.

———. and Andrew L. Ross. "Competing Visions for U.S. Grand Strategy." *International Security* 21, no. 3 (Winter 1996/1997): 5–53.

Pouliot, Vincent. *International Security in Practice: The Politics of NATO-Russia Diplomacy*. Cambridge: Cambridge University Press, 2010.

Powell, Colin and Joseph E. Persico. *My American Journey*. New York: Random House, 1995.

Powell, Nathaniel K. "Battling Instability? The Recurring Logic of French Military Interventions in Africa." *African Security* 10, no. 1 (2017): 47–72.

Press Briefing by Anthony Lake and General Wesley Clark. The White House, Office of the Press Secretary. May 5, 1994.

Press Information Bureau, Government of India, Prime Minister's Office. "Border Defense Cooperation Agreement between India and China." October 23, 2013, Accessed March 25, 2017, http://pib.nic.in/newsite/PrintRelease.aspx?relid=100178.

Pridham, Geoffrey. "The Politics of the European Community, Transnational Networks and Democratic Transition in Southern Europe." *In Encouraging Democracy: The International Context of Regime Transition in Southern Europe*, edited by Geoffrey Pridham, 212–45. New York: St. Martins Press, 1991.

Rangelov, Iavor, and Mary Kaldor. "Persistent Conflict." *Conflict, Security & Development* 12, no. 3 (July 2012): 193–99.

Rasmussen, Mikkel. *The Risk Society at War: Terror, Technology and Strategy in the Twenty-First Century*. Cambridge: Cambridge University Press, 2006.

Rathbun, Brian C. "Uncertain about Uncertainty: Understanding the Multiple Meanings of a Crucial Concept in International Relations Theory." *International Studies Quarterly* 51, no. 3 (September 2007): 533–57.

"Regionally Aligned Forces: DOD Could Enhance Army Brigades' Efforts in Africa by Improving Activity Coordination and Mission-Specific Preparation." GAO-15-568. August 2015. https://www.gao.gov/products/GAO-15-568.

"Remarks to the 48th Session of the United Nations General Assembly in New York City." *The American Presidency Project.* September 27, 1993. http://www.presidency.ucsb.edu/ws/index.php?pid=47119.

Resnick, Evan. "Defining Engagement." *Journal of International Affairs* 54, no. 2 (Spring 2001): 551–66.

Reveron, Derek S. *Exporting Security: International Engagement, Security Cooperation, and the Changing Face of the US Military.* Washington, DC: Georgetown University Press, 2016.

———. ed. *Shaping the Security Environment.* Newport Papers 29. Newport: Naval War College Press, 2007.

———. "Security Cooperation: A Key Pillar of Defense Policy," *Foreign Policy Research Institute E-Notes,* November 23, 2015, https://www.fpri.org/article/2015/11/security-cooperation-a-key-pillar-of-defense-policy/.

Ripsman, Norrin M. and T.V. Paul, *Globalization and the National Security State.* Oxford: Oxford University Press, 2010.

Risse-Kappen, Thomas. "Collective Identity in a Democratic Community: The Case of NATO." In *The Culture of National Security: Norms and Identity in World Politics*, edited by Peter J. Katzenstein, 357–99. New York: Columbia University Press, 1996.

Rogers, James and Luis Simón. "The Status and Location of the Military Installations of the Member States of the European Union and Their Potential Role for the European Security and Defence Policy (ESDP)." *European Parliament Policy Department External Policies.* Brussels: European Parliament, February 2009.

Rosato, Sabastian. "The Flawed Logic of Democratic Peace Theory." *American Political Science Review* 97, no. 4 (2003): 585–602.

Rosen, Stephen Peter. *Winning the Next War: Innovation and the Modern Military.* Ithaca: Cornell University Press, 1991.

Rosenau, William. *US Internal Security Assistance to South Vietnam: Insurgency, Subversion, and Public Order.* New York: London, 2005.

Ross, Steven T. *Napoleon and Maneuver Warfare,* Lecture at U.S Air Force Academy. Colorado Springs, CO: U.S. Air Force Academy, 1985.

Rotberg, Robert I. "Failed States in a World of Terror." *Foreign Affairs* 81, no. 4 (2002): 127–40.

Rowlett, Rick. "Joint Publication 3-0, Joint Operations." *Joint Forces Quarterly* 86, no. 3 (2017): 122–24.

Ruggeri, Andrea, Han Dorussen, and Theodora-Ismene Gizelis. "Winning the Peace Locally: UN Peacekeeping and Local Conflict." *International Organization* 71, no. 1 (2017): 163–85.

Rühle, Michael, and Nicholas Williams. "Partnership for Peace: A Personal View from NATO." *Parameters* 24, no. 4 (1994): 66–75.

Russian Ministry of Foreign Affairs. "National Security Concept of the Russian Federation." January 10, 2000. Accessed January 9, 2017. http://www.mid.ru/en/foreign_policy/official_documents/-/asset_publisher/CptICkB6BZ29/content/id/589768.

Saari, Sinikukka. "Russia's Post-Orange Revolution Strategies to Increase Its Influence in Former Soviet Republics: Public Diplomacy *Po Russkii.*" *Europe-Asia Studies* 66, no. 1 (January 2, 2014): 50–66.

Sahgal, Arun, Brigadier (ret.). "Sino-Indian Military CBMs—Reducing Tensions, Building Confidence." In *Military Confidence-Building and India-China Relations: Fighting Distrust,* edited by Dipankar Banerjee and Jabin T. Jacob, 43–54. New Delhi: Pentagon Press, 2013.

Sarkees, Meredith Reid. "Codebook for the Instate State Wars v. 4.0: Definitions and Variables." *Correlates of War Project. 2017. Online,* http://www.correlatesofwar .org/data-sets/COW-war.

Savage, Jesse Dillon, and Jonathan D Caverley. "When Human Capital Threatens the Capitol: Foreign Aid in the Form of Military Training and Coups." *Journal of Peace Research* 54, no. 4 (July 2017): 542–57.

Sayle, Timothy Andrews, *Enduring Alliance: A History of NATO and the Postwar Global Order.* Ithaca: Cornell University Press, 2019.

Scharre, Paul. "American Strategy and the Six Phases of Grief." *War on the Rocks,* October 6, 2016, https://warontherocks.com/2016/10/american-strategy-and-the -six-phases-of-grief/.

Schelling, Thomas. *Arms and Influence.* New Haven: Yale University Press, 1966.

*Security Cooperation,* US Joint Publication 3-20. Washington, DC: Government Printing Office, May 23, 2017.

Schroeder, Paul. "Alliances, 1815-1945: Weapons of Power and Tools of Management." In *Historical Dimensions of National Security Problems*, edited by Klaus Knorr. Lawrence: University Press of Kansas, 1976.

Schweller, Randall. *Unanswered Threats: Political Constraints on the Balance of Power.* Princeton: Princeton University Press, 2006.

Shalikashvili, John M. "Joint Vision 2010: America's Military—Preparing for Tomorrow." *Joint Forces Quarterly* 12 (Summer 1996): 34–50.

"The Shanghai Convention on Combating Terrorism, Separatism and Extremism," June 15, 2001. http://eng.sectsco.org/documents/.

Shanghai Cooperation Organization. "Declaration on The Establishment of The Shanghai Cooperation Organization." June 15, 2001. http://eng.sectsco.org/documents/.

Sharkov, Yuri. "'Color Revolutions': Uniformity in Diversity." *International Affairs (Moscow)* 54, no. 4 (2008): 25–31.

Silitski, Vitali. "Preempting Democracy: The Case of Belarus." *Journal of Democracy* 16, no. 4 (2005): 83–97.

———. "'Survival of the Fittest:' Domestic and International Dimensions of the Authoritarian Reaction in the Former Soviet Union Following the Colored Revolutions." *Communist and Post-Communist Studies* 43, no. 4 (December 2010): 339–50.

Silove, Nina. "Beyond the Buzzword: The Three Meanings of 'Grand Strategy.'" *Security Studies* 27, no. 1 (2018): 27–57.

Singer, J. David, Stuart Bremer, and John Stuckey. "Capability Distribution, Uncertainty, and Major Power War, 1820-1965." In *Peace, War, and Numbers*, edited by Bruce Russett, 19–48. Beverly Hills: Sage Publication, 1972.

Singh, Swaran. "China and India: Countering Terrorism." In *Military Confidence-Building and India-China Relations: Fighting Distrust,* edited by Dipankar Banerjee and Jabin T. Jacob, 119–32. New Delhi: Pentagon Press, 2013.

Snyder, Glenn H. *Deterrence and Defense: Toward a Theory of National Security.* Princeton: Princeton University Press, 1961.

———. "The Security Dilemma in Alliance Politics." *World Politics* 36, no. 4 (July 1984): 461–95.

Snyder, Jack. "Civil-Military Relations and the Cult of the Offensive, 1914 and 1984." *International Security* 9, no. 1 (1984): 108–46.

Southerland, Matthew. "The Chinese Military's Role in Overseas Humanitarian Assistance and Disaster Relief: Contributions and Concerns." *US-China Economic and Security Review Commission,* July 11, 2019, https://www.uscc.gov/sites/default/files/Research/USCC%20Staff%20Report_The%20Chinese%20Military%E2%80%99s%20Role%20in%20Overseas%20Humanitarian%20Assistance%20and%20Disaster%20Relief_7.11.19.pdf.

*Stability,* US Army Doctrine Reference Publication 3-07. Washington, DC: Government Printing Office, August 2012.

StataCorp. *Stata 14 Base Reference Manual.* College Station: Stata Press, 2015.

"Statement by the Heads of Government of the Member States of the Shanghai Cooperation Organization," September 14, 2001, http://eng.sectsco.org/documents/.

Stein, Janice Gross. "Reassurance in International Conflict Management." *Political Science Quarterly* 106, no. 3 (Autumn 1991): 431–51.

Stewart, Andrew. "An Enduring Commitment: The British Military's Role in Sierra Leone." *Defence Studies* 8, no. 3 (September 2008): 351–68.

*Strategic Defence Review: Presented to Parliament by the Secretary of State for Defence by Command of her Majesty.* United Kingdom Ministry of Defence. July 1998. http://webarchive.nationalarchives.gov.uk/20121018172816/http://www.mod.uk/NR/rdonlyres/65F3D7AC-4340-4119-93A2-20825848E50E/0/sdr1998_complete.pdf.

Taylor, Claire. "A Brief Guide to Previous British Defence Reviews." *British House of Commons Library.* October 19, 2010. http://researchbriefings.files.parliament.uk/documents/SN05714/SN05714.pdf.

*The National Military Strategy of the United States of America.* Washington, DC: Government Printing Office. January 1992.

*The National Military Strategy of the United States of America.* Washington, DC: Government Printing Office, 1997.

*The National Military Strategy of the United States of America.* Washington, DC: Government Printing Office, 2002.

*The U.S. Army Operating Concept: Win in a Complex World, 2020-2040.* TRADOC Pamphlet 525-3-1. Washington, DC: Government Printing Office, October 7, 2014.

The White House. *National Security Strategy of the United States.* Washington, DC: Government Printing Office, January 1987.

Thompson, James D. *Organizations in Action: Social Science Bases of Administrative Theory.* New York: McGraw-Hill, 1967.

Thompson, William R. "Identifying Rivals and Rivalries in World Politics." *International Studies Quarterly* 45, no. 4 (2001): 557–86.

Tzu, Sun. *The Art of War,* edited by Dallas Galvin and translated by Lionel Giles. New York: Barnes & Noble Books, 2003.

U.K. Ministry of Defence. *UK Defence Doctrine,* Joint Doctrine Publication 0-01. Fifth Edition. November 2014.

———. *Strategic Defence Review: Presented to Parliament by the Secretary of State for Defence by Command of Her Majesty.* July 1998. http://webarchive.nationalarchives.gov.uk/20121018172816/http://www.mod.uk/NR/rdonlyres/65F3D7AC -4340-4119-93A2-20825848E50E/0/sdr1998_complete.pdf.

U.S. Department of Defense. *DoD Dictionary of Military Associated Terms.* May 2017. http://www.dtic.mil/doctrine/new_pubs/dictionary.pdf.

Ucko, David H. "Can Limited Intervention Work? Lessons from Britain's Success Story in Sierra Leone." *Journal of Strategic Studies* 39, nos. 5–6 (2016): 847–77.

Uhl, Matthias. "Storming on to Paris: The 1961 *Buria* Exercise and the Planned Solution of the Berlin Crisis." In *War Plans and Alliances in the Cold War: Threat Perceptions in the East and West,* edited by Vojtech Mastny, Sven G. Holtsmark, and Andreas Wenger. London, UK: Routledge, 2006.

Vagts, Alfred. *The Military Attaché.* Princeton: Princeton University Press, 1967.

Van Evera, Stephen. *Causes of War: Power and the Roots of Conflict.* Ithaca: Cornell University Press, 2001.

———. "Offense, Defense, and the Causes of War," *International Security* 22, no. 4 (Spring 1998): 5–43.

Vertuli, Mark D., Bradley S. Loudon, and Army University Press (U.S.), eds. *Perceptions Are Reality: Historical Case Studies of Information Operations in Large-Scale Combat Operations.* US Army Large-Scale Combat Operations Series. Fort Leavenworth, Kansas: Army University Press, 2018.

Wald, Charles F. "The Phase Zero Campaign." *Joint Forces Quarterly* 43, no. 4 (2006): 72–75.

Wall, Sir Peter, General (British Army). "Transcript: Defence Engagement: The British Army's Role in Building Security and Stability Overseas." Lecture at Chatham House. March 12, 2014. https://www.chathamhouse.org/sites/files/ chathamhouse/home/chatham/public_html/sites/default/files/20140312Defence %20Engagement.pdf.

Wallander, Celeste A. "Institutional Assets and Adaptability: NATO after the Cold War." *International Organization* 54, no. 4 (2000): 705–35.

Walt, Stephen M. *The Origins of Alliances.* Ithaca: Cornell University Press, 1987.

Waltz, Kenneth. *Theory of International Politics.* Reading: Addison-Wesley, 1979.

———. "The Emerging Structure of International Politics." *International Security* 18, no. 2 (Fall 1993): 44–79.

Way, Lucan. "The Real Causes of the Color Revolutions." *Journal of Democracy* 19, no. 3 (2008): 55–69.

Williams, Nick. "Partnership for Peace: Permanent Fixture or Declining Asset?" *Survival* 38, no. 1 (1996): 98–110.

Wilner, Alex S. "Targeted Killings in Afghanistan: Measuring Coercion and Deterrence in Counterterrorism and Counterinsurgency." *Studies in Conflict & Terrorism* 33, no. 4 (March 15, 2010): 307–29.

Wilson, James Q. *Bureaucracy: What Government Agencies Do and Why They Do It.* New York, Basic Books, 1989.

Wolfers, Arnold. *Discord and Collaboration: Essays on International Politics.* Baltimore: The Johns Hopkins Press, 1962.

Wolford, Scott. *The Politics of Military Coalitions.* Cambridge: Cambridge University Press, 2015.

Yanguas, Pablo. "The Anatomy of State Building Assistance: Aid Promises and Donor Politics in War-Torn Africa." Ph.D. dissertation, Cornell University, 2012.

Yarger, H. Richard. "Toward a Theory of Strategy: Art Lykke and the U.S. Army War College Strategy Model." In *U.S. Army War College Guide to National Security Issues Vol. I: Theory of War and Strategy,* edited by J. Boone Bartholomees, Jr. Carlisle: US Army War College Press, 2012.

Yost, David S. *NATO Transformed: The Alliance's New Roles in International Security.* Washington, DC: The United States Institute of Peace Press, 1998.

Young, Crawford. *The African Colonial State in Comparative Perspective.* Yale: Yale University Press, 1994.

Zi, Sun. *The Art of War: Sun Zi's Military Methods.* Translated by Victor H. Mair. New York: Columbia University Press, 2007.

Zuber, Terence. "The Schlieffen Plan Reconsidered." *War in History* 6, no. 3 (1999): 293–96.

# INTERVIEWS

Anonymous former US official at NATO familiar with NATO's Partnership for Peace (PfP) program. Phone interview by author. July 26, 2017.

Bajwa, J.S., Lieutenant General (Indian Army, retired), former Director General of the Infantry. Phone interview by author. June 21, 2017.

Banerjee, Dipankar, Major General (Indian Army, retired), former infantry division commander in Jammu and Kashmir. Phone interview by author. June 19, 2017.

Brzezinski, Ian, former US Deputy Assistant Secretary of Defense for Europe and NATO policy and Advisor to the Ukrainian National Security Council and Foreign Ministry. Phone interview by author. September 19, 2017.

Clemmesen, Michael, Brigadier General (Danish Army, retired), former Defence Attaché to the Baltics and Commandant of the Baltic Defence College. Skype interview by author. June 12, 2017.

De Haas, Marcel, Lieutenant Colonel (Royal Netherlands Army, retired), former Professor at Nazarbayev University, Kazakhstan and current Senior Researcher at the Russian Studies Center, University of Groningen. Skype interview by author. June 29, 2017.

Dent, Mike, Colonel (British Army, retired), Military Advisor of the Ministry of Defence Advisory Team (MODAT) and Deputy Commander of IMATT. Email correspondence with author. August 20, 2017.

Gardiner, Sam, Colonel (US Air Force, retired), former NATO staff officer and Chairman of the Department of Joint and Combined Operations at the National War College. Phone interview by author. June 9, 2017.

Muddiman, Andrew, Lieutenant Colonel (British Royal Marines), served as an intelligence officer for Royal Marine's 42 Commando unit during Operation Palliser. Skype interview by author. July 19, 2017.

Skinner, Charles, former Deputy Political Advisor to US Mission to NATO. Phone interview by author. June 27, 2017.

Turner, Reggie, Lieutenant Colonel (British Royal Marines), served as a liaison officer to the UN for the Royal Marine's 42 Commando unit during Operation Palliser. Skype interview by author. June 29, 2017.

# Index

# About the Author

**Kyle J. Wolfley** is an assistant professor of International Affairs in the Department of Social Sciences at West Point and an Army strategist. At West Point, he has taught international relations, advanced international relations, the national security seminar, and a senior project concerned with great power competition and deterrence. Prior to teaching, he commanded two infantry companies in the 82nd Airborne Division and served as a platoon leader in Germany and Afghanistan. He holds a PhD and MA in Government from Cornell University and a BS from West Point; he is also a term member of the Council on Foreign Relations. Kyle has published in *Foreign Policy Analysis, The Strategy Bridge, Modern War Institute, Army Press Online Journal, and Infantry Magazine.* Kyle is originally from Pittsburgh, PA, and is the proud husband of Danessa and father of Kolson and Lydia. The views expressed in this book are personal and do not reflect the policy or position of the US Military Academy at West Point, Department of the Army, Department of Defense, or US Government.

www.ingramcontent.com/pod-product-compliance
Lightning Source LLC
Chambersburg PA
CBHW050636280326
41932CB00015B/2670